COUNTERFEIT
REVIVAL

COUNTERFEIT
REVIVAL

Hank Hanegraaff

WORD PUBLISHING

NASHVILLE

www.wordpublishing.com

A Thomas Nelson Company

Published by Word Publishing
Nashville, Tennessee

Copyright 1997, 2001 by Hank Hanegraaff.

Unless otherwise indicated, Scripture quotations used
in this book are from the Holy Bible, New International Version
(NIV). Copyright © 1973, 1978, 1984 International Bible Society.
Used by permission of Zondervan Bible Publishers.

Those marked NASB are from the New American Standard Bible
© 1960, 1962, 1963, 1968, 1971, 1972, 1973, 1975, 1977
by The Lockman Foundation.
Used by permission.

Those marked NKJV are from The New King James Version,
copyright © 1979, 1980, 1982, Thomas Nelson, Inc., Publishers

Set in New Century Schoolbook

Published in association with
Sealy M. Yates, Literary Agent, Orange, California

LIBRARY OF CONGRESS CATALOGING-IN-PUBLICATION DATA

Hanegraaff, Hank.
Counterfeit revival / Hank Hanegraaff.
   p. cm.
   Rev. ed.
Includes bibliographical references.
ISBN 0-8499-4294-2
1. Fanaticism. 2. Enthusiasm—Religious aspects—Christianity.
3. Gifts, Spiritual. 4. Revivals—History—20th century.
5. Pentecostalism—History—20th century.re. I. Title.
BR114.H36   2001
269—dc21   2001026266
                                       CIP

Printed in the United States of America
01 02 03 04 05 06 07 PHX 9 8 7 6 5 4 3 2 1

To Johannis Hanegraaff, my father,
who modeled what it means
to stand for truth, no matter what the cost.

COUNTERFEIT REVIVAL

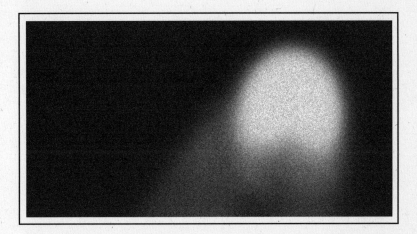

Contents

Foreword

It had never occurred to me that I could be involved with anything spiritually destructive. Yet when I reached the lowest spiritual level in my pastoral ministry, that is exactly what had happened. How could I have let things go so far?

From my perspective, serving on the board of directors of the Association of Vineyard Churches (AVC) had always been a privilege. My wife and I developed close friendships with the other leaders. Together we traveled to numerous countries, planted churches, and shared a vision for ministry. Led by a respected national leader, we considered ourselves elders of what was rapidly becoming a new denomination. We maintained a unified sense of mission and purpose as we pursued what we believed God was leading us to do.

One week, during a leadership conference in the midwestern part of the United States, several of us were invited to a private meeting. We were to be introduced to the "prophets" who were slated to have a major impact on the future of our movement. Since we were already enthusiastic about the use of spiritual gifts to enhance contemporary church life, our curiosity spurred us to accept the invitation to this landmark meeting. We entered the room, settled into our seats, and waited to see what the Lord had in store for us.

The prophets began to inform us that in the last days, the Lord was restoring the fivefold ministry of apostles, prophets, pastors, teachers, and evangelists to the church. We were challenged to accept the arrival of apostles and prophets because today's church already had plenty of teaching, pastoring, and evangelizing. The arrival of the prophets and apostles would lead to the world's last and greatest revival.

The prophets revealed that we had been chosen as the people and the movement that would lead Christians into this final display of power in the last days. We were told that one such prophet had been commissioned by God to find the apostolic leadership and apostolic ministry that, linked with the prophetic, would provide the basis for this new surge of endtime anointing. God had revealed to the "prophet" that he and our Association of Vineyard Churches were the chosen ones.

It all sounded downright intoxicating. After struggling with the daily duties of ministry and our fears of inadequacy, this was exactly what we wanted to hear. Being told that our struggles and sacrifices had made us special in God's eyes was a comfort in itself. We clung to the promise that spectacular things would follow the inauguration of this new move of God.

We listened attentively to the flattery of our new friends, the prophets. Our skepticism barely peaked above the surface of our consciousness. It disappeared entirely later in the meeting when one of the prophets singled us out and proceeded to reveal, in detail, the secrets of our lives. Now they really had our attention. How could they *not* be from God? One after another, these accurate "words from the Lord" seemed to be the perfect validation for everything they were proposing. We became completely convinced of the validity of this prophetic anointing. How else could we explain their ability to "see into" our childhoods and personal histories through their prophetic gifting?

We returned to our local churches with our minds wide open

to this new phase in the growth of our movement. During the months that followed, many of us received a plethora of "personal prophecies" predicting our future roles, positions, and successes in God's new movement. There were words of prophecy for our ministries, for their locations and growth, prophecies about the great "restoration" to come and our important part in it. "Seers" would direct people regularly to their "land of anointing." The recipients of such advice would immediately pack up and go in faith, confident that the predictions of ministry success would come true. The prophets began telephoning pastors with words straight from God directing staff changes and adjustments in church policy and practice. They anointed individuals to healing ministries and apostolic appointments. Then, instead of waiting for the prophets to call, the pastors began calling the prophets for predictions, instruction, and advice.

Ministry musicians and laypeople were promised star status if they would remain faithful to the prophetic blueprint unfolded before our movement.

Nevertheless, some of the leaders began to voice concerns and uneasiness. They had seen people uproot their families and travel great distances to the "land of their anointing," fail, and then blame God. Associate pastors and other leaders were wrongly dismissed, indicted, and convicted by nothing more than a dream or prophecy that accused them of some spiritual crime. "Fortune-cookie" faith soon became more popular than following God's clear voice in Scripture.

Some pastors began raising concerns in board meetings. Even though we were uneasy, we nervously agreed that spiritual gifts don't always operate in human beings in a perfect manner. We thought we could solve the problem by applying one of the movement's most endearing philosophies: "Don't trim the bush until it's had a chance to grow," which means, "Let's wait and see what comes of this." We put away our hedge trimmers, and the prophets continued to operate with impunity.

After only a couple of years, the prophets seemed to be

speaking to just about everyone on just about everything. Hundreds of Vineyard members received the "gift" of prophecy and began plying their trade among both leaders and parishioners. People began carrying around little notebooks filled with predictions that had been delivered to them by prophets and seers. They flocked to the prophecy conferences that had begun to spring up everywhere. The notebook crowd would rush forward in hopes of being selected to receive more prophecies to add to their prophetic diaries.

Those identified with healing ministries were holding seminars on formulas and methods for healing prayer, such as finding "hot spots" on the body. Interpreting the meaning of physical sensations or "jolts" in the bodies of those who were prayed over became a necessary part of the healers' "training."

Dreams and their interpretations soon moved to center stage as prophecy conferences taught devotees to keep a pencil and notebook on their nightstands to write down each dream as it occurred. These were later interpreted for God's message. People lived on the edges of their seats, waiting for the grandiose promises of prophecies to come true. Most waited in vain.

Not long after "prophecy du jour" became the primary source of direction, a trail of devastated believers began to line up outside our pastoral counseling offices. Young people promised teen success and stardom through prophecy were left picking up the pieces of their shattered hopes because God had apparently gone back on his promises. Leaders were deluged by angry church members who had received prophecies about their great future ministries but had been frustrated by local church leaders who failed to recognize and "facilitate" their "new anointing."

After a steady diet of the prophetic, some people were rapidly becoming biblically illiterate, choosing a "dial-a-prophet" style of Christian living rather than studying God's Word. Many were left to continually live from one prophetic "fix" to the next, their hope always in danger of failing because God's voice was so specific in pronouncement, yet so elusive in fulfillment. Possessing a prophet's phone number was like having a storehouse of treasured guidance. Little clutched notebooks replaced Bibles as the preferred reading material during church services.

Some began to fake the shaking and eye-fluttering symptoms they had been told were signs of the Holy Spirit coming upon them. They hoped the ministry team would recognize the signs of God and rush to their sides, lifting their hands and praying, "More, Lord!" Shaking, laughing, weeping, and eye twitching always ensured that the parishioner would attract the immediate attention of the leaders and their peers.

One conference speaker, addressing eight thousand people, discouraged the use of reference books, commentaries, and language tools for sermon preparation. Rather, the pastors were exhorted to determine their Sunday messages through listening for prophecies during long walks with the Lord. Something was dangerously wrong in the movement.

One of my own church board members refused to make any decision until his hands got "hot," indicating that his choice was wise. Disturbing symptoms were definitely beginning to show up in my own fellowship.

In my region of denominational jurisdiction, churches began to shrink because evangelism had been replaced by mysticism. People began to complain that church attendance would drop markedly during holiday periods because parishioners were apparently embarrassed to bring their out-of-town relatives to visit such a strange environment. Something bad was happening to the church we had planted fifteen years earlier, and I was beginning to realize that it was my fault. The "bush" was clearly growing out of control. I had reached the lowest point in my ministry, and I was staring at failure.

One of my earliest pastoral mentors had taught, "When you're not sure what God is saying, go back to what God has already said." The Bible! What a concept! I had grown weary of studying past revivals, movements, and histories of the church, vainly trying to find justification for what was happening in my own church. It seemed that as a pastor, I had given up what I *knew for sure* in exchange for what I could *never know for sure*. It was time to search *the Word* and get back to basics.

After years of pastoral training, teaching, and preaching, I knew that the bizarre changes in the fabric of our church needed biblical evaluation and correction if our flock was to survive. I was supposed to be the shepherd, but I had become a follower. My pasture was in danger of turning into a dust bowl.

Most pastors I know have bouts with insecurity, performance anxiety, and periods when they are unsure that they have made the right ministry decisions. While most might think these bouts of emotional insecurity are rare, they happen every week of the year, between Sundays. One of a pastor's greatest fears should be that he or she has not been diligent to keep the wolves out of the sheepfold. The most effective entry point into the church for any "new" teaching is through the pastor.

I remember well the first time I stepped aside and allowed false teaching in my church. I was told that we had "quenched the Holy Spirit long enough" and that it was "now time to give the church back to the Holy Spirit." I was told that the penance for the ecclesiastical felony of "quenching the Spirit" was to include an "anything goes" time during every meeting. Order would be set aside, and chaos was to be invited with prayers like, "Come, Holy Spirit!" This command to deity was typically followed by a long period of waiting to see what the Spirit would do. A mounting sense of anticipation would grow as we waited for the "manifestations" to appear. If there was any anxiety, it was dispelled by a liberal application of Matthew 7:9–11 (KJV): "Or what man is there of you, whom if his son ask bread, will he give him a stone? Or if he ask a fish, will he give him a serpent? If ye then, being evil, know how to give good gifts unto your children, how much more shall your Father which is in heaven give good things to them that ask him?"

All of this seemed very comforting at the time, but I always wondered how far the magic "Satan shield" extended—one hundred yards in perimeter? Two feet? Was there a time limit, say midnight, for example, before Satan's minions could again return to their normal attacks? How long did the bread-and-fish "kryptonite" ward off psychic duplication of God's "voice"?

Some of us were suckers for this kind of manipulation. My feelings of guilt were conjured up by suggestions that I had exerted too much human leadership and control in the church. All of my peers were confessing their sin of control and letting go, so I followed suit.

Despite the fact that Scripture nowhere advocates this misinterpretation of Matthew 7, and in fact commands order in the church (1 Cor. 14:17–19), chaos reigned in my church because I had come to believe I needed to forfeit my duty to maintain order. I had almost lost my commitment to presenting a clear gospel message to visiting nonbelievers and instead allowed subjectivity to reign over reasoning from the Scriptures. I needed to repent and become a true shepherd again.

As my wife and I prepared to attend what would be our last Vineyard board of directors meeting, we rehearsed what we would say: that we needed to eliminate the swirl of subjectivity that had entered our church, that we needed to get back to the basics of Christian evangelism and discipleship, and that we needed to restore Bible study to our members' daily lives.

We didn't want to cause trouble. We had formed close friendships with these people, loved them, and considered them an important part of our lives. But we could no longer remain silent concerning the truth.

During the series of meetings, various leadership concerns were raised about the effect "prophetic" influences were having on the core of our theology. Some of the leaders who dared to reveal their misgivings were quickly warned that the "prophet," the "one whose words never fall to the ground," had supernaturally heard our conversations and would report them to the national leader for disciplinary action. Since "Big Brother" was watching us, we were forbidden to discuss these issues with other board members.

Other directors began to share "words" that God had spoken to them for the direction of our movement. One director claimed God had told him that the pure church was the cell church and that we should abandon public Bible teaching and evangelism altogether for small group meetings. Some heralded the position that real evangelism takes place through "signs and wonders," when people are attracted to the kingdom of God through "demonstrations" of power. Some scorned the idea of evangelistic crusades. Some supported the ministry of the prophets. Others presented evidence regarding the trickery and manipulation often used by the prophets in their meetings.

Finally, after a week's worth of sometimes heated discussion, prayer, and meetings, it was all summed up by the dream someone shared the last night. The dream, related as though it were from God himself, instructed us to do nothing, to make no decisions, but to "wait and see."

Frustrated, I returned to my own church in Denver. I had just witnessed close friends, colaborers in Christ, legitimate Christian leaders being "tossed to and fro by every wind of doctrine." Our corporate ministry seemed like a laboratory test gone awry. The adoption of subjectivity as the primary source of guidance had reduced us to complete ineptitude as pastors and leaders. What had happened? Why were these Christian men and women "hearing" so many contradictory messages from God?

I knew without a shadow of doubt that it was time to begin the process of getting the church God had given me to pastor *back to basics*. At that moment, truth became more important than relationships.

My wife and I spoke with our remaining congregation. We knew that if they would commit to going back to the basics of

Christian practice with us, the Word of God guaranteed that the Lord would work more powerfully and more legitimately in our lives than ever before. The congregation agreed.

I went back to teaching the Bible in the most basic fashion I could, verse by verse. When I first announced that we were going to go through the Gospel of John for the better part of the year, the response of some was, "Why the Book of John? I read that when I was a baby Christian." Others were horrified that I would discourage shaking and twitching "in the spirit." What had been a church of forty-four hundred shrank as people left to join the "holy laughter" movement. My hate mail grew to enormous proportions. Even the movement's leader publicly denounced me, predicting that God would kill me for my "sin."

God was true to his Word in the midst of the storm that our congregation endured during what we later called "the year of slander." Within a few months, several hundred people came to a saving knowledge of Christ. Baptisms increased simply because there were new converts to baptize. People's lives were radically changing, and the church was becoming healthy again. Attendance increased almost overnight. Within a year, we added a third service to our Sunday schedule. Currently our congregation is moving past six thousand, and our struggles are with ordinary, normal issues of Christian life. All of this because of the basics. It's really that simple (see Heb. 4:12–13; 2 Kings 22:8–13; Jer. 15:16).

Books like *Counterfeit Revival* must be written and published. You see, in the day of the apostle Paul, the false prophets, heretics, and legalists resisting his ministry needed to go to considerable effort to inject the opiate of false doctrine into the church. Long travel by horseback or on foot, the heat, dust, months away from home, and painfully slow methods of copying documents all contributed to making the spread of false doctrine difficult.

Not so today—the wonders of the modern world make the spread of false doctrine deceptively thorough and quick. The urgency of biblical correction is never more pressing than now. Back in 1517, a huge contingent of the church had fallen to the ruse of a carnal monk named Johann Tetzel. He conned the believers of his day into purchasing indulgences to guarantee escape from purgatory. An outraged Martin Luther nailed his ninety-five theses of dispute on the Wittenberg door, challenging the brokerage of salvation through the exploitation of people's spiritual insecurities and illiteracy. Perhaps we have come again to such a dark age with the insurgence of false revivalism.

If this is the day, then *Counterfeit Revival* is the document. This book will be a wonderful tool in the hands of those who love true spiritual gifts and their brothers and sisters in Christ who have been confused by the influences of false revivalism. I know. I was there and back, thank God!

Only as the church experiences true reformation will it experience true revival.

Tom Stipe
Pastor, Crossroads Church of Denver
January 1997

Preface to the Updated and Expanded Edition[1]

When I first began writing *Counterfeit Revival*, the Pensacola Outpouring, with its promise of turning "into a national awakening,"[2] had not yet burst forth upon the evangelical landscape.[3] Back then it would have been hard to imagine the metamorphosis that the revival would eventually undergo. In time, "fillings in the spirit" would eclipse "fallings in the spirit" as the manifestation of choice. As one Counterfeit Revival devotee exclaimed, "Have you heard . . . there's gold in Toronto!"[4] She goes on to write:

> Wednesday night, before Dutch Sheets delivered a powerfully anointed message, there was a short video clip shown of John Arnott ministering in a South Africa meeting where people's teeth were being filled with gold. After the clip, John asked for anyone who wanted this miracle to stand and believe for it while touching the sides of their faces. After the prayer he asked that we check each others' mouths and about 10 people went forward, some yelling and all excited because they now had gold teeth and fillings which they did not previously have!
> . . . So John let a couple testify and we prayed

again . . . . this time more people received the miracle. A third time of praying came, as did more miracles!! IT WAS AWESOME!!!

Then, at just about every meeting there was prayer for this miracle and every time there would be many who would discover their mouth filled with gold! Last count that I heard was over 198 people who were leaving the conference with some gold in their mouths!

. . . One woman who had been on welfare most of her childhood had 8 new gold teeth! Another woman had 4 gold teeth and/or fillings on Wednesday and by Saturday she had 11! (I saw her at both stages of this miracle.) One man had two beautiful, perfect, shiny, gold teeth and one of them had a cross engraved on it!

. . . The drummer of the worship team received gold teeth as did one of the pastors on staff there at TACF [Toronto Airport Christian Fellowship] and while officially collecting these testimonies from the saints, the man who was recording them received gold teeth as well!

. . . And on Saturday . . . the wonderful "gold dust" started showing up on people's hands and in their tears as they worshipped![5]

A Toronto Airport Christian Fellowship official statement titled "GOLD TEETH!" reports that perhaps God was filling people's teeth with gold as "a sign and a wonder to expose the skepticism still in so many of us."[6] The statement went on to say that "reports of people's fillings turning a bright silver or gold color are coming in from South Africa, Australia, England, Mexico and across Canada and the USA. The excitement at TACF is electric with news of how these dental miracles are so rapidly spreading."

Pastors Linda and Joel Budd say they have witnessed such dental miracles firsthand. As reported by *Charisma* magazine, the Budds watched in amazement as gold crowns began to form in the mouth of Linda's eighty-one-year-old mother, Elda Munce. According to *Charisma*, Joel "saw this big glob of gold material on the top of one of her teeth. . . . The gold globule moved down the side of Elda's tooth and was covered with a translucent film that looked like clear Jell-O. . . . The gold fluid then moved to the tooth beside it." *Charisma* reports that when Joel looked into his mother-in-law's mouth an hour later, she already had five new golden crowns. The following morning the number of gold crowns had escalated to seven. Said Elda, "I had so much tartar built up—it's all gone. It's like I've been to the dentist, and it is totally clean."[7]

Even true confessions by ministry leaders have done little to diminish gold rush fever. In western Canada, Willard Thiessen, president of Trinity Television, admitted he was wrong in asserting that a gold tooth had been planted in his mouth via divine dentistry. Thiessen confessed that he was "embarrassed to tears" after disclosing that his brother Elmer had implanted the gold tooth in his mouth.[8] Likewise, during an on-air fund-raiser, TV evangelist Dick Dewert claimed, "God had implanted a gold tooth in his mouth after a bout of intensive prayer." After Dr. Jack Sherman, Dewert's dentist, revealed that he, not God, was the dentist of record, Dewert confessed, "I was sincere in what I said. When miracles appear to be happening, it's easy to get excited and, in my case, jump to conclusions."[9] In California, Rich Oliver, pastor of the Family Christian Center, was confronted with dental records after attempting to convince devotees to believe that God had implanted a glittering gold crown in his mouth. While admitting that he was "absolutely wrong," Oliver continued to "tout his congregation's 'gold rush' on the Internet." One of Oliver's followers claims that God not only gave her gold fillings but shortly thereafter "a tiny cross was divinely etched into her skin."[10]

In addition to touting gold fillings, Counterfeit Revivalists worldwide are touting an epidemic of gold fallings as well. *Charisma* magazine reported that their "offices have been flooded by fax and e-mail reports of gold dust falling on people during worship."[11] The gold dust craze hit the big time in 1998 when Ruth Ward Heflin began to host meetings for Silvania Machado, a Brazilian evangelist. *Charisma* reports, "Machado gets so much gold that it covers almost all of her face and rains from the top of her head."[12] As *Charisma* discovered, however, all that glitters is not gold. An analysis of the "gold" conducted by the U.S. Geological Survey showed that in reality it was merely plastic film.[13] Paul Crouch, founder of the Trinity Broadcasting Network (TBN), disagrees. After reportedly seeing gold dust all over healing evangelist Benny Hinn's face, Crouch exuded, "Where that gold dust came from had to be from another dimension." He went on to speculate that "heaven's door opened a crack and a little of the street dust came down on [Hinn]."[14]

Heflin saw more than gold dust falling down on Hinn. Shortly before she died the Lord reportedly spoke to her audibly and said, "Tell Benny I'm going to appear physically on the platform in his meeting."[15] According to Hinn, "Jesus, God's Son, is about to appear physically in meetings and to believers around the world to wake us up. He appeared after his resurrection and he's about to appear before his second coming." Hinn went on to say, "I know deep in my soul something supernatural is going to happen in Nairobi, Kenya. I feel that. I may very well come back—and you and Jan are coming, Paul and Jan are coming to Nairobi with me—but Paul, we may very well come back with footage of Jesus on the platform. . . . Now hear this—I'm prophesying this: Jesus Christ, the Son of God, is about to appear physically in some churches and some meetings and to many of his people for one reason—to tell you he's about to show up."[16]

Even as reports of gold fillings are pouring in from Counterfeit Revival leaders around the world, leaders at the

Brownsville Revival in Pensacola have begun citing resurrections from the dead. For seventy-five dollars, the Brownsville Revival School of Ministry will sell you a video series titled *Faith to Raise the Dead*. Brownsville leaders are claiming that David Hogan and his ministry associates have seen more than two hundred people raised from the dead.[17] The expectations of people have reached such a fever pitch that some time ago a parent who lost a child put his baby on ice and drove three hundred fifty miles to the Brownsville Assembly of God to have the baby raised from the dead.[18] To some, this father's actions may appear absurd. Yet, if, as reported, God is indeed raising hundreds from the dead in Mexico, it would be perfectly logical to think that he would raise the dead in the ongoing revival that is being touted as perhaps the greatest in the history of humanity.[19] Brownsville revivalist Stephen Hill lent particular credence to this notion when he said, "I know now that we could all get to the place where the dead are raised."[20]

While Arnott and his associates are duping people with the gold-filling ruse, and while Hogan's heroes are heralding resurrections from the dead, Rodney Howard-Browne—a prime mover in the Counterfeit Revival—attempted to make a comeback at Madison Square Garden in New York. As his following dwindled in Florida, Howard-Browne came up with a new angle. It seems Howard-Browne had "a dream from God"[21] in which Billy Graham told him about a crusade he held in New York back in 1957. Howard-Browne said that as he listened to Graham, he started weeping: "I wept so hard that when I woke up, my pillow was soaked with tears."[22] The Holy Ghost allegedly told the "Holy Ghost Bartender" that he was to launch one of the biggest soul-winning crusades ever. Through a variety of techniques, including a *Charisma* magazine advertisement, Howard-Browne began raising money and manpower for "Unlocking Heaven at the Garden."[23]

While at first blush the metamorphosis of the Counterfeit Revival may sound amusing, the consequences of such fabrications, fantasies, and frauds are often tragic. The story of the parent who took his baby to Brownsville speaks for itself. But stories of gold fillings and fallings can have equally tragic repercussions.

If or when followers catch on to the manipulations of revival leaders, they often become disillusioned and disenchanted with their deceitfulness, even calling into question the integrity of the God whom they claim to represent. As you read on you will discover that Counterfeit Revivalists have become so hypersuggestible that they seem willing to believe virtually anything that enters their minds, no matter how mundane or outlandish. Incredibly, devotees have been so indoctrinated by revivalist mantras such as "God offends the mind to reveal the heart" that they fail to ask themselves why God doesn't just restore people's teeth as opposed to filling them with gold or silver. As should be obvious, gold and silver fillings are a human solution to a decayed tooth. Surely the Creator of the universe can provide a more suitable solution to tooth decay than one fraught with side effects produced by placing metals in the mouth.[24] When Christ healed the blind man in John 9, he didn't give him a super-duper pair of spectacles; he restored his sight. Likewise, when Jesus healed the paralytic in Luke 5, he did not give him a diamond-studded gold crutch. It stands to reason therefore that if God were healing teeth, he would restore them to their natural or original state.

The tragedy of the Counterfeit Revival is that its devotees are looking for experience in all the wrong places. The real experience is not found in counterfeit fads but in Christian fundamentals. First and foremost the body of Christ must rediscover the joy of genuine worship by developing a passion for authentic prayer. The Tuesday evening prayer meetings at Brownsville Assembly of God near Pensacola, Florida, involve a practice known as "sweeping the sanctuary," in which groups of people in militaristic fashion join hands and walk throughout the sanctuary and campus to bind hindering spirits that would threaten the revival.[25] But genuine prayer is not about binding Satan or other sensationalistic ventures; it is the genuine submission of our will to the will of the Master as revealed in his Word. The Scriptures not only form the foundation of an effective prayer life, but they are foundational to every other aspect of Christian living. While prayer is our primary way of communicating with God, the Scriptures are God's primary way of communicating with us. Nothing should take precedence over getting into the Scriptures and getting the Scriptures into us.

One of the most important means of getting the Scriptures into us involves the faithful pulpit ministry of the local church. Unlike Pensacola's propensity for severe holiness preaching based on emotional anecdotes, a genuine pulpit ministry must maintain substantive Bible-centered instruction week in and week out. We need more than exposure to intensely emotional sermons in order to sustain a healthy Christian life.

As we rediscover the power of prayer and renew a passion for Scripture, we also need to rededicate ourselves to experiencing fellowship as a community of faith. We ought not think that we can find quick-fix solutions to our often distant and troubled relationships. Running off to Pensacola for an impartation to bring back to our home church is not the biblical prescription for healthy fellowship.[26] Neither is the real experience found in focusing *in* on ourselves. Rather, the genuine biblical experience is found through focusing *out* on others. The question we should be asking is not, "What can an esoteric experience in church do for me?" but, "How can I use my experiences for the edification of others?"

If more than 1.8 million[27] people have experienced the Pensacola Outpouring in some way, one would never know it from examining the immediate vicinity of Brownsville. When I was in Pensacola, I personally interviewed a number of people on the street within a block from the Brownsville Assembly of God church.[28] None of them had been positively impacted in the least by the so-called revival. Others who say they have canvassed the Brownsville neighborhood report similarly.[29]

In the revivalism of the early Christian church, one distinguishing characteristic stood out above all others. It was the passion to communicate the love, joy, and peace that only Christ can bring to the human heart. As we find ourselves entrenched in an era of esotericism, it is essential that the church awaken to the ultimate experience—the experience of being used as a tool in the hands of Almighty God in the process of transforming lives.

As you immerse yourself in the pages that follow, it is my prayer that you will become so familiar with genuine revival that when a counterfeit appears on the horizon, you will recognize it instantaneously.

Acknowledgments

As the father of nine children, I have a deep appreciation for what Kathy, my wife, goes through in bringing new life into the world. I observed this magnificent miracle once again while revising *Counterfeit Revival*. As my daughter Grace was being delivered, I marveled at Kathy's strength and stamina. She immediately expressed gratitude for her family, her friends, and her heavenly Father. Without them, the process would have been next to impossible.

While a book is not equivalent to a baby, I feel a similar sense of gratitude for my family, my friends, and my heavenly Father. This book could not have been "birthed" without them.

First, I am deeply grateful for Kathy and the kids: Michelle, Katie, David, John Mark, Hank Jr., Christina, Paul Steven, Faith, and baby Grace. They demonstrated remarkable patience during the entire research and writing process.

Furthermore, I am grateful to Gretchen Passantino for her experience as an editor and her willingness to be a sounding board as I analyzed an extraordinarily complex phenomenon; Tom Stipe for his insights into the Vineyard movement; Paul

Young, Bob Hunter, Stephen Ross, Elliot Miller, Sandy Torres, and the rest of my staff for their prayerful support.

Finally, I am grateful to my heavenly Father for giving me the strength and stamina to be of service.

Before You Begin

I can't ever remember feeling more physically worn out. I was beginning to think that something was desperately wrong. Perhaps I had contracted a dread disease. Maybe I even had cancer. For the first time in years, I felt concerned enough to do something. So I made an appointment at an internationally famous healthcare center in Dallas, Texas, that seemed perfectly suited to my needs. They promised that in less than twenty-four hours they would have me completely checked out. I had every assurance that the world-renowned founder of the clinic would be able to diagnose the problem quickly and prescribe a cure.

At the conclusion of an exhausting day of testing, I sat across from him in his office as he shuffled through the reams of test results in my folder. "Hank," he said as he looked up slowly, "I have some good news and some bad news. The good news is we haven't been able to find any major problems. You don't have cancer. You don't have diabetes. Your arteries are in relatively good condition. In short, you are fortunate that you haven't done any permanent damage to your health.

"The bad news is, if you want to live long enough to see

your children grow up, you need to start making some important lifestyle changes—now! You need more rest. You need to start eating properly. And you need to get involved in a regular exercise—"

Before he could finish his sentence, I interrupted him. "Doc," I said, "that's precisely the problem. I don't have time for all that. I'm trying desperately to condition my body to function with *less* sleep, not more. As it is, I resent how sleep robs me of time and productivity. As for eating right, you've got to remember, with my travel schedule, that's a virtual impossibility. And exercise? Get real! The only exercise I'll ever have time for is running through airports. The only way I could make the kind of lifestyle changes you're suggesting is to retire. What I need from you is something quick—a shot, a megadose of vitamins. You've got to have something."

He shook his head slowly. "Hank," he said, "there's something you need to understand. There *are* no shortcuts. For one thing, vitamins are designed to *supplement* a good diet, not to replace it. For another thing, if you don't start making permanent lifestyle changes today, you won't even make it to retirement. The bottom line is, you either get back to the basics of proper rest, proper diet, and proper exercise, or you forfeit your health."

While I should have walked out of the clinic feeling elated that my doctor had not discovered any serious problems, I departed feeling disillusioned. Perhaps, I thought, despite his reputation, my doctor was not all he was cracked up to be. Surely there must be someone who could make me feel better fast!

Dejectedly, I made the long trek back to southern California, arriving home just after dinner. I had barely kissed Kathy and hugged the kids when I heard the intrusive ring of the telephone. As Kathy left to answer it, I reminded her that I was too tired to talk to anyone.

A minute later she was back. "Hank," she said, "I know you're tired, but I think you should probably take this call."

I dragged myself to the den, picked up the telephone, and heard the familiar voice of my close friend Chuck. "I've got some great news," he exclaimed excitedly, "but first, how was your trip?" Reluctantly, I told Chuck that I had traveled all the way to Texas for nothing. Not only had I not found a solution for my fatigue, but on top of everything else, I now also had jet lag.

"It's interesting you would say that," interjected Chuck. "In fact, maybe that's the reason I felt so compelled to call you tonight! I really believe this is providential! You see, while you went all the way to Texas looking for a cure, the solution was right here in your own backyard. I'm telling you right now, yesterday was the most incredible day of my life. I honestly believe I've finally found the solution to all my problems. When I first heard about this guy, I wrote him off as a counterfeit. But somehow I got talked into going to see him. And I'm telling you, he's the real McCoy."

As tired as I was, I had to admit that Chuck's enthusiasm was becoming contagious. While I had initially hoped to cut the conversation short, my interest was piqued. I knew I had to find a more practical solution than what my doctor had given me, but already this was sounding too good to be true. If I had a dime for every person who's told me he's found the solution to life's problems, I'd be a millionaire. And the words of my doctor kept reverberating through my mind: "Hank, there *are* no shortcuts."

Chuck's words jarred me back to the present. "I'm telling you, Hank, *thousands,* no, *hundreds of thousands* of people have found what I've found. I'm telling you, it's the real thing. Truth is, you've probably already heard of him yourself. I mean, by now almost everyone has. His name is—"

Before Chuck could get the name out of his mouth, I interrupted him. "Don't even say it," I warned. "If I hear his name one more time, I think I'm going to be sick! If I've heard it once, I've heard it a thousand times. When will people wake up and realize that guys like that are phony? He's no more the answer to people's problems than a clever magician would be. Believe me, if you knew what I know, you'd never have gone to see this joker in the first place. Trust me. I know exactly how these guys fool the public. He may be from halfway around the world and have an intriguing accent, but he's definitely not the real thing."

Have you ever been shocked at the force of your own rhetoric? I was. Yet, when I paused to catch my breath, Chuck jumped back into the conversation, undaunted. As hard as I had tried to curb his enthusiasm, he appeared unfazed. "I want you to meet him," he pleaded. "He'll be in town through the end of the week. Do it for me. If nothing else, it will provide you with an amusing diversion. God knows you need it."

To this day, I don't know how Chuck convinced me. Maybe I finally realized just how badly I needed a diversion. Maybe I thought it would provide me with a tremendous illustration of how a spiritually sensitive person like Chuck could be duped. Or maybe it was his promise to arrange a private interview with the guy. Whatever it was, I was surprised to hear myself say, "Okay—I'll do it, but just for you."

After arranging to meet him for dinner Friday near the auditorium, I hung up the phone. I slowly shook my head as I reflected on the all-time low to which discernment had sunk. Chuck was the last person I thought would fall for a counterfeit. I went in search of my wife. "Kathy," I called, "guess what? We're going on a date Friday night."

"Where?" she asked in disbelief.

I responded with a twinkle in my eye, "If I told you, you wouldn't believe it. Just get a baby-sitter and be ready for a trip into the world of mental manipulation."

Over the next few days, I fell into my rigorous routine of research, radio, and reading. Before I knew it, it was Friday night, and Kathy and I, late as usual, dashed into the restaurant where Chuck and his wife were waiting nervously.

When Chuck spotted us, a look of relief flooded his face.

"Boy, am I glad to see you guys. I was beginning to think you weren't going to show up."

As we wolfed down our dinners, Chuck assured us that he had been able to arrange reserved seating in the auditorium. I wasn't sure if my growing indigestion was the result of inhaling my dinner or of Chuck's grating enthusiasm.

In the time it had taken us to finish dinner, the parking lot across the street had filled with thousands of cars. I bit my tongue, resisting the urge to voice what I was thinking. *P. T. Barnum was right: "Never underestimate the gullibility of the public"—or was it, "There's a sucker born every minute"?*

It was still twenty minutes before "show" time, but a veritable army of people flocked through the six entrances to the auditorium.

Security led us past the crowd and through a private entrance to the auditorium. As promised, our seats were front row and center. I could not help but feel conspicuous as people immediately began whispering and pointing in my direction. It didn't take a rocket scientist to figure out what they were thinking.

Surprisingly, I was also feeling uncomfortable at the stark contrast between my own hardened cynicism and the crowd's sense of expectancy. I was actually beginning to second-guess myself. Perhaps I *was* too skeptical. Why couldn't I be like everyone else and approach the evening the way they did?

All around me, people were buzzing with anticipation. Those who, like Chuck, had been to previous meetings were filling in newcomers about what they would soon be experiencing. A cacophony of sounds, splintered conversations, and random outbursts of laughter reverberated through the auditorium. I spotted a well-known local pastor across the aisle and marveled again at the apparent gullibility of so many seemingly intelligent and discerning people. Were they all just invincibly ignorant . . . or was it me?

Refrains of familiar choruses broke down my resistance

even further. The songs, interspersed with testimonials, seemed incredibly compelling. I glanced at my watch as the lights dimmed. Already the better part of an hour had flown by. The atmosphere was electric with expectation. Suddenly a voice boomed through the auditorium. It sounded amazingly like Charlton Heston delivering the commandments from Mount Sinai. "The best . . . the only . . . the unbelievable . . . the greatest . . ." I was amazed at the number of superlatives that were packed into the ninety-second introduction. The announcer paused dramatically. "And now, please join me in extending a warm southern California welcome to . . ." The name was lost in an explosion of applause.

From the start, the crowd seemed like putty in his hands. I was amazed at his commanding presence as well as by the control he exerted over the audience. Even those who, like me, were there under protest seemed genuinely impressed. The skepticism etched on their faces grudgingly gave way to smiles. Soon some of them were even laughing robustly along with everyone else. As determined as I was not to let go, I could not help smiling a time or two myself. There was no doubt about it. The laughter was downright infectious.

It wasn't long before the star of the evening began to call the more demonstrative people forward. The clamor for attention reached a fevered pitch as people strove desperately to get noticed. It was painfully obvious that the chosen few were willing to do whatever he commanded—no matter how outrageous. The pastor I had spotted earlier in the evening had thrown off all of his usual ministerial decorum and now whirled around the stage, howling like a dog. Others stumbled through the auditorium as though in a drunken stupor. One woman, who had lost all sense of modesty, thrashed around on the floor in total abandon.

I was amazed at the power this guy seemed to hold over people. His enthusiasm and encouragement seemed to egg them on to new heights of absurdity. He merely pointed in their direction, and they immediately began to jerk spasmodically. At one point he blew into his microphone, and an entire row of people keeled over in an apparent supernatural faint. As he worked the crowd, laughter echoed eerily through the auditorium.

His mental and musical manipulation was choreographed to the very last detail. One moment he would tell us, "I wouldn't dupe you"; the next he provided empirical proof that he knew just how to push people's buttons. Like a master magician, he employed embedded commands to cause even the most wary subjects to succumb to his control. Although he seemed to know every trick of the trade, he was particularly adept at using peer pressure to elicit desired responses from his willing subjects.

I was so entranced by his performance that I lost all track of time. As much as I hated to admit it, the evening's performance was among the most powerful I had ever witnessed.

By the time it was over, I was champing at the bit to meet this guy up close and personal. After the last person exited the auditorium, we met backstage. He had shed his jacket and was mopping his face with a towel, still flushed from the exuberance of a successful performance. I impatiently endured the small talk and introductions. Impulsively, I blurted out, "Over the years I've been exposed to some of the best con men, illusionists, and religious charlatans around. But you've taken this to a whole new dimension. I thought I'd seen it all, but tonight I experienced things I never even knew existed. I want to know how in the world you pulled this off!"

Although stunned by my bluntness, he recovered quickly. He methodically completed wiping his face then calmly handed the towel to his attendant. "I see your reputation doesn't do you justice," he began. "I can't remember when I've been approached more directly."

"Listen," I interrupted, "I have seen performers break the fourth wall. I've seen them use altered states of consciousness, peer pressure, expectations, and suggestion to great effect. But never before have I seen so many people completely mesmerized . . ."

Before I could finish my sentence, his broadening grin erupted into a chuckle. "That's high praise, coming from you. Truth is, however, there's nothing particularly supernatural about what I do. Quite frankly, I've done it so often it's become second nature to me. In fact, maybe that's why I'm always billed as," he gave a dramatic pause, and then his voice boomed, "TONY ANGELO—THE WORLD'S GREATEST STAGE HYPNOTIST!"

Right now you should be experiencing the full impact of what it feels like to be fooled. That was my primary purpose for crafting this elaborate con. I wanted you to know experientially just how easy it is to be fooled, given the right set of circumstances. In this case the context was the key to the con.

The context is this book, *Counterfeit Revival*. Thus, your natural assumption has been that I am writing about my experience with one of its leaders rather than my experience with "THE WORLD'S GREATEST STAGE HYPNOTIST."

Just as you were misled by the context of my story, so too you can be misled within the context of the church. You expect to be fooled by a magician or mentalist at a local carnival; you are not as likely to expect to be fooled by a missionary or minister at a local church. And that is precisely why what is happening today in the church is so alarming.

Thousands thronging into churches assume they are safe and secure. John Arnott, a leader in the Counterfeit Revival, enhances this false sense of security by urging followers not to "even entertain the thought that [they] might get a counterfeit."[1]

In stark contrast to Arnott, John the Apostle warns, "Dear friends, do not believe every spirit, but test the spirits to see whether they are from God, because many false prophets have gone out into the world" (1 John 4:1). This warning is particularly relevant today, as Christianity is undergoing a paradigm shift of major proportions—a shift from faith to feelings, from fact to fantasy, and from reason to esoteric revelation. This paradigm shift is what I call the Counterfeit Revival.

Prophets of the Counterfeit Revival claim that the entire Christian community is going to be polarized by a bloody civil war. On one side will be those who embrace new revelations. On the other will be those who obstinately cling to reason. One "prophet" went so far as to say: "God is going to renovate the entire understanding of what Christianity is in the nations of the Earth. . . . In twenty years there will be a totally different understanding of Christianity as we know it."[2]

Some of the most recognizable names in the Christian community are endorsing this paradigm shift with little or no reservation. The appeal is so staggering that churches on every continent are now inviting their people to "experience" God in a brand-new way. As of 1997, it was estimated that seven thousand churches in England alone have embraced the Counterfeit Revival.[3] And with each passing day the numbers are escalating dramatically.

Sardonic laughter, spasmodic jerks, signs and wonders, super apostles and prophets, and people being "slain in the spirit" are pointed to as empirical evidence of the power and presence of the Holy Spirit. The form and function of the church is being so radically rearranged that even the secular world has taken note.

Time magazine, in an article titled "Laughing for the Lord," pointed out that Anglican parishes across England today bear a greater resemblance to "rock concerts" and "rugby matches" than to Christian worship. The article says that sanctuaries throughout the world are littered with bodies as "supplicants sob, shake, roar like lions and strangest of all, laugh uncontrollably."[4] *Newsweek,* in an article titled "The Giggles Are for God," reported that people in churches worldwide were jerking spasmodically, dancing ecstatically, and acting like animals. The article reported that this behavior by Christians has already spread from Canada to "roughly 7,000 congregations in Hong Kong, Norway, South Africa and Australia, plus scores of churches in the United States."[5]

Newspapers from the *Orlando Sentinel* to the *Dallas Morning News* have written stories on what is termed the "fastest-growing trend within Christianity." According to the *New York Times,* this trend promotes an "experiential" Christianity that "promises an emotional encounter with God" manifested by "shaking, screaming, fainting and falling into trances."[6]

Even secular TV broadcasts around the world are exploring the shift from the age of exposition to an age of experience. Phil Donahue's vast television audience laughed in amazement as they viewed what he referred to as God's children falling for the Lord.[7]

In Australia, *60 Minutes* reported the transformation taking place within the body of Christ as "possibly the fastest growing revival in the history of Christianity."[8] In America, ABC News aired a prime-time television special titled "In the Name of God." Host Peter Jennings asked his audience to decide whether churches seeking "to attract sellout crowds are in danger of selling out the gospel." He went on to ask if the changes he had documented may be "compromising the essence of Christianity."[9]

The answer to the questions being posed by men like Jennings, tragically, must be answered in the affirmative. As secular television cameras demonstrate to a watching world, the essence of our faith is being systematically subverted. With alarming speed Christianity is taking on the barnacles of the culture. Rather than recognizing that our mandate as Christians is to conform the culture to Christ, multitudes hail the changing face of Christianity as a mighty revival. With sadness I have had to point out to Jennings and others that what they are being told is a "great awakening" is, in reality, a great apostasy. Genuine revival will not take place until the body of Christ undergoes genuine reformation.

My passion for writing *Counterfeit Revival* is best summed up by Abraham Kuyper, who more than a century ago penned the following words:

> When principles that run against your deepest convictions begin to win the day, then battle is your calling, and peace has become sin; you must, at the price of dearest peace, lay your convictions bare before friend and enemy, with all the fire of your faith.[10]

Charting the Course

With every book, either the writer or the reader struggles. As with my former book *Christianity in Crisis,* I am committed to doing all I can to ensure that the struggle is mine. My objective has been to pen *Counterfeit Revival* in a way that encourages you to read it from cover to cover, provides you with accurate documentation in context, and presents the material in a memorable format.

No admiral worth his salt would set out to sea before first charting the course. Likewise, I want you to have a clear understanding of where we are going and how we are going to get there. To make the material in *Counterfeit Revival* memorable, I've developed the acronym FLESH. This acronym will serve to distinguish the genuine work of the Spirit from the counterfeit work of the FLESH (Gal. 5:19–26):

Part One	**F**abrications, Fantasies, and Frauds
Part Two	**L**ying Signs and Wonders
Part Three	**E**ndtime Restorationism
Part Four	**S**lain in the Spirit
Part Five	**H**ypnotism

Part One: Fabrications, Fantasies, and Frauds

Leaders of the Counterfeit Revival have peppered their preaching and practice with fabrications, fantasies, and frauds, seemingly unaware of their profound consequences. Many of the followers who at first flooded into Counterfeit Revival "power centers" have become disillusioned, and some have now slipped through the cracks into the kingdom of the cults. They no longer know what to believe or whom to trust and secretly fear that the untrustworthiness of those who claim to be God's representatives translates into the untrustworthiness of God himself. When selling and sensationalism become more tantalizing than truth, the very fabric of our faith is compromised.

While the Counterfeit Revival is founded on fabrications, fantasies, and frauds, genuine revival always rests firmly on the foundation of faith and facts.

Part Two: Lying Signs and Wonders

Leaders of the Counterfeit Revival appeal to Jonathan Edwards to validate their lying signs and wonders. Edwards, however, believed that the very kind of signs and wonders to which they appeal contributed significantly to the fall of the First Great Awakening. While imprudences and irregularities were by-products in the First Great Awakening, in the Second they were the bottom line. Like Edwards, nineteenth-century circuit rider Peter Cartwright dogmatically denounced lying signs and wonders wherever he encountered them. Rather than trying to produce them, he said, "It was, on all occasions, my practice to recommend fervent prayer as a remedy."[1] The lying signs and wonders Edwards and Cartwright denounced have taken center stage in today's Counterfeit Revival. Tragically, the deceptions are not limited to revisionary history; they extend to visionary hoaxes as well.

While the Counterfeit Revival finds its validation in lying signs and wonders, genuine revival always finds its genesis in the Living Word.

Part Three: Endtime Restorationism

Endtime restorationism—the belief that at the end of the age God will restore supernatural signs, super apostles, and prophets—is a key ingredient in the mythology of the Counterfeit Revival. In the early morning hours of the first day of the twentieth century, Charles Parham laid his hand on a young woman named Agnes Ozman, and she began to speak Chinese. When she tried to write, only Chinese characters emerged from her pen. Parham was utterly convinced that Ozman's experience was a prelude to global revival and a precursor to endtime restorationism. It was believed that Christians need only receive the gift of tongues and they could go to the farthest corners of the world and preach in languages they had never learned. By the middle of the twentieth century, another hoax took center stage. Men like A. A. Allen, William Branham, and Jack Coe perpetrated the myth that a restoration of healing would lead to a final Pentecost greater than the first. In the twilight of the twentieth century, Counterfeit Revival leaders began to teach that God is restoring super apostles and prophets to the endtime church. The claim has been made that

> No prophet or apostle who ever lived equaled the power of these individuals in this great army of the Lord in these last days. No one ever had it, not even Elijah or Peter or Paul, or anyone else enjoyed the power that is going to rest on this great army.[2]

While the Counterfeit Revival presumes an endtime restoration, genuine revival is predicated on earnest repentance.

Part Four: Slain in the Spirit

Today thousands of people are being "slain in the spirit" in the name of a fashionable and palpable demonstration of Holy Ghost power. Vineyard founder John Wimber, for one, claims to have found ample validation for this phenomenon in Scripture, church history, and his own experiences. After years of observation, he has determined that while followers fall backward, leaders invariably fall forward. He even claims to have seen a man converted after he was "lifted and flung thirty feet across the floor and slammed against a wall."[3] While Counterfeit Revival leaders like Wimber attribute the "slain in the spirit" phenomenon to the Holy Ghost, in reality it has much more in common with Hindu gurus, hucksters, and hypnotists. Counterfeit Revival leaders use sociopsychological manipulation as well as a variety of Scripture-twisting tactics to dupe their devotees. Even the *Dictionary of Pentecostal and Charismatic Movements* candidly notes that "an entire battalion of Scripture proof texts is enlisted to support the legitimacy of the phenomenon, although Scripture plainly offers no support for the phenomenon as something to be expected in the normal Christian life."[4] Despite the pious attribution of this phenomenon to the Holy Spirit as well as the pragmatic addition of "catchers," multitudes continue to suffer spiritual, emotional, and physical damage from this practice. Some have even died.

While the Counterfeit Revival is fixated on sensational manifestations like being "slain in the spirit," genuine revival is focused on salvation and sanctification in the Spirit.

Part Five: Hypnotism

Today's hypnotists not only operate in carnivals and communes, they also operate in churches. What was once relegated to the ashrams of cults is now replicated at the altars of churches. Whether they are referred to as Hindu gurus or Holy Ghost bartenders, the methods they employ have much in common. They all work subjects into altered states of consciousness, use peer pressure to conform them to predictable patterns, depend heavily on arousing people's expectations, and abuse the power of suggestion to make subjects willing to accept virtually anything that enters their minds. Cynics may write off the use of altered states of consciousness, peer pressure, expectations, and suggestive powers as mere sociopsychological manipulation, but Christians must perceive an even more significant threat—these techniques are fertile soil for satanic and spiritual deception.

While leaders of the Counterfeit Revival enslave devotees through hypnotic schemes, leaders of genuine revival enlighten disciples through Holy Scripture.

———

While multitudes clamor for a massive *revival,* what the body of Christ desperately needs is a mighty *reformation.* Only as the church is reformed will the culture be revived. The real experience is not found in the works of the FLESH; rather, it is found in the basic fundamentals. First, the body of Christ must rediscover the joy of genuine worship through a passion for prayer, praise, and the proclamation of the Word. Furthermore, we must rededicate ourselves to experiencing oneness in community and confession and in the contribution of our time, talent, and treasure. Finally, we must rediscover the ultimate experience of transforming lives by bearing witness to what we believe, why we believe, and whom we believe. While multitudes look for God in all the wrong places, the real experience is found in worship, oneness, and witness—WOW!

PART ONE

Fabrications, Fantasies, and Frauds

CHAPTER 1

The Holy Ghost Bartender

The scene was surreal. It looked as if a bomb had exploded. Bodies were strewn haphazardly throughout the sanctuary. Some lay motionless on the ground. Others twitched spasmodically. Behind me a woman shrieked, "I'm hot! I'm hot!" In front of me a girl was shaking violently. A boy standing in the aisle chopped his hands feverishly at some imaginary object. Next to him a man whirled round and round in a circle. All the while waves of sardonic laughter cascaded eerily throughout the sanctuary.

A boy staggered drunkenly across the platform and collapsed at the feet of a man who called himself the "Holy Ghost Bartender." The "Bartender" screamed, "Git 'em, Jesus! Git 'em, git 'em, git 'em!" Suddenly he spun around and commanded two musclebound men to rise. "These men," he said, "are my guardian angels." Then, as if on cue, he moved deliberately in my direction. What happened next was best described by a charismatic pastor who was an eyewitness: "I witnessed a stalking [by] a barroom bully."

When the Holy Ghost Bartender (who also refers to himself as the Holy Ghost Hitman) arrived at my seat, he began threatening to have me thrown out of the sanctuary. "I'm telling you right now," he hissed, "you'll drop dead if you prohibit what God is doing!"[1] Dramatically he gestured toward the crowd and warned them that those like me, who would dare to question that what he was doing was of God, had committed the unpardonable sin and would not be forgiven in this world or the next.

The following day he crowed, "The last time I had a confrontation like that . . . was . . . with a bunch of Mormons . . . you could see their spirit, y'know . . . just a really religious, pharisaical spirit, that's what it is. Amen? . . . And I smelt it—y'know, I can smell them religious devils from about a hundred yards—I could smell them blindfolded, man. . . . You could see, last night we meant business."[2] He labeled his critics "idiots" and warned that they were about to experience either "riot or revival."[3]

The Fire Falls

What Rodney Howard-Browne refers to as "revival" had its genesis in July of 1979. At the age of seventeen, he says he gave God Almighty an ultimatum: "Either You come down here and touch me or I am going to come up there and touch You."[4] He began to shout over and over again, "God, I want your power!"[5] He shouted until he was hoarse, frightening nearly everyone present. Howard-Browne recounts that suddenly:

> The fire of God came on me. It started on my head and went right down to my feet. His power burned in my body and stayed like that for four days. I thought I was going to die. I thought He was going to kill me. . . . My whole body was on fire from the top of my head to the soles of my feet and out of my belly began to flow a river of living water. I began to laugh uncontrollably and then I began to weep and then speak

with other tongues. . . . I was so intoxicated on the wine of the Holy Ghost that I was beside myself. The fire of God was coursing through my whole being and it didn't quit. . . . Because of this encounter with the Lord, my life was radically changed from that day on.[6]

According to young Howard-Browne, the anointing he received was so powerful that he had to beg God to lift it off of him so he would live. "The best way I can describe it," he said, "is that it was as shocking as if I had unscrewed a light bulb from a lamp and put my finger in the socket."[7]

Fortunately for Howard-Browne, God lifted the full force of the anointing and spared his life. God then asked Howard-Browne for "an opportunity to move."[8] God instructed Howard-Browne to get people "saturated"[9] and not to lift his hands off people until they were "drunk in the Holy Ghost."[10] From the day Howard-Browne was "plugged into heaven's electric light supply," his "desire has been to go and plug other people in."[11]

In 1980, God supposedly gave Howard-Browne "a taste of what will come later on in your ministry."[12] A woman in a Methodist church asked him to pray for her. He lifted up his hand "like a gunslinger would draw a gun out of a holster"[13] and pointed it at the woman. Immediately:

It felt like my fingertips came off. I felt a full volume of the anointing flow out of my hand. The only way I can explain it is to liken it to a fireman holding a fire hose with a full volume of water flowing out of it. The anointing went right into her. It looked like someone had hit her in the head with an invisible baseball bat and she fell to the floor.[14]

Howard-Browne suddenly began to get nervous. Referring to his hand, he said, "I'd better look out where I point this thing. This thing's loaded now."[15] Despite his caution, Howard-Browne ended up "shooting" every member of his ministry team. Then at the prompting of God he proceeded to lay his finger on everyone in the church. "They hit the floor just like someone had slammed them in the head with a Louisville Slugger."[16]

Some of the people were pinned to the floor, some were inebriated in the spirit, and yet others began to speak in tongues.

Sometime later God allegedly spoke to Howard-Browne and said, "This is a shadow of what is to come."[17] Howard-Browne related that God was holding back because "if he gave it to me now, I would be like a four-year-old with a shotgun. I would blow everything up, including myself."[18] As Howard-Browne purportedly put it, "for an eighteen-year-old to experience that kind of anointing—it's dangerous."[19]

Thus, for the time being, God pulled the plug on the power. It wasn't until a decade later that Howard-Browne claims the power returned in full force. By this time Howard-Browne had moved from South Africa to America and, by his own admission, had a ministry that was nothing to write home about. Despite that fact, when the unusual manifestations resurfaced, Howard-Browne became indignant. Speaking to the Almighty, he said, "God, You're ruining my meetings!"[20]

God retorted, "Son, the way your meetings are going, they're worth ruining."[21]

And ruin them he did! In Albany, New York, two people were merely walking down a church aisle when God enveloped them in a "thick fog or mist" and they "fell out under the power."[22] In a meeting in New Jersey, people began to "jump out of wheelchairs without anyone touching them."[23] At times the anointing of the Holy Spirit would blow into buildings so powerfully that Howard-Browne had to hold on to the podium "because it nearly blew me flat on the floor."[24] One time the power of God hit a whole row of people, causing them to fall on their backs "before the ushers could catch them."[25]

Howard-Browne says that even he was "amazed" at what happened when he prayed for people. At times they would be "picked up and thrown over three rows of chairs like a piece of rag."[26] On one occasion, while Howard-Browne was praying for a man, the power of God allegedly came over his shoulder like a whirlwind. The man saw it coming and tried to duck, but it was too late. The whirlwind "picked him up off the ground, level with my waist," said Howard-Browne, and "then it struck him to the ground. . . . I was shocked. As the power hit him, the first couple of rows all went out. It was like a Holy Ghost tornado came in there."[27]

That was only the beginning of the unusual manifestations. In addition to becoming drunk in the spirit, being knocked down by the spirit, and getting enveloped in the mist of the spirit, suddenly people were subjected to the "glue" of the spirit.

One of Howard-Browne's books has a section titled "Holy Ghost Glue."[28] In it he recounts the story of a wealthy woman who got "stuck" in the spirit. As Howard-Browne tells it:

> She was lying there from noon until 1:30. . . . At 1:30, she tried to get up. She wanted to get up. She couldn't. All she could do was flap her hands. So she was lying there flapping away—flap, flap, flap, flap. . . . 2:30, 3:30, 4:30. . . . At 4:30 the woman was still saying, "I can't get up. I'm stuck to the floor."[29]

She flapped so long that, as Howard-Browne put it, he ended up "walking out on the Holy Spirit":

> I turned to the pastor and said, "Look, I haven't had either breakfast or lunch. It's 4:30. I'm not stuck and you're not stuck. These people are going to stay here

with her, so let's go have a meal before the night service." The ushers told us later that at 6 o'clock the woman finally peeled herself off the carpet. Then it took her an hour to crawl from the center of the church auditorium to the side wall. She had been stuck to the floor for six hours! By 7 o'clock she couldn't talk in English anymore. She tried to talk, but only tongues came out of her mouth. She couldn't help it. She was totally filled—and totally inebriated, saturated, and drunk in the Holy Ghost! The ushers put her in the back row thinking that she wouldn't disturb anyone, but she interfered with everyone who came through the door.

I've never seen anything like it. Five women were sitting around her, were struck dumb—they couldn't talk. (Their husbands were rejoicing.)[30]

Spreading the Fire

This was but a glimpse of things to come. In 1990, Howard-Browne got one of his first major breaks when Benny Hinn invited him to speak at his church in Orlando, Florida. After again giving God permission to move, Howard-Browne began to scream, "Git 'em, Jesus! Git 'em, git 'em, git 'em!" As pastors and parishioners began to fall, laugh, and get drunk in the spirit, Howard-Browne commanded God to begin dispensing double—and even triple—doses of the "new wine."

In the heat of the moment Hinn rose and declared, "This is the Holy Ghost, people, I'm telling you. Lift your hands and thank him for this. This is the Holy Ghost here!"[31] Later on, however, things degenerated to such an extent that Hinn walked out of his sanctuary, vowing never to invite Howard-Browne back.[32]

Howard-Browne enjoyed another major breakthrough approximately one year later at a Kenneth Copeland convention.

Copeland laid hands on Howard-Browne, who fell to the floor. Copeland knelt down beside him and prophesied that a spirit sent by Satan to hold Howard-Browne back would no longer hurt and hinder him. Copeland, claiming to be speaking for the Almighty, said, "The greater realm that you've been seeing all evening long is the stage set before you that I've called you to walk in, and this is only the beginning. It is only the start of the outpouring that has already begun of the former and the latter rain."[33]

The very next day, God allegedly confirmed Copeland's prophecy by speaking through Howard-Browne:

> "This is the day, this is the hour," saith the Lord, "that I am moving in this earth. This is the day that I'll cause you to step over into the realm of the supernatural. . . . The drops of rain are beginning to fall to the glory of God. Yes, yes, many of you that have sat on the threshold and have said, 'Oh, God, when should it be?' Oh, you know that this is the day and this is the hour that you'll step over into that place into my glory. For this is the day of the glory of the Lord coming in great power. . . . For I'm going to break the mold," saith the Lord, "on many of your lives and many of your ministries. And even that which was known, the way that you operated in days gone by— oh, many shall rub their eyes and shall look and say, 'Is this the same person that we used to know?' Oh, for there's a fire on the inside of them. For this is the day of the fire and the glory of God coming unto His Church. Rise up this day in great boldness. Rise up this day and be filled afresh with the new wine of the Holy Ghost. Rise up this day. . . . To drink, to drink, to drink, to drink, to drink, to drink, to drink, to drink, to drink [tongues]. We drink . . . [tongues] [he laughs]. O yea, yea, yea, yea, yea, we don't worry about what

other people say. No, it doesn't matter what they think. Ha, ha, ha, ho, oooh [tongues]."[34]

The Big Time

The "big break" that would propel Howard-Browne into international visibility happened in the spring of 1993.[35]

Charisma magazine reported that Howard-Browne's "rise to fame began . . . during a watershed meeting at Carpenter's Home Church in Lakeland, Florida."[36] Laughter in the spirit caught on there, "jetting Howard-Browne, 33, out of obscurity, whisking him from Alaska to the Pentagon."[37]

Assemblies of God pastor Karl Strader invited Howard-Browne to preach and perform at Carpenter's Home Church in its ten-thousand-seat auditorium. At the time Strader was struggling professionally through the trauma of a church split.[38] In addition he was struggling personally with what *Charisma* magazine reported as his son's arrest for racketeering charges "stemming from an alleged pyramid scheme involving more than $3.7 million."[39] Howard-Browne's revival rhetoric provided Strader with just the release he thought he needed. According to Strader's friends Charles and Frances Hunter (popular charismatic leaders known as the Happy Hunters), "he had spent six weeks on the floor of his church laughing, having the most wonderful time of his life."[40]

While Howard-Browne apparently provided Strader with a chance to laugh at his problems, Strader provided Howard-Browne with the opportunity to finally capture his claims on camera. As thousands looked on, however, Howard-Browne's claims of the miraculous did not materialize. No mighty, rushing wind blew into the auditorium, causing Howard-Browne to hold on to the podium so that he would not be blown flat on the floor. No one was picked up and thrown over three rows of chairs like a piece of rag. People did not "jump out of wheelchairs without anyone touching them,"[41] and no one was raised from the dead. Instead, Howard-Browne was relegated to re-suscitating tales of bygone miracles as well as delivering a litany of well-rehearsed jokes.

One thing Howard-Browne did produce, however, was an epidemic of "spiritual drunkenness." In response to his cries of "Fill, fill, fill! More, more, more!" or "Git 'em, Jesus! Git 'em, git 'em, git 'em!" a growing number of people began to mani-fest signs of intoxication. Some fell to the floor in uncontrol-lable laughter while others got stuck in "Holy Ghost glue." As Howard-Browne commanded God to give people double and triple doses of his "new wine," some even went "dumb in the spirit." Most notable among them was Pastor Strader, who struggled pathetically to speak but could only emit unintelli-gible grunts. Eventually, when he came to himself, Strader declared this extravaganza to be "the greatest move of God I've ever seen. It was like something in the history books." Strader went on to report that at two in the morning Howard-Browne could still be found baptizing people who were "dead drunk," having them fished from the water, and then stacking them, wet, on the platform.[42]

Despite the absence of "Holy Ghost tornadoes" and "spiri-tual levitation . . . news of Howard-Browne's success spread quickly on the charismatic grapevine."[43] The laughter that erupted in Lakeland was enough to draw thousands of spiri-tually starved saints to the church sanctuary. What was origi-nally scheduled to be a week's worth of meetings eventually stretched into three months.[44]

The wine served up by the Holy Ghost Bartender in Lake-land had only begun to ferment.

CHAPTER 2

The Party

Lakeland, Florida, had suddenly become the destination of choice. Christian leaders from America, Africa, Australia, Argentina, and elsewhere began to make pilgrimages to Florida to witness the "bizarre emotional displays"[1] firsthand. Among them was Richard Roberts, the president of Oral Roberts University (ORU), who was struggling under the weight of a forty-million-dollar debt inherited from his father, Oral. After his introduction to Lakeland's laughter, "Roberts says he ended up on the floor laughing at every Howard-Browne meeting as have members of his family."[2] Even during business meetings in which bad financial news was presented, Roberts would laugh so hard he would fall. The more he laughed, however, the more God would bring him money in mysterious ways. According to Roberts, he actually heard God say, "The same way that you're laughing now, you're going to laugh while I pay off your forty-million-dollar debt."[3] Addressing his host, Karl Strader, Roberts said, "I feel like you feel. I am going to laugh my way out of debt and into heaven in Jesus' name."[4] Roberts has continued to succumb to bouts of laughter on a regular basis. On a flight home from Lakeland, his laughter was so uncontrollable that not only the flight attendant but also the people around him thought something was wrong.[5]

Oral Roberts, who also attended the Lakeland meetings, was so enamored with Rodney Howard-Browne that he proclaimed that Howard-Browne's ministry signaled the arrival of "another level in the Holy Spirit."[6] Oral Roberts said that Howard-Browne was "raised up from a new kind of seed, with a new kind of revelation . . . yet a fresh wave."[7]

After seeing Howard-Browne perform in Lakeland, Richard and Oral invited him to come to Tulsa for a series of meetings at Oral Roberts University. There, according to Oral, Howard-Browne "touched the life of our student body, including our athletes. And nobody has *ever* touched our athletes. . . . And *all* of them got the holy laughter . . . thousands of 'em, and when he came by and said 'Fill!,' they fell in the spirit on the grounds."[8] The response, in fact, was so overwhelming that classes had to be canceled as students fell to the floor and laughed.

As Oral put it, "It's an unprecedented experience to be with this man. He has a commanding presence. He came to ORU, and at the end of his message he had the longest sustained applause in the history of ORU. . . . *No one* has ever had that kind of applause. There's no question about it. He changed my life and my son's life."[9]

Not only did Howard-Browne "change" Oral Roberts's life, but he had a dramatic impact on Roberts's nine-year-old granddaughter as well. When Howard-Browne laid hands on her, she fell to the ground and laughed for one hour and forty-five minutes. The impact of his touch was so dramatic that when her parents "tried putting her to bed, she fell out laughing," and they "finally had to put her in the bathtub."[10]

Marilyn Hickey, chairman of the board of regents of Oral Roberts University and author of *God's Seven Keys to Make You Rich,* was mightily touched by Rodney Howard-Browne in Lakeland as well. Hickey—who dispenses miracle prayer cloths, dresses in ceremonial breastplates as "points of contact," and demonstrates how Christians can create wealth by speaking to their wallets[11]—got extraordinarily excited about the laughter in Lakeland.[12] Hickey's life and that of her daughter, Sarah, were "dramatically changed"[13] as she "spent the entire time on the floor laughing."[14]

Karl Strader was so enthusiastic over the dramatic changes in the lives of these Christian superstars that he called the Happy Hunters and encouraged them "to come down and participate in this."[15] Strader told them that "Rodney Howard-Browne had been in his church for a total of thirteen weeks in one year and that not one of the people on his staff would ever be the same, because their lives were changed as a result of attending the meetings."[16] Incredibly, neither Charles nor Frances Hunter "felt anything" when Howard-Browne laid hands on them and said, "New beginnings!" Despite the fact that they experienced "no emotion, no laughter, no spine tingling sensation of having really been pounced upon by the Holy Spirit,"[17] the Hunters were impressed enough to label "holy" laughter an "End-Time Revival."[18] They concluded that in this revival

> The Spirit of God is swiftly moving in breathtaking and sometimes startling new ways, and people of every tongue and every nation are letting out what is on the inside of them. People of all races and denominations are radically falling in love with Jesus in a brand new way! They are running at a fast pace to "Joel's Bar" where the drinks are free and there is no hangover.[19]

Drinking and Driving

While the drinks dispensed by the Holy Ghost Bartender do not produce hangovers, churches, much like bars, find themselves recommending designated drivers to protect the lives of others as the spiritually inebriated go home. A large Assemblies of God church in Argentina provides a special taxi service to help people who are not fit to drive home. A large Anglican church in England (Holy Trinity Brompton) has the number of a taxi firm that understands its parishioners "are safe to have in the taxi."[20]

One woman singled out by Howard-Browne allegedly became intoxicated just listening to him on the radio. Her "drunken" driving was so pronounced that she was pulled over by a police officer. The woman apparently was so drunk that she had difficulty just rolling down her car window. When the officer tried to remove her from her car, he touched her and became so drunk himself that she had to lead him back to his patrol car.[21] Another story involves a "lady in similar circumstances asked to undertake a breathalyzer test. As she blew into the bag, the policeman fell to the ground laughing."[22]

Frances Hunter's acceptance of spiritual "drunkenness" is remarkable in light of the fact that she herself had been delivered from the "spirit of alcoholism." As she tells the story, when she was a new Christian, God took her martini sitting on the bar and "instantly turned that martini glass into a snake." When she refused to drink, "instantly the snake turned back into a martini."[23]

Since then, however, Frances, like so many others, has learned to drink "new wine" rather than martinis. Says Frances,

> More Christians are getting drunk on the Holy Spirit than anyone could ever dream possible! This new wine is filled with the genuine Holy Ghost power and everyone who has tasted it is enthusiastically encouraging everyone else to join them and have another drink, and then another drink! The world is hungry for the supernatural of God and that is the reason they are so enthusiastically and quickly jumping into this river of new wine.[24]

The Hunters dogmatically declare that we, like Jesus, must make the choice of letting "this cup pass"[25] or becoming a part of what God is doing. They urge us not merely to stick our "toe in to test the water" but to "jump all the way into this flowing river" and to follow "God into the greatest and most powerful move ever seen in the history of the church!"[26]

One pastor, who eventually jumped into the river of new wine, initially laughed at his poor wife, who "found herself stuck to the floor in the most heavenly, divine glue you could ever imagine."[27] Her husband lay on the stage, apparently enjoying himself, while watching his wife:

> Suddenly she tried to get up and got as far as a crawl position on her hands and knees, and then she froze right on the spot, completely unable to move. . . . She remained in exactly the same position for at least forty-five minutes. . . . She had stepped over into the majestic realm of the supernatural.[28]

As his "church was laughing so loudly it was impossible for him to be heard,"[29] this pastor then

> opened his Bible to 2 Cor. 9:7 and started to read about how God loves a cheerful giver. He never got beyond the first few words! He must have taken a big gulp of the new wine and it really hit him, and not only did he laugh, he discovered he was completely incapable of reading. He got so totally intoxicated with the Holy Spirit he finally had to give up. He couldn't even stand up.[30]

According to the Hunters, the laughter manifesting itself in Rodney Howard-Browne's meetings is nothing new. As they put it, their "hungry little spiritual pig hearts"[31] had drawn them to events in the past in which they had already experienced everything from lying on a "bed of Holy Ghost Glue"[32] to seeing amazing miracles through the "spirit of laughter."[33]

Lord, I Need a Miracle

One of the miracles involved a woman who allegedly grew a new breast while laughing: "I had a mastectomy last year and had my left breast removed, and while we were all laughing, God grew a new breast back on."[34]

The Hunters now admit that they do not have a shred of evidence to support this story,[35] but that has not kept them from circulating increasingly bizarre tales of other un-documented "holy" laughter healings.[36]

The Hunters claim that resisting this mighty move of God may well be futile. They recount the story of a pastor who publicly pronounced a Rodney Howard-Browne revival to be of the devil. As he "opened his Bible and started to teach . . . he fell over backwards and got stuck to the floor and started laughing uncontrollably. Then he managed to claw his way back and pulled himself over to the podium and looked at everybody and said, 'It's God, it's God, it's God, it's God!' "[37]

One of the key pastors touched by the Hunters was Colin Dye, touted as the pastor of "the largest church in England."[38] Dye not only "exploded with the greatest outburst of holy laughter"[39] the Hunters had ever seen, but also got drunk in the spirit and stuck in Holy Ghost glue. So impressed was Dye with his experience that he eventually "leaped up and said, 'Can I do the same thing and impart this laughter?' "[40] The Happy Hunters granted his wish and anointed Dye. Thereafter, the Hunters report, Dye was used by God "in one of the greatest demonstrations of Holy Spirit power we have ever seen."[41] The manifestations that went on inside one of the largest churches in England that day were allegedly so spectacular that church authorities "bolted the doors to keep the people out who were trying to break down the doors to get into this great move of God."[42]

One lady lucky enough to have gotten out of the snow and into the sanctuary that day was "an osteopath" who "had a brain tumor, excruciating pain and paralysis on her forehead and was blind in one eye."[43] After being ministered to by Charles Hunter, "the pain and the paralysis disappeared, and in just a few seconds, her sight returned."[44]

The Hunters claim that a group of twenty people from Ireland was so impressed with their power that they began to scream, "We want this anointing to take back to Ireland!"[45] The Hunters "anointed" people from Scotland, Switzerland, and Germany as well.[46]

When the Hunters flew to Holland, they "discovered that the Holy Spirit had jumped over the English Channel and arrived before we did, or at exactly the same time."[47] The Good News Centrum in Rotterdam was the site of further excitement:

> The air was electric with expectancy. News about London had traveled fast, and there were thirty people from Belgium at the meeting—they all came expecting! The head of the Hispanic churches of all Europe was there as well. . . .
>
> Sparks began to fly once again which struck the heart of *all* those in attendance! Holy Laughter broke out and Pastor John Howard ran up and asked us to anoint all the staff members of his church. . . . He was so hungry he wanted that anointing "right now."[48]

The Hunters reported that "the people from Belgium, all thirty of them, rushed forward and asked to be anointed to take the spark of revival back to their country." In fact, say the Hunters, the "power of God caused us to know that another spark had been ignited in another nation."[49]

No doubt even Karl Strader was later amazed at what resulted from simply picking up his phone and asking his close friends the Hunters to participate in what *Charisma* magazine dubbed "Laughter in Lakeland."

The Vatican of the Faith Movement

While the Holy Spirit allegedly was using the Happy Hunters to spread "holy" laughter throughout Europe, back home in America "holy" laughter got a powerful shot in the arm as well. Rodney Howard-Browne, himself a former associate pastor of a Word of Faith church in South Africa, was summoned to speak at the "Vatican" of Faith theology—Kenneth Hagin's Rhema Bible Training Center (located near Tulsa, Oklahoma).

Rodney Howard-Browne was tailor-made for Rhema. The parallels between his preaching and practice and those of Rhema's founder, Kenneth Hagin, are striking. Like Howard-Browne, Hagin is quick to pronounce divine judgment on those who dare to question his prophetic ministry. Hagin has gone so far as to predict the untimely death of a pastor who doubted his false doctrine. According to Hagin, "The pastor fell dead in the pulpit . . . because he didn't accept the message God's Spirit gave me to give him."[50]

Unlike Hagin, who claims to have received his techniques directly from Jesus, Rodney Howard-Browne appears to have copied his techniques from Smith Wigglesworth, whom Howard-Browne describes as "a wild man."[51] For example, Howard-Browne recounted one healing by Wigglesworth of a man who was dying of cancer: "Wigglesworth punched him in the stomach so hard he flew through the air and hit the floor, dead! He killed him!" His rendition of the story does not end there, however. According to Howard-Browne, ten minutes later the man was running around the church, healed.[52] Taking a page out of Wigglesworth's playbook, Howard-Browne once slapped a deaf person so hard the person fell flat on the floor. And it worked! The deaf person then got up totally healed.[53]

Years before Howard-Browne began popularizing "holy" laughter, Hagin preached and practiced "holy" laughter at Rhema. Thus, when Rodney Howard-Browne came to this "mecca" of Faith theology in August 1993, most of the people were well prepared for what he brought. One person, however, was not.

CHAPTER 3

The Vineyard Connection

Randy Clark had traveled to Rhema discouraged, disillusioned, and close to a complete breakdown. He was a burned-out pastor who, during the twenty-four years of his ministry, had gradually lost the fervency of his faith. The Bible no longer spoke to him, he no longer wanted to pray, and he did not like going to church. He was at Rhema for Rodney Howard-Browne's appearances only because of the persistent urging of a friend "who moved in power" and in "the gift of discernment."[1]

Clark's friend Jeff had discovered during a phone call with Clark how spiritually drained Clark was. Jeff knew just the solution. Jeff knew firsthand how powerfully the Holy Spirit moved when Rodney Howard-Browne preached. Jeff, at his own crisis point, had challenged God, "If I can't experience you . . . I don't want to live." Under Howard-Browne, Jeff had been spiritually "refreshed" and "refilled."[2]

Reluctantly, Randy Clark gave in and decided to attend Howard-Browne's next appearance. He was dismayed when he found out it was to be at Rhema. Clark was passionately opposed to the Faith movement; his agreeing to go to Rhema was like Daniel asking to be thrown into the lion's den. He was so against everything Rhema and Kenneth Hagin stood for that, as he later confessed while teaching in his church, "out of my mouth this demon would come forth and would say 'if you've come here to name it and claim it, blab it and grab it, confess it and possess it, you're in the wrong church.'"[3]

Clark now says that in the midst of his spiritual disillusionment, God rebuked him, saying, "You have a . . . denominational spirit if you think you can only drink of the well of your own . . . group."[4] God then asked Clark a very pertinent question: "How badly do you want me?"[5] Thus chastened by the Almighty, Clark made his pilgrimage to Rhema.

Randy, Rodney, and Rhema

To his own amazement, at Rhema Randy Clark "fell under the power" as Howard-Browne prayed for him. At first he doubted that the experience was real because he was not "shaking" and "hurting from electricity"[6] as he had during a similar experience at a Vineyard in 1989. However, the accompanying phenomena convinced Clark that this was a genuine encounter with the Holy Spirit. While he was "pinned to the floor," says Clark, "two bodies down from me there was somebody oinking!"[7] Clark immediately began laughing in the spirit and then got drunk in the spirit. In time, Clark got so drunk that he was actually afraid the police would arrest him on his way home.[8] Clark was uncomfortable with being drunk in the spirit because he worried that his earlier Baptist vow never to touch alcohol was in some way compromised by his drunken behavior—even though it came from God, not from a bottle.[9]

Despite his mixed feelings, Clark became convinced that it was vitally important that he be "touched" by God in a dramatic way during the meetings. He began to fast and gave God an ultimatum, telling him: "I'm not going to eat until you touch me."[10]

During one meeting, which Howard-Browne called a "Holy

Ghost Blowout," Howard-Browne prayed for each of the forty-five hundred attendees individually. Clark waited his turn in line, but was disappointed when Howard-Browne's command to "Fill, fill, fill!" produced no discernible reaction. He wasn't ready to give up, however, and so he got back in line for a second "blessing." Again, Howard-Browne blessed him. Again Randy Clark felt nothing. Clark managed to get in line a third time and finally a fourth time, encouraged by Howard-Browne's brother, Basil, who said, "That's all right; you look hungry."[11] The fourth time Howard-Browne blessed him, he fell down and later got up realizing that "he was emotionally healthy for the first time. Because of this, he realized that God was working, even though he wasn't experiencing any shaking."[12]

Clark's associate pastor, Bill Mares, who had accompanied him and received the blessing as well, couldn't wait to bring the Rhema experience back home. Clark, however, did not want to bring the manifestations into his church until he had spent six months preparing his people. When Mares said, "I can't wait that long," Clark pulled rank and countered, "I'm the senior pastor." God allegedly intervened then by impressing Clark with the words, "I'm God, and I'll do it when I want."[13]

We All Fall Down

And do it he did. Their first Sunday back, while the congregation was worshiping God, a woman on the worship team fell, knocked over a guitar stand, and began to laugh uncontrollably. As Clark pointed out, "she just didn't fall and lie still, she's laying there, doing this—Laughing!—Ha! Ha! Ha! Ha! Ha! Ha! Ha! Ha! All the way through forty-five minutes of worship, just continues to do this."[14] Although none of his people had ever fallen in church before, by the end of the service virtually everyone enthusiastically rushed forward to be touched by Clark, who recounted later, "WHOOOMP! Wall to wall people. . . . BOOOM! Boy, this is fun! BOOOM! BOOOM!

BOOOM!"[15] As Howard-Browne had touched Clark, Clark now touched his people, and they all fell down.

All, that is, except for one skeptical Christian named Daryl. Daryl stubbornly refused to laugh and would go forward to the front of the church only when it was time to partake of the Lord's Supper. During communion, however, God intervened in the life of Doubting Daryl—God froze him in the spirit, stuck him to the floor, and emotionally healed him as he suddenly remembered being sexually molested as a child. The floodgates of blessing had been opened, and for sixteen months Clark's church experienced exotic manifestations every single Sunday.[16]

The initial impact of Clark's visit to Rhema was merely a harbinger of things to come. A woman in his church who had been touched received a vision in which she saw Toronto, Canada. In her vision Toronto was "on fire and little blades of fire [were] going three-hundred-sixty degrees all over Canada."[17] Sure enough, not long after this vision, Clark received a call from a Vineyard pastor named John Arnott, whose church was located in Toronto, Canada.[18]

Arnott had heard about Clark's participation in a regional meeting of Vineyard churches in which every pastor, as well as all of their wives (except one), were touched by "drunkenness and partying."[19] Arnott wanted Clark to export these experiences to Canada.

A Wing and a Prayer

Pastor Clark, however, was afraid to step out as a guest leader because, as he put it, he had only "a testimony and maybe one other sermon."[20] Once again God intervened. This time, instead of speaking directly to him, God sent him a prophetic pronouncement through an intermediary. The pronouncement did not come through a Vineyard prophet, most of whose antics Clark classified as "weird." Instead, it came through a Baptist friend named Richard Holcomb, whose record of prophetic accuracy in the past was allegedly 100 percent.

Repeating himself three times, presumably for emphasis, God said (through Holcomb):

> Test me now. Test me now. Test me now. Do not be afraid. I will back you up. I want your eyes to be opened to see my spiritual resources in the heavenlies for you just as Elijah prayed that Gehazi's eyes would be opened. And do not become anxious, because when you become anxious you can't hear me.[21]

Expressing astonishment that the media had not yet picked up on the significance of this spiritual phenomenon, Clark later announced "that prophetic word" to be the very thing that "changed my life." Not even his emotional "healing" from a near-nervous breakdown when he had first seen Rodney Howard-Browne at Rhema could compare with its significance.[22] Randy Clark is now convinced that without this prophecy, he would not have made the transition from being an emotionally disturbed pastor to becoming the conduit through which the new wine of the Spirit would be dispensed to people who until now had never even conceived of Holy Ghost glue or divine drunkenness.

Within hours of the prophecy, Clark was in a van, headed to the airport on a mission that would forever change his life and the lives of multiplied millions of other people later touched by the "Toronto Blessing" as well. As he exclaimed to his traveling companions, "I want you guys to know we're going on an apostolic mission trip to another country. We're going to Canada and we're gonna see things like we have never seen before."[23]

Revival historian Richard M. Riss best summed up the significance of the prophetic phone call that changed Randy Clark's life: Without it, "the Toronto Revival would never have happened."[24]

The Runway in Toronto

Long before Randy Clark's January 1994 trip to Canada, Toronto Airport Vineyard Pastor John Arnott was being conditioned for what was to follow. As his wife, Carol, explains, "God also spoke to John and said, 'I want you to hang around people that have an anointing.'"[25]

According to Carol, God directed them back to an old friend named Benny Hinn, whom John "had ministered with in the early years."[26] Hinn had prayed for the Arnotts "fifty times, maybe,"[27] and his impact on their lives began to escalate dramatically. When Hinn would get through ministering to them backstage, Carol would be so drunk that John would have to carry her home. As he explained it during a pastor's conference, "I'd have to undress her and put her to bed, she was so out of it."[28] John, however, did not "feel anything."[29] While he would fall on the floor in front of Hinn just like everyone else, he was not really sure why. "It's like, I didn't know if he slammed me on the head or if the ushers pulled me back, or if I actually fell down, or if I just cooperated, or if there was so much psychological pressure in front of that many people that I just simply went with it."[30]

In June of 1993 John Arnott was prayed for by Rodney Howard-Browne, but the results were the same. Arnott lamented, "Two hundred and forty-eight people fell down, but I was still standing."[31] While he did not fall down, he did not give up in his quest for a supernatural experience with the Holy Spirit.

The Quest

In November of 1993 Arnott embarked on an expedition to Argentina, where he was prayed over by a Pentecostal pastor named Claudio Freidzon. If anyone could have identified with Arnott, it was Freidzon, who himself had undertaken a spiritual pilgrimage through which he received "an impartation of spiritual anointing from both Benny Hinn and Rodney Howard-Browne."[32]

After being touched by both Hinn and Howard-Browne, Freidzon started a crusade ministry characterized by manifestations of "uncontrollable laughter,"[33] the same kind of phenomenon that would eventually impact the lives of millions of people through the "Laughing Revival." Among those who were ministered to personally by Freidzon and who later became leaders of the Laughing Revival was John Arnott.

During an Argentinean pastors' conference organized by Luis Palau's brother-in-law, Ed Silvoso,[34] Claudio Freidzon asked Arnott "if he wanted this new empowerment, and if so to take it." While Carol, as John puts it, "went flying,"[35] John didn't know whether "to stand, fall, roll or forget it."[36] Suspecting that he might just be "going along with it" again, John fell down as he had so many times before. When John got up from the floor, Freidzon walked over to him and said, "Do you want it?"[37] He then slapped John on both of his hands and immediately Arnott felt God prompt him with the message, "For goodness' sake will you take this? It's yours."[38] With those words Arnott finally gave in and received the breakthrough he had been seeking so desperately.

While Freidzon was the agent through whom John Arnott finally received "the fire," Carol Arnott is correctly credited with fanning the spark into a flame. Any time John would have a hard time "feeling it," he would simply call Carol over, and "Boom, I'd go down and she'd soak me awhile."[39]

The Toronto Blessing

The Arnotts traveled back from Argentina with great expectations. When they heard that, like them, Randy Clark had been touched, they invited him to speak. On January 20, 1994, he gave his testimony before one hundred twenty attendees at the Toronto Airport Vineyard. In short order "almost 80 percent of the people were on the floor."[40] As John tells the story, "It was like an explosion. We saw people literally being knocked off their feet by the Spirit of God. . . . Others shook and jerked. Some danced, some laughed. Some lay on the floor as if dead for hours. People cried and shouted."[41]

Like the congregation, the staff of the Toronto Airport Vineyard was dramatically impacted. Arnott reported that the sound man got "drunk, drunk, drunk."[42] The church receptionist could not speak for three days and after that "could only speak in tongues."[43] Delighted, Arnott described how "our staff loves to get me on the floor, you know, they all run over, 'Hey he's down,' you know. They come 'More, Lord!' [and] they try to get me to shake or jerk or something. It just makes their day."[44]

Despite the encouragement of his spouse and his staff, John Arnott continued to have difficulty receiving all that God had in store for him. One day, while he was attempting to "receive," the Holy Spirit suddenly began to "backfire" on him. As John recalls, he was asking Carol:

> "Is it flowing in, you know?" And she'd say, "Oh, yeah, oh, yeah, oh, yeah, it's going in, it's going in, you're receiving." And I'm going, "Really? Okay, I'll take your word for it." And then she'd all [of a] sudden go, "Oops! Where did you go?" And I'd say, "What do you mean, 'Where did I go?' I'm right here, still." She said, "No, you went somewhere, because what I felt flowing into you suddenly backfired and backwashed on me."[45]

Arnott soon came to understand that the Holy Spirit would "backfire" if he lost his focus or attention. Suddenly he would find himself distracted with such thoughts as needing "to get the car fixed" and "vroom, it would backfire."[46]

During one sermon Arnott pointed out that his tendency to get distracted during encounters with the Spirit was much like the tendency of some men to think about such things as football while kissing a woman. He presented an analogy of how God must feel when our minds wander while he is touching us physically. Arnott pointed out how negatively he would be affected if, while he was vulnerable to Carol during intimate relations, she suddenly started asking for such things as money or a new fur coat. That kind of behavior, says John, is why God is so hard to find. God left no doubt that John had correctly analyzed the situation, speaking to him, saying, "When I reveal my heart to people, I become very vulnerable."[47]

Arnott argues that as God is vulnerable when he reveals his heart to people, we too should become vulnerable to God's power in our lives. Vulnerability is not something we should dread but rather something we should discover, as did Pastor Paul Reid from Belfast, Ireland. "To see what God did to him and taught him about humility and vulnerability, it was just a wonderful thing to see," John recalled. During ministry time at the Toronto Airport Vineyard, this prim and proper pastor had been, as Arnott put it, "laughing out loud with his fist down his throat." In fact, remembered John, by the end of the meeting:

> he was actually "surfing." He'd never "surfed" in his life. But he's up there in the spirit, just kind of o-o-o-o-o-o, you know, he's just "riding the wave." We said, "Paul, what was going on?" He says, "I don't know! I was having a vision. There was just this, I was catching the wave and I'd never surfed in my life, and I was on the wave of God and I was just going for it!"[48]

Arnott believes that many have been kept from riding the wave of the spirit because they simply would not let go of their emotions. The reason he himself had such a hard time getting drunk and falling in the spirit was, as Carol clarified, "You control your emotions. You control your responses."[49]

Controlling emotions is not only harmful to an individual, but doing so can also have a significant impact on others. John explains:

Many times Carol and I will be praying for people, we're soakin' 'em, soakin' 'em, soakin' 'em, feel the anointing going in. Next thing you know the guy that's supposed to be catching goes flying back 'cause it just kind of, it's got to go somewhere. If the person doesn't take it, it goes to the catcher, or it rebounds back on the person praying, or something where they can't take it.

This dilemma can be solved, Arnott says, if he and the other leaders "break those controls off of people and boom! They'll take it just like that."[50]

Arnott is quick to point out that controlling one's reactions is not the only roadblock to receiving. Sometimes the mistake people make is as simple as "praying in the spirit" instead of "soaking in the power." Arnott warns, "Many times people think, when we talk about the Holy Spirit, that they need to pray; pray in tongues or pray out loud or something, and so when we come to them and start to pray, 'Oh, fill them, Holy Spirit,' they'll immediately start praying in tongues. Now that will hinder what we're trying to do."[51] Instead he encourages people to be completely open: "It's like if there's a room full of the Holy Spirit, like we have here tonight, all you gotta do is be a sponge and just get down into the moisture and just [slurping sound] soak it up."[52]

Another reason for failing to receive is people's fear of deception. The antidote, says Arnott, is not to become a good discerner, but instead, when you come "asking to be filled with the Holy Spirit, I don't want you to even entertain the thought that you might get a counterfeit."[53] Arnott notes that, in the past, Vineyard leaders made mistakes regarding the supernatural: "We used to think when people shook, shouted, flopped, rolled, etc., that it was a demonic thing manifesting and we needed to take them out of the room. That was our grid, that's what our experience had taught us, that demons could be powerful."[54] Now he thinks these kinds of situations should be handled simply by enjoying the experiences and checking the "fruit" later. He explains:

> And so it's like, well, why would we focus, then, on "Yeah, but I don't like the way he fell and shook and got stuck to the floor and everything!" Listen! Who cares whether he did or he didn't? Who cares? If he thinks it's God and he likes it, let him enjoy it! Because you can test the fruit later.[55]

Caution would be a big mistake. "If you play it safe with this thing, the Holy Spirit, you know what? You're never going to get anywhere."[56]

Throwing Caution to the Wind

Arnott uses his wife as a graphic illustration of what people might experience if they would just let God have his way. One night while Carol was doing what is described as "carpet time," she asked God what he wanted her to do. God spoke to her and said:

> "Just stay there. Let me come on you." And so, you know, five, ten minutes went by and she asked him again. "No, just wait on me. Just long for me. Just desire me to come." And then as she did, He began to come, she began to feel this presence, this tingling, electricity, just coming all over her body and filling and intensifying and more and more and more, and just washed over her and refreshed her and strengthened her.[57]

John provides a rich assortment of examples of those who wisely throw caution to the wind and reap the consequent spiritual benefits. He describes how Swiss pastor Martin Bullman showed up in Toronto, walked right up to Arnott, and said,

"Hi, I'm Martin Bullman from Bern, Switzerland, and, you know, we've come because we want more of God."[58]

Arnott responded, "I can't talk now, 'cause we're right in the middle of ministry. The Lord bless you." Immediately, Bullman "felt like a hand grabbed him by the face and pulled him to the floor. There he was, wham, on the floor." When he got up, "he was so cranked and so turned on, I mean he's a wild man anyway, but [when] he went back to Switzerland, his church doubled in about two or three months."[59]

Although many of the people who have fallen at Arnott's feet have accused him of pushing them to the ground, Arnott steadfastly maintains, as do Benny Hinn and Rodney Howard-Browne, that "God pushed them." Arnott does confess that when he gets a little "drunk" while ministering, he may get a little heavy-handed. "In a busy night I'm kind of staggering around, you know, a little bit drunk, and I put my hand on somebody, and I think, 'Aw, I'm pushing on them a little heavy there, you know? Just keep it light, keep it light.' Imagine if a heavy hand is on you and the guy's staggering around like this, what does that feel like, you know?"[60]

Don't Push Me

While people have accused John Arnott of pushing them in the physical dimension, God supposedly once accused Arnott of pushing him in the spiritual dimension. Arnott attributes this to his faulty assumptions regarding God's purpose in revival:

> We didn't think it was going to look like this. We were praying for God to move, and our assumption was, when God moves we'll see more people saved and more people healed, and there would be the excitement that that would generate. We didn't think he would come and throw a massive party.[61]

Arnott is quick to admit that in the beginning he had no "theological framework for parties."[62] He adds, "I had no desire for Christians to fall down, roll around and laugh." Instead he says he wanted God to "save the lost, heal the sick, and expand the kingdom."[63] Today, however, he proudly promotes parties during which Christians get "thoroughly blasted" while "Jesus picks up the tab."[64]

While he is happy to "marinate"[65] Christians in the Holy Spirit, he complained when God began bringing "animal sounds" and "strange prophecy"[66] to the party. When the Almighty allegedly asked, "Would you like me to take it away?" Arnott quickly acquiesced.[67] He may well have remembered that, without the "oinking"[68] heard by Randy Clark at Rhema, the Toronto Blessing may have remained an unfulfilled fantasy.

Arnott's assumption that God was more interested in evangelism than experiences led to another unexpected revelation as well. As he preached salvation messages, he began to sense a "quenching of the Spirit." He went to the Lord in prayer and asked, "Well why, why is this hard, like I would have thought you would have liked it if I'd have preached on that." To his astonishment, the Lord replied, "It's because you're pushing me." And then God said, "Is it all right with you if I just love up on my church for a while?"[69]

Arnott not only discussed this issue with God, he also discussed it with Randy Clark. Clark, like Arnott, came to the conviction that, rather than giving people "the heavy message of holiness to start with,"[70] it was wise for God to throw "a party first."[71] Clark later elaborated: If God had not first thrown a party, "the church couldn't even have responded" because "most of the people in church already feel so icky about themselves."[72]

Clark's emphasis is personified in a woman by the name of Janis Chevreau. If ever there was someone who had felt icky about herself, it was Chevreau. She later explained on

The Phil Donahue Show that she and her husband were copastors of a Baptist church where things were not going particularly well.

By the time she heard about the party God was throwing at the Toronto Airport Vineyard, she had become "too desperate to be skeptical,"[73] so she joined in on the fun. For four hours she laughed while "rolling under chairs." Chevreau explained her emotional release to an incredulous Donahue: "It didn't matter what I was doing . . . everything was funny."[74]

Janis Chevreau not only rolled around under the chairs in the Toronto Airport Vineyard, but as her husband, Dr. Guy Chevreau, explained, she also became "hysterical with laughter."[75] Dr. Chevreau wrote in his book *Catch the Fire,* chronicling the Toronto experience, that John Arnott "prayed that she would stay in this state for forty-eight hours. She was that, and more—at times unable to walk a straight line, certainly unfit to drive, or to host guests that came for dinner."[76]

The "party" attributed to God at the Toronto Airport Vineyard had such a powerful impact on Janis Chevreau that, as she proudly pointed out to Donahue and his audience, she ended up doing some "throwing" of her own. During what she described as a "very serious meeting" with members of her congregation, she ended up throwing fish.

Her husband, who holds a Th.D. in historical theology and now travels internationally to spread the revival, explained, "On my return, our guests were already seated at the table. Without any place settings, Janis proceeded to toss hot, greasy fish to each of us; she dumped the box of French fries in the middle of the table, and then pushed little piles in our respective directions, all the while finding *everything* VERY funny."[77]

Choose, Choose, Choose

As attractive as the "party" is, Laughing Revival leaders seem convinced that the day is coming when critics will polarize in opposition to those who know how to enjoy the party. Vineyard prophets Wes and Stacey Campbell point out that after people "throughout the entire Christian community of the world" find out about the party, "there will come a polarization."[78] The Campbells warn that this is "no laughing matter."[79] A horrendous "time of bloodshed" is coming in which "there won't be a house that escapes weeping."[80] God himself (using Stacey Campbell as his mouthpiece) called upon those gathered at the Toronto Airport Vineyard:

> Grab all you can while you can get it. Take what you can while you can have it. For the days are coming, says the Lord, when a great division will begin in the church, and a man's enemies will be those of his own household. And your parents will criticize you, and speak evil of you and say they have lost you to a cult. And your sons and daughters will say, "My parents have gone crazy." And there will be mourning in the house of God.
>
> And I tell you there are those even among you now who are here simply to spread discord among the brethren. . . . And for the one who comes to bring division, to divide the church of Christ, to cut off his arms and his legs, and the toes from his feet, the Lord says it would be better for Sodom and Gommorah [sic] than it will be for that one on that day. But I tell you, nonetheless, that division will come, and it is even now brewing like a leaven in the church.
>
> For the Lord calls you right now, this day, seeing what you are seeing, hearing of the miracles you are hearing of, seeing the fruit of God that you are seeing, to call it God, endure to the end and be saved, or to follow after human wisdom and reasoning that kills the word of faith and brings division and justifies in self-righteousness the dividing of the church.

The Lord wants you to purpose in your heart this
night—is it God or isn't it?—and to stand by your commitment as you are called to stand by your confession
of faith.[81]

God Almighty then summed up his sentiments in just three
words—"Choose! Choose! Choose!"[82]

John Arnott likens the choice God is calling for to that which
faced the Israelites while they were wandering in the desert
three thousand years ago. Says Arnott, "God came along with
a once-in-a-lifetime opportunity." However, "due to fear and
unbelief," the Israelites failed "to possess the kingdom of God."[83]
According to Arnott, God is once again giving us an opportunity to "enter the promised land." The question is, will we be
"radical enough to go for it"?[84]

CHAPTER 4

The Pensacola Outpouring[1]

Like Arnott, John Kilpatrick, pastor of the Brownsville Assembly of God in Pensacola, Florida, saw "the party" God was throwing in Toronto as "a once-in-a-lifetime opportunity."[2] Leaving little doubt that he was "radical enough to go for it," Kilpatrick determined to import the party from Toronto to Pensacola. Church officials traveled to Toronto and indulged in the new wine of the Spirit firsthand;[3] various church members were treated to a video of their counterparts in Toronto getting "thoroughly blasted";[4] and Brenda Kilpatrick began to display such bizarre manifestations as being "frozen in the spirit."[5] Kilpatrick, however, had only begun to prime the pump.

Father's Day 1995

On Father's Day, June 18, 1995, pastor Kilpatrick invited an evangelist named Stephen Hill to fill his pulpit.[6] Hill, who had been personally prayed for by Carol Arnott, had called the Kilpatricks and told them about the "impartation" he had received at Holy Trinity Brompton in England. As Brenda Kilpatrick recalls, "we were so excited and said maybe this will bring revival."[7]

Hill began a time of teaching, replete with miracle stories. As a veteran of a seven-year Argentinean revival, he witnessed everything from the lame walking to the blind receiving their sight. He went so far as to say he had physically witnessed God filling cavities in people's teeth. "But something more has happened," said Hill. "If you don't believe there is more, then you've got a boring God."

God affirmed to Hill that he was anything but boring. Speaking to Hill, the Almighty said, "Steve, you're gonna learn something, and you're gonna learn it or nothin's gonna happen: I am spontaneous." Father's Day 1995 would be different, however. Rather than God moving spontaneously, Hill informed his audience that the Almighty had spoken to him the Wednesday before at 4:00 in the afternoon and revealed that every person who arrived at the meeting dry would be "drenched with a heavenly rain."

After going through a litany of the great people he had worked with in revival, Hill launched into a time of personal testimony. He told of his own conversion—a conversion that, if true, would be unprecedented both biblically and historically. According to Hill, he was converted *completely apart from the gospel*. As a junkie, mainliner, and thief, Hill says he encountered a Lutheran vicar who claimed that all he had to do to be set free was to "say the name Jesus." Despite the fact that he did not believe in God, Hill complied. In unbelief he repeated the word "Jesus" over and over again for thirty seconds. Thus, says Hill, he was miraculously converted into "a brand-new person" without so much as even "the four spiritual laws."[8]

That, however, was only the beginning. Hill went on to relay the story of how as a seasoned believer he went to England and was touched by an Anglican vicar at Holy Trinity Brompton. Said Hill, "When he touched me the power of God swept through my body. I fell to the ground. I don't ever do that, ever! For twenty minutes rivers were flowing through me. A river. Just a river. I've been filled with the Holy Ghost, friends. I've seen everything a man can see in missions. I got up twenty minutes later transformed. I was brand new. I was brand new. Brand new." After his experience Hill says he felt like a kid at Toys 'R' Us. He began running up to people and asking them to touch him and experienced getting knocked down repeatedly. Said Hill, "Little did I know how dry I was until God soaked me."

Hill's time of testimony eventually led into a time of ministry in which he attempted to soak the spiritually dry as he himself had been soaked. He asked that a chorus be sung over and over again and proceeded to holler into people's ears, "Now, Jesus!" "More, Lord!" "Now, Holy Ghost!" "Fire! Fire! Fire!" "Now! Now! Now!" As the hours rolled on, Hill, followed by "catchers," moved about the church continuing to shout, sweat, and slay subjects in the spirit. All the while the music droned on in the background.

While a videotape of the proceedings documents that nothing out of the ordinary took place that day, the storm clouds of revivalism had drifted from Toronto and gathered over Pensacola, Florida. In time they rained down on the Brownsville Assembly of God in what would come to be known as the Brownsville Revival or the Pensacola Outpouring.

Pastor Maul Ely, speaking from the pulpit of the Brownsville Assembly of God, declared to raucous applause that no less an authority than God himself specifically revealed the direct connection between the Toronto Blessing and the Pensacola Outpouring. As Ely put it:

> The Lord said, "Son, draw the tabernacle on a piece of paper." So I just opened up my notebook and I drew the tabernacle. Nice rectangular lines.
>
> And the Lord said, "Now, put there at the western side of the tabernacle," he said, "write down Azusa."
>
> I said, "Okay." How many know you need to do what he tells you to do, whether you understand it or not?

He said, "Now, go all the way across to the eastern part of the tabernacle, the entrance," and he said, "write Cleveland, Tennessee." So I wrote Cleveland, Tennessee.

He said, "Now, go to the northern side and write Toronto." Oh, oh! I feel it.

He said, "Now, go to the southern side of the tabernacle and write down Brownsville." You ain't heard nothin' yet!

He said, "Now, draw a line from Azusa to Cleveland, Tennessee"—how many know that the first wave of the Holy Spirit came to America started on the western coast and went across to the eastern coast?—he said, "Now draw a line from the northern side at Toronto to Brownsville.". . . He said, "The lines that you have drawn have made a cross across the tabernacle." And he said, "Now look at America. I have made a spiritual cross across America."[9]

The Pensacola Spin

Hearing Pastor Kilpatrick's recollection of what happened Father's Day 1995, one would think he was talking about an entirely different event. His rendition bears little resemblance to the video of the proceedings that day. Kilpatrick said he suddenly heard what he first thought was a mighty wind but later discovered was a river of the Holy Ghost. The force of the river was so pronounced that Kilpatrick claimed, "My ankles flipped over." After being pulled up to the platform by his pant legs, Kilpatrick shouted, "Folks, this is it! Get in! Revival's come!" He went on to exclaim:

And man, when I said that it was like dynamite exploding [explosion sound]. And it looked like somebody had taken a machine gun and mowed people down. Even out in their pews. Even out in their pews [*sic*]. I mean, they were falling out of the pews; they were falling down between the seats; they were falling out up here without anybody even touching them. A little like [machine gun sound], you know, somebody just cut 'em down.

Man, I hit this floor up here. And evangelist [Steve Hill] saw me up here by the pulpit, and I was looking about half-drunk, you know. And he just waved his hand like that and said, "More, Lord." And I said, "Whap!" And I hit the floor and I stayed there from 12:30 to 4:00. . . . I was laying there thinking, you know. It felt like I weighed ten thousand pounds. It didn't feel like you was pinned to the floor or nothing like that, but you're just so heavy. Just felt so heavy. It felt wonderful.

I thought, *Dear God, whatever this is, don't take it off of me.*

But one of our worship team ladies that fell in my arms—long after revival broke out, a lady came up to me during the revival and she said, "Brother Kilpatrick, your wife is so sweet. She sings so good in that worship team."

And I thought, *Worship team?*

She said, "You know, the black-headed one that was laying in your arms up there on the platform."

I said, "That's not my wife."

She said, "It's not?"

She just fell out under the fire too and just happened to land in my arms. And so I said, "Lord, this don't smell like Brenda here."[10]

The trance state John Kilpatrick said he experienced on that Father's Day in 1995 was merely a harbinger of things to come. As the years rolled on, his followers would experience manifestations ranging from sardonic laughter to spasmodic jerks.

One man in particular experienced such unusual convulsions on the platform in Pensacola that he became the center of attention. Stephen Hill, no doubt realizing that he was losing his audience, turned to the man and said:

> Now some of you are watching this young man up here. I want to tell you exactly what he is doing, and then I want you to turn your eyes from him. He's interceding for your soul. Some of you are on the verge—it's like we've got you with a thread and you're hanging over hell. It's intercession in the deepest form right here. It's moanings and groanings, words that can't be uttered. God's put it on him. You can't tell me God doesn't love you, friend. You can't tell me God doesn't love you when he will stricken [*sic*] another young man who loves God with all his heart, cause him to fall to the ground and experience the moanings and groanings and the birth pains. He's giving birth to you, friend. He's giving spiritual birth to you. He's dying for you right now. He's dying that you might have life.[11]

Pensacola promoters claim that "in less than two years Evangelist Steve Hill has won hundreds of thousands to Christ."[12] Hill identifies two out of the "hundreds of thousands" as alleged drug dealers. As reported on the Brownsville Web site, "Police officers had arrested three men in the Brownsville area for suspected drug dealing. For some reason, the police officers brought these men to one of our revival services instead of jail. Two of the three men responded to the altar call and were saved."[13]

Not only does Hill assert that police officers have brought suspected drug dealers to the revival instead of to jail, but also he claims that congressmen are weeping under the power of God in Pensacola:

> We're having politicians come in here now. Congressmen. I'm talking about Washington DCers are coming

into this place now. It's getting serious. Would you sa,
that with me? It's getting serious. When it gets to Washington, it's getting serious. One of the congressmen that
was with us from up north, his statement was this—I
believe he made it to Charlie, or somebody—He said,
"I'm bringing back twelve." So we proclaim that in a
very short while our Congress, our Senate is ablaze with
the power of the gospel, that they're on fire! That they're
on fire with the power of the gospel, that their lives are
changed and transformed. Those of you that have that
kind of doubt, would you open your eyes and watch
what's happening? You still can't see it. We're telling
you, we've already had them here. The congressmen
are here. They're weeping under the power of God.
They're already here. We're not dreaming. They've already been here.[14]

In addition, Pensacola promoters proclaim that they are having an impact on crime in Pensacola. They point out that "crime
in the city of Pensacola [has] dropped off significantly," and that
"the driving force behind the declining crime rate" is "the revival."[15]

Pensacola spin doctors use salvation statistics, converted
congressmen, and crime conditions to draw a distinction between the Toronto Blessing and the Pensacola Outpouring.
Michael Brown, an apologist for Pensacola, has gone so far as
to deny any relationship between the two: "The bottom line is
that there is no formal or informal relationship between
Toronto and Pensacola, and the spirit and thrust of the meetings are very different."[16]

Manifestation Mania

As Pensacola promoters endeavor to spread their movement
worldwide, they dogmatically declare that, unlike Toronto, bizarre manifestations are not the focus of their revival. The
facts, however, say otherwise.

One of the videos used by Pensacola promoters is entitled "Honey, Where Are We From?" It features the testimony of a pastor and his wife who become so spiritually inebriated that they can't remember where they are from. First, the wife becomes incoherent, and her husband intervenes to explain what she is attempting to say. Then he too becomes disoriented and is unable to think or speak rationally.[17]

The sensational physical manifestations of Alison and Elizabeth Ward are also strategically utilized to arouse people's expectations for similar experiences. The sisters have been brought up before the entire congregation to describe and display their mysterious experiences, thus giving the people a sense that they are having a close encounter with the divine. Peer pressure is brought to bear as Elizabeth tells prospects, "After standing there so long watching those people being touched by God, I guess my spirit got hungry." When she finally threw caution to the wind, she said, "The shaking went on for about three days. . . . I couldn't eat and I would shake in my sleep. My family had to feed me through a straw. My whole body was convulsing for three days."[18] Her sister, Alison, says she shakes in the sanctuary because "it feels good."[19]

Baptisms at Brownsville are used as yet another promotional gimmick. In a widely used promotional video, some of the baptized jerk so violently that baptizers can no longer control their behavior. In one clip the subject shakes so severely that someone is actually kicked in the face.[20] Physical danger is part and parcel of the process. Pensacola leaders point out that "the power of God falls during the Friday night water baptisms, and sometimes even the workers are overcome by the spirit and have to be carried out of the water."[21] Ironically, a word of caution has come from the Brownsville pulpit about not sitting too close to other people during the time of ministry out of concern that someone under the influence of a manifestation might injure nearby worshipers.[22]

Thousands who have viewed the videos and subsequently

experienced the manifestations testify to radically changed lives. Nevertheless, my then eleven-year-old son David and I attended a Christian convention during which the manifestations of Pensacola were promoted. He rode on an elevator with a couple of ladies who were still glowing from their spiritually intoxicating experience. They were delirious over the life-transforming work that the manifestations had produced in them. Suddenly, one of the ladies noticed my son's nametag. Instantly she began shrieking, "I know who you are. You're the son of the Bible Answer Man. You are a cursed child."

David is not the only child who has tasted the fatal spiritual fruit of Pensacola. Several children from a youth group traveled to Pensacola and experienced such severe twitching that when they returned to their classrooms, they were unable to do their schoolwork. After these children were dismissed from school, their pastor encouraged them to view their expulsion as persecution for the sake of Christ. [23]

CHAPTER 5

The Fatal Fruit[1]

More bizarre than the physical manifestations themselves are the biblical pretexts that are used to validate them. As a case in point, *Charisma* magazine ran a series of articles designed to undermine my credibility and integrity.[2] One article was titled "They Called Jesus a Counterfeit, Too." Even more telling than the misrepresentations contained in the article were the texts author Jon Ruthven used to legitimize the manifestations of counterfeit revival hot spots, such as Pensacola. Ruthven, an Assemblies of God minister and associate professor of systematic theology at Regent University, Virginia Beach, Virginia, wrote:

> Hanegraaff demands proof for the biblical grounds of charismatic revivalism. Yet he seems to ignore that many times in Scripture people who were influenced by the Holy Spirit acted in unusual ways.
>
> When the Spirit "rushed" upon Saul in 1 Sam. 19:20–24, he stripped off his clothes, prophesied before Samuel and "lay down naked all that day and all that night" (v. 24 NKJV). Ezekiel displayed even more bizarre behavior after God told him to lie on his side,

put "the iniquity of the house of Israel" on himself for 390 days, burn his hair and cook his food over human excrement! (Ezek. 4:4–5, 12; 5:1–2, 4). Isaiah was told by God to walk naked through Jerusalem for three years proclaiming judgment on the city (Is. 20:2–3). . . . We can only imagine how Hanegraaff would react to these types of behavior if they were to appear today. He seems to assume that Christian orthodoxy is a rationalistic, sterilized Calvinism that functions entirely on an intellectual level—devoid of the subjective spiritual dimension.[3]

Before examining Ruthven's abuse of Scripture, it should be noted in passing that his stereotyping of me in this review as an anticharismatic Calvinist and an antispiritual rationalist is best disingenuous. A closer look at my background or a careful reading of my books would forever dispel this myth.

As for his use of the Bible, while at first blush his arguments from 1 Samuel, Ezekiel, and Isaiah may appear compelling, a careful examination will expose their absurdity. Let's take a closer look:

1 Samuel 19:20–24. The fact that Saul stripped off his clothes, prophesied before Samuel, and laid down naked all day and night (v. 24) provides no validation for the peculiar manifestations in places like Pensacola.

First, as should be obvious, Ruthven's interpretation of Saul's nakedness cannot be used as normative behavior for Christians today. If it were, we would be compelled to endorse Counterfeit Revivalists who decided to parade around naked as a sign of spiritual enlightenment!

Furthermore, as a professor of systematic theology, one would presume that Ruthven is aware of the basic hermeneutical principle that narrative passages must always be interpreted in light of didactic or teaching passages (e.g., Scripture *records* Judas hanging himself, but it *teaches* that suicide is wrong).

Finally, this passage clearly reveals God's judgment against Saul, not his blessing. In context, Saul is seeking to destroy David but instead is humiliated by the Holy Spirit. While the Holy Spirit had once come upon Saul to minister through him, on this occasion the Spirit came upon Saul to resist his evil intentions.

Ezekiel 4–5. Professor Ruthven claims that Ezekiel displayed even more bizarre behavior than Saul. By this reasoning, the precedent is in place for today's revivalists to push the envelope beyond even nakedness.

First, the very fact that Ezekiel was engaged in an unusual process is precisely why it should *not* be considered normative for us today. If, indeed, it were the norm, it would not be much of a sign.

Furthermore, what Ruthven labels "bizarre behavior" is in reality extraordinarily meaningful. One need only take the time to read this passage in context to grasp God's explanation for the symbolism of Ezekiel's behavior. While unusual, it is neither random nor bizarre.

Finally, as with Saul, Ezekiel's actions represent God's judgment, not his blessing.

Isaiah 20. In yet another vain attempt to justify the radical behavior of today's Counterfeit Revivalists, Ruthven uses the fact that God told Isaiah to walk naked through Jerusalem for three years.

First, as should be obvious to Professor Ruthven, the wording in Isaiah does not necessitate the notion that the prophet was stark naked. Complete nakedness would have been considered religiously, as well as socially, unacceptable, particularly in light of Middle Eastern culture.

Furthermore, as Hebrew scholars Keil and Delitzsch point out, "With the great importance attached to the clothing in the East, where the feelings upon this point are peculiarly sensitive and modest, a person was looked upon as stripped and naked if he had only taken off his upper garment. What Isaiah was directed to do, therefore, was simply opposed to common custom, and not to moral decency."[4]

Finally, as previously noted with regard to Saul, if God had instructed Isaiah to walk around stark naked and if that is justification for Pensacola proclivities today, then if they really do start stripping, God can be blamed for setting the precedent for their bizarre behavior.

Tragically, Ruthven's reasoning process is the norm rather than the exception for Counterfeit Revivalists. One need only scan books by Pensacola leaders, such as John Kilpatrick, Steve Hill, and Michael Brown, to find even more outrageous examples of texts taken out of context and used as pretexts for Pensacola extravagances.

Aping the Practices of Pagan Spirituality

Out of all the bizarre manifestations I have witnessed in today's Counterfeit Revival, one scene has been indelibly etched into my consciousness. One Sunday morning I sat in the sanctuary of the Brownsville Assembly of God and watched in horror as a woman in the choir began to jerk her head spasmodically from side to side. An hour went by, then another. All the while the shaking continued unabated as intermittently she bent spasmodically at the waist.

A church member noting the look of concern on my face quickly attempted to assure me that this woman was merely under the influence of the "Holy Ghost." When I asked if she was certain it was the Holy Ghost, she seemed incredulous. "What else could it be?" she snapped. "We're in church, aren't we?" She went on to report that this woman had been shaking wildly in the sanctuary for more than a year and a half.

Several months later on CNN's *Larry King Live*, King asked me if there was a substantial difference between the kingdom of Christ and the kingdom of the cults. In response I pointed out that Christianity was historic and evidential—not a blind leap into a dark chasm, but faith founded on objective fact. I went on to say that in sharp distinction, cult leaders attempt to subjugate their followers' critical thinking faculties because the mind is seen to be the obstacle to enlightenment.

Sadly, I had to acknowledge that what was once practiced only in cults is now present in our churches, as Christians mimic the practices of pagan spirituality. What heightens the danger of this kind of activity in churches is that Christians do not expect a counterfeit. While virtually the same methods employed in cultic communes can now be experienced in Christian churches, there is a significant difference. At the altars of Pensacola, these practices are cloaked in Christian terminology and attributed to the Holy Ghost rather than, say, to a pantheon of Hindu deities.

Pensacola practices, such as jerking spasmodically, laughing uncontrollably, and falling backward into trance states, are conspicuous by their absence in the ministry of Jesus Christ and the apostles. Conversely, they are commonplace in the world of the occult. Peter warned believers to be wary of just such pagan practices. He admonished believers to "be clear minded and self-controlled" (1 Pet. 4:7).

It should also be noted that these practices are harmful and characteristic of neurological diseases such as palsy. Dr. Oliver Wilder-Smith warns, "[For] somebody who's shaking their head violently for a long period of time, the potential for physical damage is massive because your cervical spine, which is a very delicate organ, is just not built for that sort of activity. I'm sure she'll be having degenerative changes of all of the joints in her cervical spine very rapidly. . . . The purely physical consequences of shaking your head for hours on end are very, very damaging from a purely medical point of view."[5]

The spiritual consequences can be even more damaging. My concern for this woman and scores of others like her prompted me to plead with Pensacola pastor John Kilpatrick to consider the physical and spiritual consequences. While acknowledging that the woman I identified in his church "shakes like she has palsy," he defiantly paraded her across his platform as a trophy of the "Pensacola Outpouring." Ominously he shouted, "If you don't want your head to start shaking—you make fun of someone in the choir shaking—come here a minute, girl. Come down here a minute. Hurry up. Hurry up. If you don't want your head to do like this, you better lay your mouth off of her."[6]

Separating Fact from Fabrication

The fatal fruit of the Counterfeit Revival is not only evident in its torture of Scripture and dangerous manifestations, it is also evident in its propensity to fabricate stories. As already noted, revivalist renditions of what happened on Father's Day 1995, at the Brownsville Assembly of God is directly contradicted by the videotape of the proceedings. Let's take a closer look at a small sampling of Pensacola fabrications masquerading as facts.

Fabrication: "Police officers had arrested three men in the Brownsville area for suspected drug dealing. For some reason, the police officers brought these men to one of our revival services instead of jail. Two of the three men responded to the altar call and were saved."[7]

Fact: While salvation statistics vary wildly from source to source,[8] the men referred to above are two of the "hundreds of thousands" who were supposedly saved as a result of the Pensacola Outpouring.[9] However, the Pensacola Sheriff's Department has stated unequivocally that this did not happen and, moreover, that it could not happen.[10] When Pensacola promoters were confronted with this fabrication, they promised to remove it from their Web site.[11] Sadly, however, they continued to circulate this fabrication as a testimony to the authenticity of the Pensacola Outpouring.[12]

Fabrication: "We're having politicians come in here now.

Congressmen. . . . So we proclaim that in a very short while our Congress, our Senate is ablaze with the power of the gospel . . . that their lives are changed and transformed. . . . We've already had them here. . . . They're weeping under the power of God."[13]

Fact: Despite Steve Hill's dogmatic declaration that congressmen are in Pensacola "weeping under the power of God," he has not provided a shred of evidence to support his claim. His proclamation that congressmen will be changed and the Senate ablaze with the power of the gospel is at best an unrealized fantasy.[14]

Fabrication: "Crime in the city of Pensacola [has] dropped off significantly. . . . The driving force behind the declining crime rate [is the revival]."[15]

Fact: According to the Pensacola Police Department, this widely circulated story has no basis in reality. As the police pointed out, total crimes have, in fact, risen from 83,849 in 1995 to 85,581 in 1996 (a total increase of 1,732 crimes). "Forcible sex" was up from 52 to 69; "assault" was up from 623 to 656; "drug possession" was up from 647 to 660.[16] As Assistant Chief Jerry Potts reported, "Contrary to a widely circulating rumor, crime rates in Pensacola have not decreased dramatically."[17] By way of contrast, as reported in the *Orange County Register*, 13 March 1997, the crime rate in Orange County, California (home of the Christian Research Institute) has dropped at least 23 percent.[18]

Fabrication: "There is no formal or informal relationship between Toronto and Pensacola, and the spirit and thrust of the meetings are very different."[19]

Fact: In sharp contrast to this denial by Pensacola's Michael Brown, evangelist Steve Hill confessed, "We've received a lot from the Toronto church on how to pray with people and care for folks . . . we model a lot of what is going on here from them."[20]

It is also significant to reiterate that prior to Father's Day 1995, Brenda Kilpatrick and staff members of the Brownsville

Assembly of God had made pilgrimages to Toronto and received "an impartation." In addition, Pensacola revivalists, such as Steve Hill, have candidly acknowledged that they have been prayed for by John Arnott in Toronto and that Arnott and members of the Toronto staff have been to Pensacola.[21]

While much more could be said, unmasking all of the fabrications of Pensacola spin doctors would be an endless project. In fairness it should be noted that the fabrications emanating from Toronto are equally devastating.

The Best One So Far

Of all the miracles claimed by the Counterfeit Revival, Arnott calls the healing of Sarah Lilliman "the best one so far." Arnott not only tells his unsuspecting audience that the healing was "documented," but he also makes a point to chide those who may not have the kind of faith it took to facilitate the miracle.

Lilliman, says Arnott, was "like a vegetable . . . totally incapacitated, paralyzed, and blind." Her friend, "out under the power [at the Toronto Airport Vineyard] has a vision: Jesus said, 'Go pray for Sarah, your friend, I'm going to heal her.'" To enthusiastic applause, Arnott continues, "That girl, totally incapacitated, paralyzed, and blind, after two and a half hours of soaking prayer, got up seeing."[22]

Sadly, however, Arnott's story plays fast and loose with the truth. An examination of the facts shows just how wildly Arnott has embellished his story:

+ Sarah was *not* totally incapacitated, paralyzed, and blind; Sarah Lilliman's doctors had diagnosed significant psychosomatic emotional problems underlying her physical problems.

+ Jesus did *not* heal Lilliman as he supposedly promised her friend he would.

+ When Arnott's associate (who allegedly documented the

case) was interviewed, he acknowledged that he had not done any investigation.[23]

Two months later, during a visit to the Toronto Airport Vineyard, Sarah Lilliman's friend claimed that God once again had a word for her. This time the Almighty told her (through her friend) that if she "would go to the front of the church and testify, He would heal her eyes."[24] An Arnott associate then promised Lilliman that God was not only going to heal her eyes but would heal her emotions as well.

Today despite the broad circulation of this story by Arnott and his associates as evidence of God's power in the Toronto Blessing, *Sarah Lilliman is still, as before, legally blind.* Unfortunately, just as before, she and her family are continuing to struggle with her physical and psychosomatic disorders.[25]

As you read on, you will become painfully aware that this fabrication on the part of John Arnott is not unique. Fellow Counterfeit Revivalists pepper their appearances with fabrications, fantasies, and frauds, seemingly unaware of the disastrous consequences. Followers who at first crowded through the front doors of their churches often become disillusioned and fall out the back door, some even becoming vulnerable to the kingdom of the cults. They no longer know what to believe and secretly fear that the untrustworthiness of those who claim to be God's representatives may indicate the untrustworthiness of God himself.

The Bible Answer Man *Broadcast*

One disillusioned follower of the Counterfeit Revival called me on the *Bible Answer Man* broadcast, May 1, 1996. Just before signing off that day, I squeezed in one last phone call. The female voice on the other end of the line was obviously shaken and scared. She told me that her pastor had traveled to the Toronto Airport Vineyard and had "brought this thing back with him." While he had gone a skeptic, he had returned a believer, convinced that the power he had personally encountered was real. He convinced his parishioners to let him pray over them, and they too began to experience what he had experienced. Kristy, however, did not experience anything but frustration.

If this was from God, as her pastor claimed, she desperately needed his touch. "Why, God?" she pleaded. "Why are you leaving me out?" She sat down on the floor and began to cry bitterly as people all around her continued to laugh, shake, and be slain in the spirit. Suddenly, she realized she was flat on the floor, unable to move. Instantly her frustration turned to fear.

Although she was recounting this to me more than a year later, I could still hear the fear in her voice. I was convinced she needed to understand exactly what had happened to her. I began by explaining why the experience she had been subjected to was unbiblical and dangerous. I described some of the common consequences of such behavior: wild swings of emotion, depression, anxiety, anger, irrational outbursts, prolonged trances, feelings of alienation and confusion. As I spoke, she began to weep.

"That's what happened to me!" she said between sobs. As she struggled to regain her composure, Kristy confessed that she was still reeling from the effects of her experience. She said that after she had finally gotten up off the ground, she felt like she had "just run a hundred-mile marathon." In fact, the physical effects of her depression became so severe that her physician had to place her on antidepressant medication.

The spiritual consequences were equally severe. She began to question Christianity altogether. The happiness she had sought so desperately through an esoteric experience had turned into a living hell:

> My relationship with the Lord is totally turned upside down. I am afraid to pray. I am afraid to find out what that experience really was because I know it

wasn't of the Lord. I'm afraid to go to church, afraid of God. I've seen things that go against every good thing I learned in the Bible as a new Christian. It terrifies me. It's so scary to me. I'm afraid this has done something to my husband and me forever.

It has taken both of us so long to get back into the discipline of Bible study and prayer. It's almost like we don't understand salvation anymore. I remember days when it was so clear, and now it seems so confusing. I'm still scared. We read and we pray, but still the relationship we had just doesn't seem to be what it used to be. I don't call this a "blessing"! It was a nightmare that is just now beginning to lift from me, my husband, and our marriage. It makes me so angry to see how much this has hurt our family and messed up our relationships.

I can't believe where I'm at now spiritually. I have no desire for the Lord. I am now so critical and so skeptical that I don't know who to trust.

I know there are so many believers like me who don't know. It was so gradual. When the leadership you've trusted, the leadership that seemed to be so grounded in the Word endorses this stuff, you feel guilty going against it.

As I continued to talk with Kristy, she began to understand how she, like her pastor, had succumbed to the sociopsychological manipulation tactics described in part 5 of this book. She also began to comprehend that these manipulation techniques provide the fertile soil in which satanic and spiritual deception grow.

Understanding brought closure, and suddenly she began to see the silver lining in this ominous cloud. "My story has to help others," she said. "Otherwise it is a waste. I can speak from both sides now. I experienced the numbness in my body, but now I know it wasn't from God. If I can help someone, then it will be worth all the pain. I know the experience was real; now I also know how it was produced. Now more than ever, I know it wasn't from God."

Truth or Consequences

While Kristy *almost* abandoned Christianity, multitudes are, in fact, doing just that. Millions more look on in amazement and dismiss Christianity as little more than a succession of hoaxes. If Christians are willing to embrace current mythology, they reason, Christians must be just as prone to embracing mythology that is two thousand years old.

When Christian standards have more in common with those of the *National Enquirer* than the New Testament, it is time for us to examine ourselves. If selling and sensationalism become more tantalizing than truth, the very foundation of our faith is compromised. As followers of the One who proclaimed himself to be not only "the way and the life," but also *"the truth,"* we must set the standard for the world, not vice versa. We would do well to heed Blaise Pascal's words (in *Pensées*) as they ring down through the ages with prophetic poignancy: "Truth is so obscure in these times and falsehood so established, that unless we love the truth, we cannot know it."

PART TWO

Lying Signs and Wonders

CHAPTER 6

Animals, Animation, Advertisements, and Athletics

Counterfeit Revival leader James Ryle[1] said that the voice he heard was the kind that "stops you in your tracks and makes your hair stand on end. It came from above me and had an unmistakable air of authority about it. The Voice simply said, 'This is the mantle of Zechariah.'"[2] After three thundering knocks the voice spoke once again: "James, it is the Lord!" Suddenly James Ryle understood. The "vast purple mantle" that had fallen upon him in a dream was the mantle of a "seer."

In his book *A Dream Come True,* Ryle says the mantle that fell on him was enormous—"more than any one person could handle."[3] Thus, according to Ryle, this blind world soon would be enlightened by an "army of seers."[4] Ryle believes that God not only commissioned him directly but also called upon Vineyard founder John Wimber to pray that he be "released as a seer." "From that time forward," says Ryle, "the frequency, scope, accuracy, and fulfillment of dreams, visions, and prophetic words has been staggering."[5]

In a book titled *Hippo in the Garden,* Ryle recollects many of the "staggering" revelations given to him by God. His book derived its title from a dream in which Ryle watched God bring his pet hippo into a garden.[6] God subsequently revealed to Ryle the meaning of the dream.

Animals

The hippo represents modern-day seers, while the garden represents the church. In vivid detail, God revealed that as the aroma of hippo manure was offensive in a garden, so too his seers would be an offense to unbelievers.[7] As his pet hippo had a big mouth, so his seers would have big mouths;[8] and as the hippo ranks first among the works of God (at least according to Ryle), the prophetic ministry will rank first in authority within the body of Christ.[9] Ryle made it clear that his revelation was not merely the figment of a fertile imagination, saying, "I know what I saw in my dream and I am equally certain that the Lord showed me what it meant."[10]

Animation

The signs and wonders chronicled by Ryle run the gamut from creatures to cartoon characters. On one occasion, Ryle says, a lady in his audience suddenly caught his eye. Superimposed on her face was the cartoon character Olive Oyl. As hard as he tried, Ryle says, he could not shake this image.

Through what he characterized as "remarkable insight," Ryle received information on the lady. It was revealed to Ryle that "like the cartoon character Olive Oyl, she had been fought over by the brute Bluto but that 'Popeye' had come to the rescue." Adding a humorous twist, the Lord permitted Ryle to turn Popeye "into a pun that carried special meaning for her." He emphasized the word *Popeye* so that it came out as "Pop's Eye," which signified that this lady was the apple of the Father's eye.[11]

"Olive Oyl" was evidently so touched that she divulged her deeper connection with the cartoon characters in Ryle's vision.

Apart from being nicknamed "Olive Oyl" and having been divorced from a man like "Bluto," God had blessed this lady with a husband who was nicknamed "Popeye." Ryle concludes that it was an "unspeakable privilege to have been used by the Lord in such an unusual and unforgettable way."[12]

The signs and wonders recounted by Ryle are at times so incredible that even the apostle John's visions on the Isle of Patmos seem to pale by comparison. Ryle says he once dreamed he "was literally inside the Lord."[13] And from the vantage point of "seeing through the eyes of Jesus,"[14] he was enabled to unravel myriad mysteries for the people of God. As a classic case in point, God revealed to Ryle his purpose for placing a special anointing of music upon the Beatles (despite the fact that none of them were committed to Christ). As the Almighty allegedly articulated, "It was my purpose to bring forth, through music, a worldwide revival that would usher in the move of my Spirit in bringing men and women to Christ."[15] Because the Beatles used their anointing for Satan's kingdom instead, Ryle says the Lord lifted his anointing, "kept it unto himself and is about to release it again."[16]

Advertisements

The meaning of Ryle's revelations are not always self-evident. On one occasion God gave him an esoteric message via a pig and a billboard. At first Ryle thought Jesus might be telling him that "there would be demons in the meeting tomorrow, and I was to cast them into pigs" or that he shouldn't teach the next day "because it would be like casting my pearls before swine." He even thought that Jesus might be telling him "not to look at any pretty girls who were there, because they would be like a gold ring in a pig's nose." Ryle said he felt foolish after God had to show him the vision a second time and explain to him what the vision really meant: "I am speaking to my people in 'billboards' all of the time, but they are so distracted by the little pigs that they seldom notice what I am saying."[17]

Athletics

Ryle's revelations are not limited to animals, animation, and advertisements. They also extend to athletics. On August 22, 1989, the Almighty gave Ryle a dream about football. In the dream, Ryle saw "something like an energy field" encircling the University of Colorado Buffaloes football team. He then heard a voice that said, "This will be their golden season!"[18]

The next day Ryle shared the dream as well as its interpretation with Bill McCartney, who was then the Colorado Buffaloes' coach and who later founded the national Christian men's group Promise Keepers. Ryle said, "The Lord will now fulfill promises which He has made to you by empowering the players with His Spirit. This will be the golden season!"[19] At the end of the golden season, before the championship game, Ryle says, "I felt certain that we would win and be crowned the national champions of college football—we were already firmly locked in the number-one position in the polls. I was *sure* that we would win; my confidence was unshakable!"[20]

Minutes before the national championship game, however, the Lord gave Ryle a tragic revelation through a female buffalo named Ralphie. Via the omen[21] of Ralphie's broken horn, God revealed that the power of his Spirit had departed from the team.[22] This time, however, Ryle kept the revelation to himself until after the game.

As he stood stunned in the stadium, contemplating Colorado's crushing 21 to 6 loss to Notre Dame, the Holy Spirit told Ryle to turn to Isaiah 21:6.[23] While the content of Isaiah 21:6 has no correspondence to football games, Ryle says, "My curiosity was awakened."[24]

After the tragic ending to the Buffaloes' "golden season," God revealed to Ryle that he would "reach out His hand a second time" (Isa. 11:11).[25] And, sure enough, the following year, the Colorado Buffaloes were again pitted against Notre Dame in the national championship game. Prior to the game, Ryle once again checked for a sign, using Ralphie's horns as an omen. This time they were intact; thus, Colorado went on to win the national championship of college football. Astonishingly, the omen was confirmed for Ryle by the season win-loss-tie record (11-1-1), which matched the passage (Isa. 11:11) that the Holy Spirit had prompted him to consult.[26]

A brief review of Ryle's own testimony reveals that astounding encounters with the divine are commonplace. Ryle was merely fourteen years of age when he was first contacted by the Sovereign Ruler of the universe as he attempted to escape from an orphanage. Four years later God spoke a second time when Ryle was selling drugs so he could pay an attorney to defend him on manslaughter charges. God spoke to Ryle a third time after he had successfully transitioned from prison to pulpit. This time the Lord told Ryle to forgive the senior pastor of his church for allegedly being involved in "gross sexual misconduct" with Ryle's wife.[27] Today Ryle says that God speaks through him with staggering frequency, scope, and accuracy. As a modern-day seer, he now not only functions as a pastor, but also "helps provide biblical direction for men through Promise Keepers."[28]

All That Glitters Is Not Gold

While at first blush Ryle's revelations appear to be solid gold, a closer look exposes them for what they really are—fool's gold. Take his "golden season" prophecy, for example. While Ryle claims that God communicated to him via the omen of a buffalo horn, Scripture clearly denounces any such interpretation of omens.

God makes it clear that he does not want his people to "learn to imitate the detestable ways" of paganism. In Deuteronomy 18:10, he specifically warns against practicing divination and interpreting omens. It is significant to note that even though the slave girl (in Acts 16) "who had a spirit by which she predicted the future" may have been communicating accurate information, she was still rebuked by the apostle Paul.[29] While the slave girl may have conveyed facts, even a cursory investigation of Ryle's "revelations" demonstrates that he conveys fabrications. Ryle's revelations concerning "Olive Oyl" provide a perfect example.

Ryle claimed that his vision was a "wonderful" word of prophecy that "deeply" touched "Olive Oyl's" heart. In sharp contrast, "Olive Oyl" herself told me that Ryle's vision was a "weird" word of prophecy that was deeply distressing to her. When I interviewed her, she recounted that she had never believed it was a genuine prophecy from the Lord. She told me how she had felt:

> My first reaction was, I'm trapped. I'm a staff person and I'm in front of everyone and I can't afford to react in any way. I can't get out of this. I felt trapped and manipulated. . . . I had no doubt that what was happening through James was *not* from God. . . . I was disgusted. I almost could not believe that I was hearing this. It was so weird. I felt trapped and wished I could get out of the room. I was being impacted, but not the way he says. I was impacted by the way I was trapped into validating his manipulation.[30]

Furthermore, what Ryle characterized as "remarkable insight" derived through revelation, "Olive Oyl" characterized as insider information derived from her pastor. Since she was the church administrator, she was well aware of her pastor's usual "preparation" for a visiting prophet. As she put it, "I worked closely with the pastor, so I knew precisely how the manipulation worked in that church." "Olive Oyl" lived with the guilt of feeling as though she had betrayed her Lord because she did not expose the manipulation.[31]

Finally, it should be noted that Ryle's revelation is riddled with factual errors. Among them is the fact that "Olive Oyl" was never beaten by the "Bluto" of Ryle's revelation, nor did she ever marry anyone nicknamed "Popeye." In addition, when Ryle recounts this story (as he does in *Hippo in the Garden*), he conveniently omits the portion of the prophecy in which God revealed to him that "Olive Oyl" would be a "prophet like unto Daniel and would receive an anointing ten times greater than any of her associates"—a prophecy that never materialized.

Today, many years after her recovery from the devastating impact of Ryle's lying signs and wonders, "Olive Oyl" (whose real nickname is "Sal") warns others not to lose faith because of such cons:

> I can tell you of people who have walked away from Jesus and no longer believe themselves to be saved, because they have discovered the manipulation and deceit and so they just give up on Christianity altogether. . . . A lot of people die a very ugly spiritual death due to false prophecies; it's just very tragic. . . . So many Christians have become spiritual heroin addicts who eventually end up wasted, dead, and empty.[32]

CHAPTER 7

A Jack with a Lantern

James Ryle and the "army of seers" by whom, he says, "this blind world would soon be enlightened" are aware that their failed prophecies have not gone unnoticed. They attempt to seduce devotees into believing that both New Testament prophets and today's endtime prophets operate under a different standard than did the prophets of the Old Testament.[1]

Vineyard pastor David Ravenhill says that seers should not be tested by the accuracy of their predictions but by the character of their lives: "I believe the test of a prophet is not whether his word comes to pass; it's his lifestyle. It's the character of the individual. That is how you test a prophet. . . . It's not a matter of whether the word comes to pass or not; it's the nature of that person's life."[2]

Contrary to Ravenhill's assertions, biblical prophets were clearly authenticated by absolute accuracy (Deut. 18:21–22). Nevertheless, Counterfeit Revival prophet Bob Jones says, "I figure if I hit two-thirds, I'm doing pretty good."[3]

Counterfeit Revival leader Jack Deere also believes that it is wrong to hold modern-day seers to the test of 100 percent accuracy. Deere recounts the story of a prophet who, in front of eight hundred peers of a nineteen-year-old, falsely accused the young man of having a problem with pornography. The seer in Deere's story called out the young man and said, "You're into pornography. And the Lord says you have to repent!" Deere says the young man began to weep because the truth was that he was not into pornography. As Deere elaborates, "He was publicly humiliated before eight hundred high school kids. We had to go back to his church, apologize to his whole church, apologize to the whole conference. It was a horrible mess."[4]

Despite the mess, Deere concludes, "But you know what? God is in the process of offending our minds in order to reveal our hearts. And I don't know any place where he's going to give us a pure ministry. I don't know any place where it's going to be 100 percent right. There's going to be stumbling blocks in every ministry *that the Holy Spirit is really responsible for*"[5] (emphasis added).

Attacking Agabus

Like Deere, James Ryle attempts to convince his devotees that the prophets of the Counterfeit Revival should not be held to the standard of a biblical prophet. The tack he takes is to impugn the credibility of New Testament prophets. He attempts to prove that Agabus (who gained "credibility by prophesying a great famine that occurred during the reign of Claudius Caesar"—Acts 11:28) blew it when he prophesied that the apostle Paul would be "bound by the Jews in Jerusalem" (Acts 21:11). According to Ryle, Agabus failed the test of 100 percent accuracy when he mistakenly predicted that the Jews, rather than the Romans, would bind Paul.[6]

By Ryle's method of interpretation, Luke's writings would be untrustworthy as well. In Acts 1:18, Luke writes that Judas purchased the potter's field while Matthew 27:7 asserts that the chief priests purchased it. Furthermore, if Ryle's understanding is correct, the Old Testament prophet Jeremiah should have been stoned for incorrectly prophesying that the purchase of the potter's field would be by the chief priests rather than by Judas.[7] Like Jeremiah, the Old Testament prophet Zechariah (whose mantle allegedly fell on Ryle) would have received the death penalty for prophesying that Jesus would be pierced by inhabitants of "the house of David,"[8] when in reality Jesus was pierced by the Romans.

In fact, if Ryle were right in asserting that New Testament prophets were fallible when they asserted "the Holy Spirit says,"[9] then it necessarily follows that the New Testament is fallible as well.

In truth, however, the basic principles of biblical interpretation militate against Ryle's reasoning. Scripture often speaks of a person performing an action when in reality that person is merely the cause or agent of the action. Thus, Agabus is perfectly accurate in saying that the Jews bound Paul because the Jews were the cause for which Paul was bound.[10] Likewise, according to this principle, Luke, Matthew, Jeremiah, and Zechariah are perfectly accurate in both their proclamations and predictions.

The Omen

Ryle's assertion that God speaks to him about such things as the outcome of football games via the medium of a broken buffalo horn is equally outrageous. While divination—obtaining knowledge about the future through the interpretation of omens—is standard fare in the kingdom of the cults, it is singularly foreign to the kingdom of Christ.

From the early Christian church to the present, divination has been uniformly discouraged as a magical art and a morbid addiction. Eighteenth-century theologian and preacher Jonathan Edwards (1703–1758) put it well when he said, "As long as a person has a notion that he is guided by immediate direction from heaven, it makes him incorrigible and impregnable in all his misconduct."[11]

It is also safe to say that when James Ryle alleges that he received "direction from heaven" to read Isaiah 21:6 (after the Colorado Buffaloes lost to Notre Dame 21 to 6), he is merely communicating the delusions of his own mind. We can also be assured that Ryle is presumptuous in alleging that the Holy Spirit revealed to him a year in advance that Colorado would win the national championship of college football by directing him to read an esoteric meaning into Isaiah 11:11.

More than two hundred years ago, Jonathan Edwards addressed this sort of "Bible Roulette" when he said:

> Some that follow impulses and impressions indulge a notion, that they do no other than follow the guidance of God's word, because the impression is made with a text of Scripture that comes to their mind. But they take that text as it is impressed on their minds, and improve it as a new revelation to all intents and purposes; while the text, as it is in the Bible, implies no such thing, and they themselves do not suppose that any such revelation was contained in it before. . . .
>
> If such things as these are revealed by the impression of these words, it is to all intents a new revelation, not the less because certain words of Scripture are made use of in the case. Here are propositions or truths entirely new, that those words do not contain . . . wholly different from those contained in the text of Scripture. . . .
>
> This is quite a different thing from the Spirit's enlightening the mind to understand the words of God, and know what is contained and revealed in them . . . and to see how they are applicable to our case and circumstances; which is done without any new revelation, only by enabling the mind to understand and apply a revelation already made.[12]

Rather than indulging impulses and impressions, Edwards advises Christians to "take the Scriptures as our guide." Without the final standard of Scripture, the body of Christ lies open to "woeful delusions and would be exposed without remedy to be imposed on and devoured by its enemies."[13] Edwards implores Christians "to be contented with the divine oracles—that holy pure word of God, which we have in such abundance and clearness":

> Why should we desire to have any thing added to them by impulses. . . . Why should we not rest in that standing rule that God has given to his church, which the apostles teach us [2 Pet. 1:12–21] is surer than a voice from heaven?
>
> They who leave the sure word of prophecy—which God has given us a light shining in a dark place—to follow such impressions and impulses, leave the guidance of the polar star to follow a Jack with a lantern.[14]

Tragically, James Ryle is not alone in leaving "the guidance of the polar star" to follow "a Jack with a lantern." A host of others have followed in his footsteps.

CHAPTER 8

A Great Apostasy

James Ryle's deceptions are not limited to visionary hoaxes. They extend to revisionary history as well. As Ryle has exchanged God's enduring revelation for his own erroneous revelations, so too he has exchanged historical realities with historical revisionism.

In this too Ryle is not alone. In teachings, transcripts, tapes, and television appearances, men like John Arnott (Toronto Airport Vineyard), Dr. Guy Chevreau *(Catch the Fire)*, Gerald Coates (Holy Trinity Brompton), Patrick Dixon *(Signs of Revival)*, and a host of other Counterfeit Revival proponents are deceiving devotees by revising history. Their primary ploy is to persuade people that sardonic laughter, spasmodic jerks, slaying in the spirit, and other "enthusiasms" were not only pervasive in the First Great Awakening but were also promoted by such historical heavyweights as Jonathan Edwards (popularly cited as one of the greatest theological minds produced in America).

One of the most brazen examples of historical revisionism comes from the lips of Arnott. At an international pastors' conference, Arnott tried to dupe devotees by denouncing the theology of John Calvin while in the same breath affirming the theology of Jonathan Edwards. Arnott was attempting to refute "cessationists," whom he believes were "shutting down the Holy Spirit" by questioning the practice of "acting like lions and oxen and eagles and even warriors." His basic argument was that since "God himself has no hesitation of comparing himself to an animal," we shouldn't either. Thus, according to Arnott, Calvinists and cessationists would be "far better advised to refer to Jonathan Edwards and his theology on discernment."[1]

While Arnott no doubt knew that Edwards was a Calvinist and a cessationist (believing that such supernatural gifts as tongues and prophecy had ceased), he apparently banked on the fact that his followers did not. Arnott, however, is not alone in this deception. Counterfeit Revival "historian" William DeArteaga, for example, uses the Toronto Airport Vineyard as his bully pulpit to simultaneously *condemn* Calvinism and *commend* the theology of Jonathan Edwards. DeArteaga compounds the deception by telling devotees that Edwards's contemporary critic Charles Chauncy "ensured the defeat of the Awakening" by "using the assumption of Calvinist theology."[2]

In truth, far from using Calvinism to ensure the defeat of the Great Awakening, Chauncy was an Arminian who *opposed* "the resurgence of Calvinistic theology—especially as preached by Jonathan Edwards."[3]

The most disturbing deception of all is that the leaders of the Counterfeit Revival have coopted one of the church's true spiritual giants and dishonestly claimed him for their own. In the words of DeArteaga, "The Lord has already chosen the predominant theologian of this revival. It's not me! *It's Jonathan Edwards*"[4] (emphasis added).

Nothing, however, could be further from the truth. The theological focus of Edwards was on eternal verities such as sin, salvation, and sanctification. In sharp contrast, the temporal fixation of men like John Arnott is on such earthly vanities as sardonic laughter, spasmodic jerks, and being slain in the spirit.

While Edwards personified a passion for piety, Arnott personifies a priority for parties.

Dr. Nick Needham has well said that anyone who believes that Edwards would have approved of this paradigm shift "must surely have kissed a final farewell to his mind."[5]

Jonathan Edwards

Other leaders of the Counterfeit Revival have appealed to Jonathan Edwards. Thus, to Edwards we shall now go. Nowhere is there a more compelling contrast between counterfeit and genuine revival than in Edwards's manuscript titled *The Distinguishing Marks of a Work of the Spirit of God.*[6]

He identifies nine characteristics that critics seize upon to negate the Great Awakening as a genuine work of the Spirit. Edwards draws a clear line of demarcation between Great Awakening and great apostasy. The signs identified by Edwards are so significant that I have alliterated them to make them easy to review and easy to remember.[7]

Extraordinary Enthusiasms

What the church has been used to, is not a rule by which we are to judge; because there may be new and extraordinary works of God.[8]

In *Catch the Fire,* Counterfeit Revival historian Dr. Guy Chevreau goes to great lengths to "prove" that the "new and extraordinary works of God" to which Edwards referred are precisely what he experienced when he first visited the Toronto Airport Vineyard. Chevreau confesses that he was "too desperate to be critical"[9] when he first encountered the "uncontrollable laughter and inconsolable weeping; violent shaking and falling down; people waving their arms around, in windmill-like motions, or vigorous judo-like chopping with their forearms."[10]

Thus, when John Arnott prayed that Chevreau's wife, Janis, would remain in a drunken stupor for forty-eight hours, he did not attempt to intervene. Instead, Chevreau proudly proclaimed that Arnott's prayer had been abundantly answered. As described earlier, for more than two days Janis fell "repeatedly," was "hysterical with laughter," and was "unable to walk a straight line."[11] So severe was her spiritual drunkenness that Janis was completely unfit to drive.

On worldwide television Janis witnessed to the "new and extraordinary works of God" by telling Phil Donahue that for four hours she had rolled around under chairs at church. She went on to testify that the very next day she began to "toss hot, greasy fish" at parishioners during a very serious dinner meeting. Dr. Chevreau spends almost a third of his book attempting to convince readers that these were precisely the kinds of new and "extraordinary enthusiasms" that Edwards defined and defended.

In doing so Chevreau corrupts the clear intention of Edwards's words. When Edwards spoke of the "new and extraordinary works of God," he was referring to the Spirit's "ordinary work of converting sinners, but carried on at certain points in history in an extraordinary way as far as numbers and community-wide consequences were concerned."[12]

Chevreau also blurs the distinction between the experiences of his wife and those of the wife of Edwards. In clear contrast to the "very flaky"[13] beliefs and behavior of Janis Chevreau, Edwards points out that his wife, Sarah, experienced the glory and grandeur of God.[14] Dr. Nick Needham points out that what Jonathan and Sarah Edwards approved of was

the complete mirror-image of such fun-drunk spiritual "parties." Perhaps Edwards was wrong. Perhaps he was spiritually deficient in his sense of humor. But it is profoundly dishonest to appeal to Edwards' name to give credibility to a spiritual ethos he would have abhorred with every fibre of his lofty and reverent soul.[15]

While Chevreau couches Edwards's comments in the context of Counterfeit Revival chaos, in truth his commentary is clearly communicated within the context of Great Awakening conversions. Perhaps this distinction is best personified by the experience of a non-Christian reporter named Mick Brown, who traveled to Toronto on assignment for a secular magazine.

For the most part Brown was singularly unimpressed by what he experienced. He described the sermons as "turgid enough to tax the most devout believer."[16] At one point he even left the spiritually intoxicated gathering for a quick beer in a nearby bar. His account, however, concludes with a startling revelation:

> Perhaps it was the heat, or the air of febrile intoxication coursing through the air, but I could feel myself growing giddy. . . .
>
> I didn't even see [Pastor John Arnott's] hand coming as it arced through the air and touched me gently—hardly at all—on the forehead. "And bless this one, Lord. . . ." I could feel a palpable shock running through me, then I was falling backwards, as if my legs had been kicked away from underneath me.
>
> I hit the floor—I swear this is the truth—laughing like a train.[17]

In a subsequent interview, Brown said, "I'm not and I wasn't a practicing Christian before going to Toronto, but I've always had an interest in all sorts of different religious experience."[18] He went on to say that in his estimation "every culture and every faith expresses an understanding of God, or the divine, in their own particular way, and the divine does not discriminate between different cultures, [or] between different religions."[19]

Brown's account of his Toronto Vineyard experience bears an eerie resemblance to a previous encounter he had with a Hindu avatar named Mother Meera:

> I went to see her, took *darshan* with her. *Darshan* means (literally) an audience with a teacher, and it was a very powerful experience. What it actually involved was her taking my head in her hands for about a minute or so, and then lifting my head up and holding my gaze for another minute or so. The immediate effect was an extreme warmth on my face, a burning sensation, which lasted for a few hours afterwards. . . . The feeling of euphoria lasted for two or three days.[20]

Brown says he did not experience long-term change as the result of either his encounter with Mother Meera or with John Arnott. He didn't change his reservations about Christianity, nor did it make him think "that Buddhism, Hinduism, Islam, Red Indian Shamanism or whatever other kind of manifestation of faith could go out with the bathwater." After leaving the Toronto Airport Vineyard, Brown was more convinced than ever that Christ was merely "a sort of man, someone through whom God was working."[21]

Tragically, after a prolonged visit to the Toronto Airport Vineyard, Brown had experienced sardonic laughter but had not encountered a single sermon on salvation. Instead of being saved by the Spirit of the Lord, he had merely been slain by the spirit of laughter. As Dr. Needham rightly observed:

> There is something slightly sinister about Christians having a self-indulgent spiritual "party" while the world around them is sliding into the outer darkness, where there is weeping and gnashing of teeth, where the worm never dies and the fire is never quenched. Edwards teaches us that we need to confront the soul-

destroying idolatry of entertainment and fun that dominates our society, and appears to be hypnotizing and seducing the Church.[22]

Effects on the Body

The misery of hell is doubtless so dreadful, and eternity so vast, that if a person should have a clear apprehension of that misery as it is, it would be more than his feeble frame could bear.[23]

"One night I was preaching on hell," boasts Counterfeit Revival leader Rodney Howard-Browne, when suddenly laughter "just hit the whole place. The more I told people what hell was like, the more they laughed."[24] This was not an isolated incident. An associate confirmed Howard-Browne's account by announcing that as he told his parishioners the story of God's judgment on Ananias and Sapphira, "everyone ended up on the floor laughing."[25]

Edwards provides a completely different perspective. When leaders of the Great Awakening preached on the terrors of hell and impending judgment, people were moved by the Spirit and experienced weakness and weeping. The reality of hell and the brevity of life so engaged their minds that they experienced corresponding effects in their bodies. Rather than being deliberately produced by the laying on of hands or loud shouts of "More, Lord!" these responses were the spontaneous results of a vivid encounter with eternal verities. As Edwards elaborated:

If we should suppose that a person saw himself hanging over a great pit, full of fierce and glowing flames, by a thread that he knew to be very weak, and not sufficient to bear his weight, and knew that multitudes had been in such circumstances before, and that most of them had fallen and perished, and saw nothing within reach, that he could take hold of and save him, what distress would he be in! How ready to think that now the thread was breaking, that now, *this minute,* he should be swallowed up in those dreadful flames! And would not he be ready to cry out in such circumstances? How much more those that see themselves in this manner hanging over an infinitely more dreadful pit, or held over it in the hand of God, who at the same time they see to be exceedingly provoked! No wonder that the wrath of God when manifested but a little to the soul, *overbears human strength.*[26]

Edwards made it crystal-clear that a true valuation of the judgment of God and the terror of hell produces such powerful inner emotions that corresponding effects on the body are only natural.

Likewise those who get even a glimpse of the glory and grandeur of God may well also experience effects in their bodies. Edwards exuded, "A true sense of the glorious excellency of the Lord Jesus Christ, and of his wonderful dying love, and the exercise of a truly spiritual love and joy, should be such as very much to overcome the *bodily strength.*"[27]

The effects on the body described by men like Edwards were never random or ridiculous but were the result of spiritual awakening. The effects on the body produced through men like Howard-Browne are largely the result of sociopsychological manipulation (see part 5).

Leaders of the Counterfeit Revival proudly promote bodily effects such as sardonic laughter, spasmodic jerks, and "surfing in the spirit" and perceive preaching as virtually pointless. As Howard-Browne has acknowledged, "As to what you're preaching on, it's almost irrelevant."[28] In sharp contrast, leaders of the Great Awakening believed that powerful preaching on sin, salvation, and sanctification was paramount. Dr. Nick Needham poignantly added:

The idea that true spiritual joy can be expressed by laughter, or by any kind of lightness (what we might call fun or clowning), has never had a more determined opponent than Jonathan Edwards. Those Toronto apologists who appeal to him to justify such modern-day phenomena are either speaking out of a profound ignorance, because they have not troubled to read Edwards at all, or are irresponsibly and deceptively misrepresenting Edwards' clear and forceful teaching on the subject.[29]

Endorsements

When Christ's kingdom came, by that remarkable pouring out of the Spirit in the apostles' days, it occasioned a great stir every where.[30]

"The fire is blazing out of control,"[31] boasted Arnott. The "world-wide spread" is so dramatic that "opposition to this move of God is becoming very much like a fly on an elephant."[32] Despite the fact that "tens of thousands of pastors"[33] and hundreds of thousands of participants have been impacted, Arnott contends we haven't seen anything yet: "We are currently in a time similar to the ministry of John the Baptist and will soon be coming into a time resembling the ministry of Jesus where powerful signs, wonders and miracles will take place."[34]

Arnott's words are a common refrain among leaders of the Counterfeit Revival. Rick Joyner goes so far as to prophesy that the "faithful will soon walk in unprecedented power and authority":

In the near future we will not be looking back at the early church with envy because of the great exploits of those days, but all will be saying that He certainly did

save His best wine for last. The most glorious times in
all of history have now come upon us. You who have
dreamed of one day being able to talk with Peter, John,
and Paul, are going to be surprised to find that they
have all been waiting to talk to you![35]

Leaders of the Counterfeit Revival cite the widespread acceptance of their movement as proof that it is a work of the
Spirit. Leaders of the Great Awakening did not. While Edwards
acknowledged that the outpouring of the Spirit in the days of
the apostles caused a great stir, he resisted the notion that the
expansion of a movement was an endorsement from God. If
size, scope, and spread were validations for a religious movement, one would be compelled to accept the counterfeit Christ
of the New Age movement.

Edwards knew full well that the record of history bore elo-
quent testimony to the fact that a great apostasy can spread
as rapidly as a great awakening. In the days of Athanasius
(295–373), the Arian apostasy[36] spread so swiftly that it threat-
ened to pervert the Christian church into a cultic commune.
The endorsement of Arianism by the emperor escalated the
spread of this egregious error throughout the empire.
Athanasius, however, stood against the tide. While the endorsement of the world stood against Athanasius, Athanasius stood
against the endorsement of the world.

Esoteric Imaginations

*It is no wonder that many persons do not well distin-
guish between that which is imaginary and that which
is intellectual and spiritual; and that they are apt to
lay too much weight on the imaginary part, and are
most ready to speak of that in the account they give of
their experiences, especially persons of less understanding and of distinguishing capacity.*[37]

In *A Dream Come True,* James Ryle characterizes a dream or a vision as "a puzzle waiting to be solved, a promise waiting to be realized, or a premonition waiting to happen."[38] To validate his "peculiar fascination," Ryle turns to a priest and Jungian analyst named Morton Kelsey (a devotee of occult practices) who describes Jesus Christ and his disciples as shamans (sorcerers).

Ryle quotes Kelsey as saying that after a ten-year study on dreams and visions, "I discovered that my dreams were wiser than my well-tuned rational mind.... These strange messengers of the night offered suggestions on how to find my way out of my lostness."[39] Ryle dismisses those who disagree as "arrogant and ignorant."[40]

Rather than dismissing dissenters, Ryle should have warned devotees about the dangers inherent in Kelsey's worldview. Kelsey believes that "almost all Christians who were true disciples were something like shamans in the style of their master."[41] As he put it, "Jesus not only used these powers [of the shaman] Himself but He passed the same powers of superhuman knowledge, healing and exorcism on to His followers."[42]

Kelsey not only recasts Christ in the image of a shaman, but he also turns Christians on to such committed occultists as Carlos Castaneda[43] (dubbed by the *Los Angeles Times* as one of the "godfathers of the New Age movement"[44]). This despite the fact that Castaneda classifies the art of dreaming as the most vital method of the sorcerer's armory and the most dangerous. After indulging in this practice for many years, Castaneda recalled, "In my daily state I was nearly an idiot, and in the second attention [altered state of consciousness] I was a lunatic."[45]

Ironically, while Bill McCartney enthusiastically endorses the practices and principles of James Ryle in his foreword to Ryle's book *A Dream Come True*, Castaneda warns devotees of the dangers inherent in the world of visions and dreams in his book *The Art of Dreaming*. From his vantage point as a New Age guru, Castaneda writes, "Everything in the sorcerer's path is a matter of life or death, but in the path of dreaming, this matter is enhanced a hundred fold . . . that's why you have to go into their realm exactly as if you were venturing into a war zone."[46]

As personified by the life of Ryle, once one is immersed in the world of dreams and visions, it becomes increasingly difficult to distinguish fact from fantasy. Nevertheless, many continue to endorse the esoteric imaginations of men like Ryle.

In clear contrast, Edwards was convinced that esoteric imaginations are at best human hallucinations and at worst demonic deceptions. He stood fast against those who attempted to elevate their esoteric experiences to the status of divine revelation. As Edwards explained, "Some are ready to interpret such things wrong, and to lay too much weight on them, as prophetical visions, divine revelations, and sometimes significations from heaven of what shall come to pass."[47]

Edwards further explains that imaginary ideas are the natural by-product of a powerful religious experience. As he put it, "Such is our nature, that we cannot think of things invisible, without a degree of imagination. I dare appeal to any man, of the greatest powers of mind, whether he is able to fix his thoughts on God, or Christ, or the things of another world, without imaginary ideas attending his meditations."[48] Edwards goes on to warn his hearers of supposing that their imaginations are "of the same nature with the visions of the prophets, or St. Paul's rapture into paradise."[49]

Unlike the oracles of Ryle, the oratory of Edwards always focused followers on such biblical realities as the felicities of heaven and the fires of hell. This is precisely what happened when Edwards preached the sermon for which he is most noted, "Sinners in the Hands of an Angry God." His oratory aroused in his audience visions of what it would be like to experience an eternity away from the grace and goodness of God. Thus, far from their visions being esoteric imaginations, they were instead eternal illuminations.

Examples

Not only weak and ignorant people are much influenced by example, but also those that make the greatest boast of strength of reason.[50]

Carol Arnott claims the Almighty spoke to her husband, saying, "I want you to hang around people that have an anointing." According to Carol, God directed them to a man named Benny Hinn, whom John had "ministered" with in the early years. Carol heeded the word of the Lord and began "to hang around" with Hinn. As a result, she says, "I just got absolutely buzzing with the anointing of God."[51] According to the Arnotts, Hinn prayed for them some "fifty times." And the effects of his example are today being experienced around the globe.

Edwards was fully aware of the contagious power of example. Thus, he reminds us of Paul's instruction to young Timothy: "Don't let anyone look down on you because you are young, but *set an example* for the believers in speech, in life, in love, in faith and in purity. Until I come, devote yourself to the public reading of Scripture, to preaching and to teaching" (1 Tim. 4:12–13; emphasis added). Edwards insisted that Scripture was the principle means through which the power of example is made effectual:

> Even the sacraments have no effect but by the Word. *And so it is that example becomes effectual.* For all that is visible to the eye is unintelligible and vain without the Word of God to instruct and guide the mind.[52]

One can only imagine what Edwards might have said had he encountered the example of Hinn slaying supporters in the spirit by casting his coat at a crowd or blowing on believers. Imagine how he would have reacted had he witnessed a member of Wimber's family leading by example as she jerked spasmodically in what Wimber fondly refers to as the "chicken walk." While Edwards clearly maintained that it was "agreeable to Scripture that persons should be influenced by one another's *good example,*" he would have surely resisted such ghastly examples with every "fibre of his lofty and reverent soul."

Excessive Zeal

Lukewarmness in religion is abominable and zeal an excellent grace; yet above all other Christian virtues, this needs to be strictly watched and searched; for it is that with which corruption, and particularly pride and human passion is exceedingly apt to mix unobserved.[53]

Counterfeit Revival leader Larry Randolph, speaking at the Toronto Airport Vineyard, declared that there are only "two groups of people in the church today." He categorized them as

Those that are affected by what God's doing and those that are offended by what God is doing. There is not a lot of neutral ground. The neutral ground is dissipating by the hour. You can't stand in the middle anymore and say, "Well, I don't know. Maybe it's God, maybe it's not." You're going to get rolled over.[54]

Randolph says that in his estimation, the song the Holy Spirit is currently singing is "I'm a Steam Roller, Baby, and I'm Going to Roll Right over You."[55] Counterfeit Revival leaders Bob Jones and Ryle agree. They predict that the party God is presently throwing for his people will soon give way to a bloody civil war. On one side of the war will be "blues" who readily accept new revelations from God. On the other will be "grays" who rely solely on the revelation God has already given. According to Rick Joyner, the grays (whom he labels "spiritually ruthless and cruel"[56]) will "either be converted or removed from their place of influence in the church."[57]

Joyner dogmatically declares that both "believers and unbelievers alike will think that it is the end of Christianity as we know it, and it will be."[58] When the "grays" are finally eliminated, there is going to be "an entirely new definition of Christianity."[59]

While leaders of the Counterfeit Revival predict a great battle in which those who stand against them will be eliminated, Edwards warned against just such a "holy war." He made it clear that even in a cause as crucial as the Reformation, kindness rather than killing should be the order of the day. As he sadly reflected, even "in that glorious revival of religion, at the reformation, zeal in many instances appeared in a very improper severity, and even a degree of persecution."[60]

In place of excessive zealousness that predicts a bloodbath in which those who refuse to accept new revelations are eliminated, the life of Edwards personified the maxim "In essentials unity; in non-essentials liberty; and in all things charity."

Endtime Revelations

However great a spiritual influence may be, it is not to be expected that the Spirit of God should be given now in the same manner as to the apostles, infallibly to guide them in points of Christian doctrine, so that what they taught might be relied on as a rule to the Christian church.[61]

In a vision concerning the endtime harvest, Joyner says Jesus revealed to him that there would be "a great reaping among the Jehovah's Witnesses, Mormons, Seventh Day Adventists, and other sects in which there is a doctrinal mixture." Jesus allegedly went on to point out that these sects would "be won by love, not truth."[62] According to Joyner, Jesus is about to "enormously increase" our understanding on even such basic truths as "salvation and being born again."[63] He even predicts that the endtime church will rise above differences in doctrine and "worship Him in unity."[64] Ominously, he warns that anyone who resists this new "tide of unity" based on love rather than doctrine will be disqualified or removed from leadership:

> Some who are presently in leadership that resist this move will become so hardened they will become opposers and persecutors of the church. Others will be changed and repent of their hardness of heart, even though, in some cases, their resistance to the Holy Spirit will have disqualified them from leadership. This growing tide of unity in the church will reveal the true nature of those in leadership.[65]

Counterfeit Revival historian DeArteaga goes even further. He denounces those who make essential Christian doctrine a prerequisite for unity. According to DeArteaga, such people are guilty of "Pharisaism," which he defines as "the heresy of orthodoxy."[66] He explains that the "core problem with the Pharisee is that he cannot recognize the present work of the Holy Spirit."[67]

One could imagine Edwards not only turning over in his grave at such bizarre notions but also going into high rotation. Pharisaism cannot be correctly defined as orthodoxy, nor should orthodoxy be denounced as heresy. Edwards would have blanched at the mere mention of unity at the expense of essential Christian doctrine.

While Joyner sees no need for the absolute, external, objective standard of Scripture by which to test his endtime visions, Edwards was firmly committed to the principle of *sola scriptura*. He warned that even some godly men during the Great Awakening had been deluded by imagining that their impulses and impressions were infallible revelations:

> Many godly persons have undoubtedly in this and other ages, exposed themselves to woeful delusions, by an aptness to lay too much weight on impulses and impressions, as if they were immediate revelations from God, to signify something future, or to direct them where to go, and what to do.[68]

Erroneous Judgments

And it is particularly observable, that in times of great pouring out of the Spirit to revive religion in the world, a number of those who for a while seemed to partake in it, have fallen off into whimsical and extravagant errors, and gross enthusiasm, boasting of high degrees of spirituality and perfection, censuring and condemning others as carnal.[69]

Ryle likens those who speak out against the "extravagant errors" of the Counterfeit Revival to those "who crucified Jesus Christ." He not only condemns critics as carnal but also characterizes them as the corrupt Pharisees of Christ's day. Not content to cast judgment upon their eternal destiny, he judges their present motivations as well:

> What motivates them to tear down another church? The answer is pride, jealousy, fear, hatred, or ignorance. Take your pick. You can be sure one of these factors is at the heart of this present contention.[70]

Likewise, Trinity Broadcasting Network president Paul Crouch does not hesitate in "censuring and condemning" those who criticize the teachings that are regularly featured on TBN.

His judgment is swift and severe: "I think they're damned and on their way to hell, and I don't think there's any redemption for them."[71] He ominously warns critics to "get out of God's way. Quit blocking God's bridges, or God's gonna shoot you if I don't."

Like Crouch, Toronto Airport Vineyard pastor Marc Dupont warns critics of the Counterfeit Revival that their fate may well be as severe as death:

> There is a judgment that's coming against many lead-
> ers and against the church that despises what God is
> doing in the nineties. . . . I believe judgment this year
> is radically increasing, especially leaders that are go-
> ing to stand in a strong pharisaical stance and are
> going to attack what God is doing. . . . I believe that
> many leaders who are fighting what the Spirit of God
> is doing and saying, God is going to take them out of
> ministry. I believe some of them, I know this isn't a
> new revelation, other people have said this, but I do
> believe that it's true, that God is actually going to be
> taking some leaders home to heaven, rather than to
> continue to allow them to mislead God's people.[72]

Edwards cautioned against just such judgments. He pointed out that even though Judas was a devil, "he had been treated by Jesus himself, in all external things, as if he had truly been a disciple."[73] While we may rightly judge a person's doctrines and deeds in light of Scripture (Acts 17:11; 1 Thess. 5:21–22; Gal. 1:6–10; 2 Cor. 11:4 ff.), we must never pass judgment on their eternal destiny. That is the sole prerogative of God, who alone can search our hearts and who alone has the power to sentence one to hell. As Edwards said of Judas:

> Though Christ knew him, yet he did not then clothe
> himself with the character of omniscient Judge, and

searcher of hearts, but acted the part of a minister of the visible church; (for he was his Father's minister); and therefore rejected him not, *till* he had discovered himself by his *scandalous practice;* thereby giving an example to guides and rulers of the visible church, not to take it upon them to act the part of searcher of hearts, but to be influenced in their administrations by what is visible and open.[74]

Eudaemonism

The main work of ministers is to preach the gospel.[75]

During the first anniversary celebration of the Toronto Blessing, a pastor stood up and asked Randy Clark why the Counterfeit Revival, unlike historical revivals, had not placed a strong emphasis on the holiness of God and the depravity of man. Clark responded by saying that in the current revival, God decided to throw a party for his people because they "already feel so icky about themselves."[76] Like other leaders of the Counterfeit Revival, Clark seems convinced that God's present priority is entertainment rather than evangelism. In sharp contrast to Edwards's thinking, he is convinced that God's purpose is to make us happy as opposed to making us holy.

J. I. Packer sums up such notions with the word *eudaemonism,* which is the "basic principle of hot tub religion."[77] Webster defines *eudaemonism* as the doctrine of happiness, or the system of ethics that considers the moral value of actions in terms of their ability to produce happiness. In stark contrast to Clark, Packer bemoans the fact that this is "a false principle. It loses sight of the place of pain in sanctification whereby God trains his children to share his holiness (see Heb. 12:5–11)."[78]

Leaders of the Counterfeit Revival believe "this recent move of the Spirit is the Lord *romancing* His church."[79] Leaders of the Great Awakening believed that the move of the Spirit was the Lord *reforming* his church. As in our day, eighteenth-century Christianity had assumed the barnacles of the Enlightenment and had come to believe that the pursuit of happiness was the loftiest human goal. In his book *The Scandal of the Evangelical Mind,* Mark Noll pointed out that "the intellectual achievement of Jonathan Edwards was his refusal to admit that these assumptions were in fact the starting points of thought." Edwards "resisted the idea that the pursuit of happiness was the highest purpose of human life."[80] Unlike Clark, he was convinced that the reason the church needed reformation was not because Christians "feel so icky about themselves" but rather because they don't feel icky enough. Rhetorically, he asked:

> Is it really grievous to you, that you have fallen, or do fall into sin; and are you ready, after the example of holy Job, to abhor yourself for it, and repent in dust and ashes, and like Paul to lament your wretchedness, and pray to be delivered from sin, as you would from a body of death?[81]

If you do, then according to Edwards, "you have the evidence that your grace is of the kind that tends to holy practice, and to growth."[82]

It is the height of irony that Counterfeit Revival leaders compare themselves to Great Awakening revivalists, who were criticized not for serving intoxicating Holy Ghost laughter, but for "insisting very much on the terrors of God's holy law, and that with a great deal of pathos and earnestness."[83] Far from discrediting the Great Awakening as a work of God, Edwards made it clear that warnings about the reality of hell were an indispensable part of proclaiming the gospel. Without knowing how desperately "icky" we really are, we will never fully grasp the greatness of our salvation. As Edwards passionately proclaimed:

If there be really a hell of such dreadful and never-ending torments, as is generally supposed, of which multitudes are in great danger . . . then why is it not proper for those who have the care of souls to take great pains to make men sensible of it? . . . If I am in danger of going to hell, I should be glad to know as much as possibly I can of the dreadfulness of it. If I am very prone to neglect due care to avoid it, he does me the best kindness, who does most to represent to me the truth of the case, that sets forth my misery and danger in the liveliest manner.[84]

The Paradigm Shift

Nowhere is the paradigm shift that has taken place in Christianity and our culture more obvious than in the contrast between the ministry of Edwards and the message of the leaders of today's Counterfeit Revival. The ministry of Jonathan Edwards was characterized by dynamic expositional preaching. The message of the Counterfeit Revival is characterized by delusional experiential pandering.

While the Great Awakening was an era of exposition, the Counterfeit Revival is an era of esoteric experience. Today thousands are being deceived into believing that reality can be transformed into a personal experience of enlightenment—a transformation of consciousness that initiates them into true spirituality. The very thing that Edwards wanted people to be saved *from* is what Counterfeit Revival leaders are inducing people to indulge *in*.

CHAPTER 9

A Great Awakening

The passion for a great awakening has reached fever pitch. Leaders spanning the spiritual spectrum predict that the greatest awakening in human history may be just around the corner. Rodney Howard-Browne in *The Coming Revival* wrote, "The coming revival will be the culmination of all other revivals."[1] Bill Bright in his book also titled *The Coming Revival* said the Holy Spirit assured him "this awakening will result in the greatest spiritual harvest in history."[2] Billy Graham's associate Robert Coleman in *The Coming World Revival* suggested that "we may be the generation that will see the greatest revival since the beginning of time."[3]

In their haste to embrace a great awakening, many Christians have instead become ensnared in a great apostasy. Rather than testing experience by the objective standard of Scripture, they have subjectively embraced esoteric experiences. Jonathan Edwards warned against such "woeful delusions." He urged believers to "take the *Scriptures* as [their] guide" (emphasis added). Pointing them to the First Epistle of John, he outlined five essential principles of genuine revival. These principles are so significant that I have alliterated them to make them easy to remember and review.

As you read on, the contrast between the counterfeit (promoted by men like Howard-Browne) and the genuine (prayed for by men like Bright and Coleman) will become self-evident. The counterfeit replaces esteem for Christ with esteem for self, eternal verities with earthly vanities, expositional preaching with wild enthusiasms, essential Christian doctrine with esoteric biblical interpretations, and ego-effacing love with egocentric proclivities.

Esteem for Christ

No man, speaking by the Spirit of God . . . will show an ill or mean esteem of [Christ].[4]

In *The Father's Blessing,* Counterfeit Revival leader John Arnott conveys a conversation he had with Jesus Christ. During the dialogue, Arnott asked the Almighty what he would like to do when they met. Christ allegedly responded, "Oh, John, I just want to wash your feet."[5]

Edwards warned against just such delusions. While Christ once (on earth) humbled himself as a suffering servant, he is now exalted to the highest place so that at the name of Jesus every knee should bow (Phil. 2:5–11). Rather than expecting Christ to bow and wash our feet as he once did with the disciples during his earthly sojourn, true disciples bow at Christ's feet in awe of his majesty and glory. As Edwards so eloquently elaborated, "Humility doth primarily and chiefly consist in *a sense of our meanness* as compared with God, or a sense of the infinite distance there is between God and ourselves. . . . There is no true humility without somewhat of this spirit. . . . We are not truly humble unless we have a sense of our own nothingness as compared with God."[6]

One of the marks of true revival, as Edwards consistently communicated, is esteem for Christ rather than esteem for self. By contrast, Counterfeit Revival leaders like Howard-Browne denigrate the deity of Christ to elevate themselves. Howard-Browne goes so far as to say, "Nothing Jesus did was because He was the Son of God. The Bible says He laid aside His royal robes of deity and when He walked the earth He did so as a prophet under the Abrahamic covenant."[7]

Scripture, however, does not support this diminished view of Christ. Nowhere does the Bible say that Jesus "laid aside His royal robes of deity." While Christ, in his incarnation, took on the limitations of humanity, he was undiminished deity. If Christ were divested of a single attribute of deity, he would not be fully God. Without *both* his divine and human natures, Christ's passion on the cross would have been insufficient to pay the penalty for our sins. In his humanity, Christ was our representative, the second Adam (Rom. 5:18). In his deity, Christ's death was sufficient to provide redemption for all of the sins of humankind (1 John 1:7).

Far from being an apologist for the Counterfeit Revival, Edwards warned against the dangers of embracing an imaginary Christ like the Christ imagined by leaders of the Counterfeit Revival. The result, he says, is that "in their rejoicings and elevations, hypocrites are wont to keep their eye upon themselves; having received what they call spiritual discoveries, their minds are taken up about their own experiences; and not the glory of God, or the beauty of Christ."[8]

Eternal Perspective

The influence of the Spirit of God is yet more abundantly manifest, if persons have their hearts drawn off from the world and weaned from the objects of their worldly lusts.[9]

Nowhere is there a more clear-cut contrast between genuine and counterfeit revival than when it comes to an eternal versus an earthly perspective. While the preaching of the Great

Awakening was focused on eternal verities, the promises of the Counterfeit Revival are focused on earthly vanities.

Benny Hinn, who has had a profound impact on such Counterfeit Revival leaders as John Arnott, is a classic case in point. Personifying the epitome of an earthly perspective, Hinn exclaimed:

> I'm sick and tired of hearing about streets of gold. I don't need gold in heaven, I gotta have it now! I mean, when I get to glory, all my bills will be paid, brother. I won't have bills in glory! I won't need to worry about bills in glory. I gotta have it here! You say, "Well, Benny Hinn, isn't it wonderful to have streets of gold in heaven?" Well, of course, but if I hear the thing one more time of how it will be and how it was, I'm gonna kick somebody![10]

Hinn not only says that he's "gotta have gold," but also we're "gonna have good health":

> The day is coming, I tell you this, I know it like I know my name, the day is coming there will not be one sick saint in the body of Christ. Nobody will be, nobody's gonna be, no one will be raptured up out of a wheelchair. No one will be raptured out of a hospital bed. You're all gonna be healed before the rapture.[11]

Like Hinn, endtime prophet Paul Cain promises prospects that "all the sick are gonna be healed, the dead are gonna be raised, and nations are gonna turn to God in a day."[12] In fact, says Cain, national news broadcasts will have nothing to report but good news.[13] Cain promises that God is now raising up a Christian army to take over the sociopolitical systems of the day. In his words, "Not even Elijah or Peter or Paul or anyone else enjoyed the power that is going to rest upon this great army."[14]

Rick Joyner raised expectations of devotees to fever pitch by exuding:

> Angelic appearances will be common to the saints and a visible glory of the Lord will appear upon some for extended periods of time as power flows through them. There will be no plague, disease, or physical condition, including lost limbs, AIDS, poison gas, or radiation, which will resist the healing and miracle gifts working in the saints during this time. Food will be multiplied day after day where there is no other provision. At times the Lord will provide abundant supplies from heaven like He did with Israel in the wilderness.[15]

Not only will individual Christians be empowered from on high, but God will also allegedly raise up super apostles and prophets who will pack arenas and stadiums to overflowing. These prophets and apostles "will stand up to bless fields and cities in the name of the Lord and to remove every trace of radiation from them." And that's just for starters. Joyner goes on to promise:

> No one will look back at the early church as a standard; all will be saying that the Lord has certainly saved His best wine for last. The early church was a firstfruits offering, truly this will be a harvest! It was said of the Apostle Paul that he was turning the world upside down; it will be said of the apostles soon to be anointed that they have turned an upside down world right side up. Nations will tremble at the mention of their name, but they will also be healed by them.[16]

Howard-Browne points out that not only will the nations tremble, but also national talk-show hosts will be terrified:

One of these days, a true prophet, anointed of God, will be a guest on one of these television talk shows. When they start to mock him, he will simply look at them and say, "That you may know there is a God who lives—that you may know that He shall not be mocked—you will be blind for three days as a sign to you and this audience." The talk show host will scream, "Oh, my God, I can't see! I can't see! I'm blind!" And the telephone lines will be jammed; signs and wonders will be made manifest.

He goes on to say that in his estimation we "slipped over the edge into this great outpouring in 1990." Thus it will soon be commonplace to see awesome manifestations of the glory of God. Says Howard-Browne, "Creative miracles will happen; eyeballs will form, legs and arms will grow out, people will leap out of wheelchairs."[17]

Kenneth Hagin summed up Howard-Browne's sentiments well when he asserted: "Yes, sin, sickness and disease, spiritual death, poverty, and everything else that's of the devil once ruled us. But now, bless God, *we rule them*—for this is the Day of Dominion!"[18]

The more you listen to these messages, the more crystal-clear their common refrain becomes. Leaders of the Counterfeit Revival demand the kingdom now!—in this life, with all of its attendant material wealth, public accolades, physical health, and earthly power. Jesus, however, said, "My kingdom is not of this world. . . . My kingdom is from another place" (John 18:36). When his followers heard this, the shout, "Hosanna! . . . Blessed is the King of Israel!" (John 12:13) became the scream, "Crucify him! . . . We have no king but Caesar" (John 19:15).

Like leaders of the Counterfeit Revival, their sights were focused on earth, not eternity. In sharp contrast, Edwards was utterly convinced that in genuine revival the Spirit of God was at work "to lessen men's esteem of the pleasures, profits, and honors of the world, and to take off their hearts from an eager pursuit after these things; and to engage them in a deep concern about a future state and eternal happiness which the gospel reveals—and puts them upon earnestly seeking the kingdom of God and his righteousness."[19]

C. S. Lewis, like Edwards, understood the utter folly of aiming at earth. As he so poignantly put it, "Aim at heaven and you get earth thrown in. Aim at earth and you get neither."[20]

Expositional Preaching

We see it common in enthusiasts, that they depreciate this written rule and set up the light within or some other rule above it.[21]

Counterfeit Revival leader John Wimber, in a message on supernatural healing, expressed concern that evangelical Christians today are placing far too much emphasis on Scripture: "Evangelicals all over the country are worshiping the book. They have God the Father, God the Son, and God the Holy Book. They took the very workings of the Holy Spirit and placed it in the Book."[22]

Wimber expressed particular concern for the Calvary Chapel movement, well known for teaching people verse-by-verse through the Scriptures:

Calvaryites are sometimes a little too heavily oriented to the written Word. I know that sounds a little dangerous, but frankly they're very pharisaical in their allegiance to the Bible. They have very little life and growth and spontaneity in their innards. Sometimes they're very rigid and can't receive much of the things of the Lord.[23]

Edwards's concern was quite the opposite. He could not have fathomed someone being "too heavily oriented to the written Word." On the contrary, he was convinced that "the spirit that operates in such a manner, as to cause in men a greater regard to the Holy Scriptures, and establishes them more in their truth and divinity, is certainly the Spirit of God."[24] He expressed disgust for "enthusiasts" who depreciated Scripture and instead turned for revelation to the "light within."

The "light within" that Edwards scorned was, as he put it, "the spirit the Quakers extol."[25] He abhorred the notion propounded by Quaker founder George Fox that "ultimate and final authority for religious life and faith resides within each individual."[26] Edwards most certainly would have resisted the Quakerism of Wimber (a Quaker pastor for five years[27]), just as he resisted the Quakerism of Fox. He was fully aware of the danger of abandoning the objective standard of scriptural exposition for the mystical inner light of subjective experience.

Predictably, what Edwards condemned as error, Todd Hunter (national coordinator of the Association of Vineyard Churches) commends as "thoroughly evangelical":

> Evangelicals get so mad when we say we're one of you. Oh, it drives them nuts! But we are! I've showed you tonight we're historically, directly linked. John was a Quaker. You don't get any more evangelical than Quakerism.[28]

While there are unquestionably Quakers who are evangelicals, Quakerism itself has historically compromised the evangelical essential of *sola scriptura*. The "evangelicalism" championed by Edwards was committed to the principle that "ultimate and final authority" resided in Scripture alone. What leaders of the Counterfeit Revival described as "light," the leader of the Great Awakening denounced as darkness:

If they speak not according to this word, it is because there is no light in them. . . . The devil has ever shown a mortal spite and hatred towards that holy book, the Bible: he has done all in his power to extinguish that light and to draw men off from it: He knows it to be that light by which the kingdom of darkness is to be overthrown. . . . He is enraged against the Bible and hates every word in it: And we may be sure that he never will attempt to raise persons' esteem of it or affection to it.[29]

Essential Christian Doctrine

Whatever spirit removes our darkness, and brings us to the light, undeceives us, and, by convincing us of the truth, doth us a kindness.[30]

In a message titled "Receiving the Spirit's Power," Counterfeit Revival leader Carol Arnott claims she had a conversation with the Holy Spirit. During the dialogue, the spirit that spoke with her communicated sorrow over being separated from Jesus:

"You know, the Father, and Jesus and I have been together for all of eternity. But when Jesus went back to heaven to be with God the Father, I came to earth." And he said, "I am so lonely for Jesus." He said, "So that when people really, really love Jesus, and really honor him, and really worship him," he said, "I love to be around those kinds of people." . . . He misses Jesus, and he misses the Father.[31]

Edwards warned against just such delusions. He passionately exhorted his followers to test the spirits by taking "the Scriptures as our guide."[32] Edwards pointed specifically to the warning of John the Apostle: "Do not believe every spirit, but test the spirits to see if they are from God" (1 John 4:1).

Instead of listening to the warning of John the Apostle, Carol chose to listen to the warning of John Arnott: "If you play it safe with this thing, the Holy Spirit, you know what? You're never going to get anywhere. . . . I don't want you to even entertain the thought that you might get a counterfeit."[33]

This kind of foolishness was completely contrary to all that Edwards held dear. Without the Scripture as a guide, Edwards warned, the church would "lie open to woeful delusions." Had Carol Arnott consulted the canon of Scripture, she would have readily recognized that the spirit that communicated with her was not the Spirit of God. The Holy Spirit revealed in Scripture is not separated from Jesus Christ. Nor is the Holy Spirit lonely. If he were, he would be incomplete and thus imperfect. The localized god described by Arnott is finite and divided. The omnipresent God of Scripture is infinite and one in essence. As codified by the Creed of Athanasius, "We worship one God in Trinity, and Trinity in Unity . . . the whole three Persons are coeternal together, and coequal."

It should be noted that Carol Arnott is not alone in her revelation of a finite and imperfect god. In a message titled "Close Encounters of the God Kind," Jesse Duplantis said that during one of his mystical trips to heaven, he learned that the Holy Spirit is separated from Jesus Christ and God the Father:

> I actually understand the Trinity physically now. I've seen Jesus come out of Jehovah-Elohim-God. And I asked that angel, now, you know, kind of a dumb question. I said, "Where's the Holy Spirit?"
>
> And that angel looked at—and I could see it in his eyes, like, "This boy ain't got a lot of sense."
>
> I said, "I see God the Father, I see Jehovah-Elohim-Yahweh. I seen Christ come out of him. Where's the Holy Spirit?"

And he just said, "Jesse, he's on the earth."
I said, "Yeah, that makes sense."[34]

What is true for Carol Arnott is true for Jesse Duplantis. If he had tested his experience in light of Scripture, he would have come to the inevitable conclusion that his revelation was a counterfeit.

Edwards warns that there is both the "Spirit of truth" and the "spirit of error" (1 John 4:6 KJV). The Spirit of truth leads us to the light of essential Christian doctrine and "represents things as they truly are."[35] The spirit of error leads only to darkness. Says Edwards:

> There are undoubtedly sufficient marks given to guide the church of God in this great affair of judging of spirits, without which it would lie open to woeful delusions, and would be remedylessly exposed to be imposed upon and devoured by its enemies. And we need not to be afraid to trust these rules. Doubtless that Spirit who indicted the Scriptures knew how to give us good rules, by which to distinguish his operations from all that is falsely pretended to be from him.[36]

Ego-Effacing Love

Indeed there is a counterfeit love, that often appears among those who are led by a spirit of delusion. There is commonly in the wildest enthusiasts, a kind of union and affection, arising from self-love.[37]

The final characteristic of genuine revival cited by Jonathan Edwards is the emulation of ego-effacing love. In sharp contrast, counterfeit revival is characterized by the elevation of egocentric love. Rather than exalting Jesus Christ, the Counterfeit Revival effectively reduces Christ to a means to its ends.

Devotees are urged to come to the Master's table, not in devotion to the Master but rather to devour what is on the Master's table.

The egocentric refrain sung by Counterfeit Revivalists is that God is finally going to elevate us to the top echelon of society. Their magic mantra is that he will soon make us the head and not the tail, the lender and not the borrower. Repeatedly they promise prospects that "the wealth of the wicked is laid up for the righteous."

While the Great Awakening was focused on evangelistic priorities, the Counterfeit Revival is focused on egocentric parties. John Arnott even asserts that God accused him of being pushy when he tried to preach evangelistic messages. As I mentioned earlier, the Almighty allegedly admonished Arnott with the words: "Is it all right with you if I just love on my church for a while?"[38] At one Counterfeit Revival party, Arnott recounted, one man "got blasted, just totally blasted—there's no other word—by the Spirit. He fell; he shook; he yelled; he thrashed; he did it all." When he returned home, his wife extolled the virtue of the party, enthusing, "I sent this worn-out machine to Toronto and a lover came back home to me."[39]

Rarely is the self-gratifying orientation of Counterfeit Revivalists more prominent than in Arnott's book *The Father's Blessing*. In a section titled "Jesus Wants a Love Affair with You," Arnott describes how Jesus appeared to a woman and fulfilled all her fantasies. Jesus laughed with the woman as together they ran around with arms stretched out like airplanes; Jesus lay on the ground with the woman and played Legos; then Jesus played with her hair and met her deepest needs and desires.[40]

Similarly, in one of Carol Arnott's visions, Jesus brings her a bouquet of lilies after which they "run and play and have a wonderful, intimate time together." Carol and Jesus then get married. At the wedding feast, Carol said, she "was standing in an open spot when Jesus walked up and said, 'Carol, may I have the first dance?'" Carol exuded that cardinals and blue jays "picked up my veil, and I danced with Jesus."[41]

Edwards cogently contrasted the selfless love of genuine revival with the selfish love of counterfeit revival:

> The surest character of true divine supernatural love—distinguishing it from counterfeits that arise from a natural self-love—is that the Christian virtue of *humility* shines in it; that which above all others renounces, abases, and annihilates what we term *self*. Christian love, or true charity, is an humble love.[42]

Edwards's characterization of selfish love was emphatic:

> Indeed there is a counterfeit love, that often appears among those who are led by a spirit of delusion. There is commonly in the wildest enthusiasts, a kind of union and affection, arising from self-love, occasioned by their agreeing in those things wherein they greatly differ from all others, and from which they are objects of the ridicule of all the rest of mankind. This naturally will cause them so much the more to prize those peculiarities that make them the objects of others' contempt.[43]

The Demise of the Great Awakening

In the end the "peculiarities of wild enthusiasts" spelled the demise of the Great Awakening. The powerful expositional preaching of men like Edwards, with its emphasis on esteem for Christ, an eternal perspective, essential Christian doctrine, and ego-effacing love, was replaced by excesses, errors, and extremes. The turning point, in Edwards's estimation, came when enthusiastic endorsers of the revival began to entertain and encourage such lying signs and wonders. According to biographer Iain H. Murray:

He came to believe that there was one principle cause of the reversal, namely, the unwatchfulness of the friends of the Awakening who allowed genuine and pure religion to become so mixed with "wildfire," and carnal "enthusiasm," that the Spirit of God was grieved and advantage given to Satan.[44]

As lying signs and wonders took center stage in the Great Awakening, division arose between those who resisted "imprudences and irregularities" and those who promoted them. Perhaps the most deplorable demonstration of discord and division took place when James Davenport led a group of revivalists onto a town wharf and proceeded to burn the works of such great Puritans as John Bunyan. "By 1743 America's clergy were evenly split over whether the revivals were a work of God or a work of the devil."[45]

Despite the divisiveness and short duration of the First Great Awakening, the colonies had been greatly impacted. In addition to spurring conversions and spawning churches, the revival resulted in the founding of five significant colleges, including Princeton and Dartmouth.

By the beginning of the American Revolution (1776), however, Christianity was once again on the decline. The emotional excitement and spiritual effects of the Great Awakening had deteriorated into apathy and indifference. Multitudes had been converted to complacency, and prominent people such as Thomas Jefferson and Thomas Paine renounced Christianity and embraced deism. As Os Guinness noted, however, "the real struggle in the period 1780–1830 was not between evangelicals and deists, but between those who took theology seriously and those who did not."[46]

While the First Great Awakening had emphasized the rational understanding of essential Christian doctrine, "it remained for the Second Awakening, the next great wave of

American revivalism, to advance almost purely emotional Christianity to a central position in popular American religion."[47] In the First Great Awakening, excesses had been the by-product of revival; in the Second, they would be the bottom line.

CHAPTER 10

A Muddy Mixture

Lying signs and wonders had felled the first great revival, but revivalism had only just begun. While widespread revivals were absent between 1745 and 1795, local awakenings kept the revival flame from completely dying out. In 1796 the embers were once again ignited by the fiery frontier preaching of a Presbyterian named James McGready. It wasn't until 1800, however, that the Second Great Awakening would be set ablaze.

The First Great Awakening took place primarily within the context of formal church services. The Second Great Awakening took place primarily within the context of frontier campsites. The extemporaneous manner of men like James McGready resonated with frontier people who "lived, worked and died hard" and "were impatient with the fine theological points that interested Eastern congregations."[1] Revival historian Keith Hardman describes the scene at McGready's meetings in June of 1800:

> On that occasion, four or five hundred members of McGready's three congregations gathered for a communion service at Red River. For many this was the third year that they had prayed for a display of God's

power. Three Presbyterian ministers (McGready, William Hodge, and John Rankin) were joined by two brothers, the Presbyterian William McGee and the Methodist John McGee. The first three days of the meetings were solemn and reverent. On the final day, John McGee exhorted the people that "there was a greater than I preaching" and that they should "submit to him." At this insistence that God was at work, the congregation joyously and frantically began to shout and cry.[2]

While some called for order, McGee said the power of God was so strong upon him that he "went through the house shouting, and exhorting with all possible ecstasy and energy, and the floor was soon covered with the slain; their screams for mercy pierced the heavens."[3]

McGready and his associates were so convinced that God was at work that they organized another meeting the following month at Gasper River. To their amazement people traveled from as far as one hundred miles away to attend what was to become known as the first true camp meeting.[4] In the ensuing months, similar revival meetings were held throughout Kentucky and Tennessee.

The Cane Ridge Revival

In 1801 the fire of the famous Cane Ridge Revival, for which the Second Great Awakening is best remembered, was sparked. According to Vanderbilt historian Paul Conkin, Cane Ridge became "arguably the most important religious gathering in all of American history. It ignited the explosion of evangelical religion, which soon reached into nearly every corner of American life. For decades the prayer of camp meetings and revivals across the land was 'Lord, make it like Cane Ridge.'"[5]

The unlikely leader of what "quickly became one of the

best-reported events in American history"[6] was a man named Barton W. Stone, who denied such essential Christian doctrines as the Trinity.[7] When Stone, the Presbyterian pastor of the Cane Ridge meeting house in Bourbon County, Kentucky, heard about the "McGready revivals," he traveled across the state to witness them firsthand. Intrigued by the extraordinary enthusiasms and excitement, Stone determined to organize a revival of his own.

What happened next dwarfed anything that had taken place thus far. At times more than twenty thousand people listened to revival rhetoric amid songs and shouts. Pentecostal historian Vinson Synan provides an apt description of the sights and sounds of Cane Ridge:

> Those who attended such camp meetings as Cane Ridge generally expected their religious experiences to be as vivid as the frontier life around them. Accustomed to "braining bears and battling Indians," they received their religion with great color and excitement. Their "godly hysteria" included such phenomena as falling, jerking, barking like dogs, falling into trances, the "holy laugh." . . .
>
> In the light of the blazing campfires hundreds of sinners would fall, "like dead men in mighty battle." Others would get the "jerks" and shake helplessly at every joint. Peter Cartwright reported that he once saw five hundred jerking at once in one service. The unconverted were as subject to the "jerks" as were the saints. . . . [8]

Peter Cartwright

Cartwright, himself a product of the revival, became an authority on its excesses. Although he confessed that he often laughed upon seeing "proud young gentlemen and young ladies, dressed in their silks, jewelry, and prunella, from top to toe, take the jerks," he was also aware of the inherent danger.

He told the story of one unrepentant sinner who got such a bad case of the jerks that it actually killed him:

This large man cursed the jerks, and all religion. Shortly afterward he took his jerks, and he started to run, but he jerked so powerfully he could not get away. He halted among some saplings, and although he was violently agitated, he took out his bottle of whiskey, and swore he would drink the d——d jerks to death; but he jerked at such a rate that he could not get the bottle to his mouth, though he tried hard. At length he fetched a sudden jerk, and the bottle struck a sapling and was broken to pieces, and spilled the whiskey on the ground. There was a great crowd gathered around him, and when he lost his whiskey he became very much enraged, and cursed and swore profanely, his jerks still increasing. At length he fetched a very violent jerk, snapped his neck, fell, and soon expired, with his mouth full of cursing and bitterness.[9]

Drinking and disorderly conduct were such problems during the revivals that some states prohibited the sale of alcohol within a few miles of the campsites.[10] Some meetings degenerated to the point that "watchmen carrying long white sticks patrolled the meeting grounds each evening to stop any sexual mischief. Enemies of camp meetings sneered that 'more souls were begot than saved.'"[11]

As a circuit riding preacher, Peter Cartwright was all too familiar with this unbridled decadence. He dogmatically denounced both licentiousness and lying signs and wonders wherever he encountered them. Rather than trying to produce them, he said, "It was, on all occasions, my practice to recommend fervent prayer as a remedy." He went on to say:

From these wild exercises, another great evil arose from the heated and wild imaginations of some. They professed to fall into trances and see visions; they would fall at meetings and sometimes at home, and lay apparently powerless and motionless for days, sometimes for a week at a time, without food or drink; to have seen God, angels, the devil and the damned; they would prophesy, and, under the pretense of Divine inspiration, predict the time of the end of the world, and the ushering in of the great millennium.

This was the most troublesome delusion of all; it made such an appeal to the ignorance, superstition, and credulity of all the people, even saint as well as sinner. I watched this matter with vigilant eye. If I opposed it, I would have to meet the clamor of the multitude; and if any one opposed it, these very visionists would single him out, and denounce the dreadful judgments of God against him. They would even set the very day that God was to burn the world, like the self-deceived modern Millerites.

They would prophesy, that if any one did oppose them, God would send fire down from heaven and consume him, like the blasphemous Shakers. They would proclaim that they could heal all manners of diseases, and raise the dead, just like the diabolical Mormons. They professed to have conversed with spirits of the dead in heaven and hell, like the modern spirit rappers. Such a state of things I never saw before, and I hope in God I shall never see again.[12]

The lying signs and wonders that Peter Cartwright prayed he would never see again are today center stage in the Counterfeit Revival. While multitudes clamor for revival, what the church sorely needs is reformation. Only when the church experiences reformation through esteem for Christ, an eternal perspective, expositional preaching, essential Christian doctrine, and ego-effacing love will the world experience revival.

PART THREE

—

Endtime Restorationism

CHAPTER 11

Endtime Restoration of Tongues

Endtime restorationism had its genesis in the early morning hours of the first day of the twentieth century. A twenty-seven-year-old preacher from Topeka, Kansas, named Charles Parham placed his hands on the head of his young student Agnes Ozman. Suddenly, a "halo seemed to surround her head and face"[1] and Agnes began to speak Chinese. For three solid days she was utterly incapable of speaking a single word in English. Even more incredibly, when she tried to write, only Chinese characters emerged from her pen.[2]

Ozman's experience became the catalyst for other students in Parham's class to seek the gift of tongues.[3] It wasn't long before many of them, like Agnes, began to speak in languages they had never studied. According to Parham, his students, "Americans all, spoke in twenty-one known languages, including French, German, Swedish, Bohemian, Chinese, Japanese, Hungarian, Bulgarian, Russian, Italian, Spanish, and Norwegian."[4]

Parham told a *Kansas City Times* correspondent that "his students had never studied these languages and that natives of the countries involved had heard them spoken and verified their authenticity." Parham proudly proclaimed that while missionaries throughout church history necessarily studied foreign languages, this would no longer be the case. As a result of the endtime restoration of tongues, "one need only receive the baptism with the Holy Spirit and he could go to the farthest corners of the world and preach to the natives in languages unknown to the speaker."[5]

Pentecostal historian Vinson Synan candidly points out that when Parham's theory was put to the test, the result was a "fiasco." He recounts the tragic tale of Alfred Garr, pastor of the L.A. Burning Bush Mission. Garr received the gift of tongues, moved to India, and began preaching to the natives in what he believed to be their own languages. Synan concludes, "This was the outstanding attempt at carrying out Parham's teaching concerning the missionary use of tongues and it ended in failure."[6]

Parham was so convinced that tongues was a prelude to global revival and a precursor to endtime restorationism that he "closed his school at Topeka and began a whirlwind tour of revivals which lasted for four years."[7] In 1905 he moved to Houston, Texas, and opened a school to propagate his newfound theology. It was at this school that Parham taught a man "given to dreams and visions"[8] who was to become the "Apostle of Azusa Street."[9] His name was William Seymour.

The Apostle of Azusa Street

Synan describes the "Apostle of Azusa Street" as "a short, stocky man, minus one eye," a "poverty stricken Southern Negro with little or no knowledge of religious history."[10] Because of his ethnic status, Seymour was not permitted to sit in Parham's classes. Rather, he was relegated to sitting in a hallway and listening to Parham's doctrines through a doorway.

While Seymour roundly rejected Parham's teaching that Anglo-Saxons were God's chosen race,[11] he uncritically embraced

Parham's theology on tongues. Seymour was so convinced of Parham's position that even before he personally spoke in tongues, he told parishioners of a Los Angeles Holiness church that tongues, not sanctification, was evidence of the baptism in the Holy Ghost. Mrs. Hutchinson, the pastor who had invited Seymour to preach in her church, was so upset that she "padlocked the church door the next night to keep Seymour out."[12]

Several days later, however, Seymour experienced the breakthrough he was looking for. He and seven devotees "fell to the floor in a religious ecstasy, speaking with other tongues."[13] News spread like wildfire, and before long curious onlookers beheld such sights as Jennie Moore (Seymour's future wife) singing in what was at the time believed to be the Hebrew language. Curiosity swelled the size of the crowds so much that Seymour rented an old, abandoned African Methodist Episcopal Church at 312 Azusa Street in which to conduct revival meetings.

Weird Babel of Tongues

On April 18, 1906, subscribers to the *Los Angeles Times* were startled by the headline "Weird Babel of Tongues." The article proclaimed: "New Sect of Fanatics Is Breaking Loose; Wild Scene Last Night on Azusa Street; Gurgle of Wordless Talk by a Sister."[14] The notoriety only served to fan the flame. As news spread, people from across America headed to Azusa Street to "catch the fire."

The endtime restoration of Pentecostal power proved to be so compelling that Christians and cultists alike suspended their meetings and headed to 312 Azusa Street. Together they engaged in the "jerks" and in "treeing the devil." It wasn't long before "spiritualists and mediums from the numerous occult societies of Los Angeles began to attend and to contribute their seances and trances to the services." In time things got so out of hand that "Seymour wrote Parham for advice on how to handle 'the spirits' and begged him to come to Los Angeles to take over supervision of the revival."[15]

When Parham arrived, he was outraged at the spiritual pandemonium he encountered. He forcefully denounced the "hypnotists and spiritualists who seemed to have taken over the services."[16] While Seymour was sympathetic to Parham's concerns, he refused correction, and the two pillars of Pentecostalism suffered an irreparable falling out. Seymour barred Parham from ever preaching at Azusa Street again. Parham, in turn, denounced Seymour as "possessed." Pentecostal historian Synan aptly summed up Parham's sentiments:

> For the rest of his life, Parham continued his denunciation of the Azusa Street meetings as a case of "spiritual power prostituted" to the "awful fits and spasms" of the "holy rollers and hypnotists."[17]

The man whom Seymour extolled as his "father in the Gospel of the Kingdom"[18] went on to spend "the later years of his life as an avid supporter of the Ku Klux Klan."[19] For his part, Seymour stayed the course in his unique preaching and practice, "hurling defiance at anyone who did not accept his views."[20]

While the racial and religious rift between Charles Parham and William Seymour was never repaired, the twin pillars of Pentecostalism did succeed in setting the stage for endtime restorationism. Through their ministries, the baptism of the Holy Ghost with the evidence of speaking in tongues was restored to the endtime church.

Recovering Lost Truth

Counterfeit Revival leader Rick Joyner points out that while other reformers and revivalists also spoke in tongues, Parham's "experience came at what could be called 'the fullness of time' or a time that was ripe for the harvest of a recovered truth."

While he refers to Parham as a "true spiritual father . . . of the modern Pentecostal Movement,"[21] he regards Seymour's "remarkable leadership at Azusa"[22] as the key to giving the Holy Spirit the freedom that he needed in the recovery of lost truth:

> In spite of almost constant pressure from world-renowned church leaders, who came from around the globe to impose what they perceived to be needed order and direction on the revival, for over two years Seymour held the course and allowed the Holy Spirit to move in His own, often mysterious ways.[23]

Joyner says that "understanding how true moves of God begin is crucial." He tells devotees that if they are to grasp what a movement will look like when it is full-grown, they must go back to its genesis: "Just as the genetic code that determines what a grown man will look like is set at conception, the genetic code of entire movements is usually set even before their birth."[24]

CHAPTER 12

Endtime Restoration of Healing

Todd Hunter, national coordinator of the Association of Vineyard Churches, believes that from "Azusa Street to today, the Pentecostals have been *the* largest, most dynamic force of Christians on the earth."[1] Thus, says Hunter, "I'm sick and tired of being impugned about being called a Pentecostal."[2] After extolling the virtues of Azusa Street, he turns the attention of devotees to "the renewing influences" of three Pentecostal healing evangelists: A. A. Allen, William Branham, and Jack Coe. According to Hunter, these men may have emerged from Pentecostal ranks, but "they had some renewing influences in mainline Christianity"[3] as well.

In sharp contrast, denominational leaders within Pentecostalism candidly acknowledged the reprehensible influences these men had on the Christian cause. Rather than commend them, they condemned the flamboyant lifestyles and fantastic lies of these endtime restorationists.

Asa Alonso Allen (1911–1970)

The Assemblies of God denomination in particular was horrified by the antics of A. A. Allen, whose dogmatic and undocumented claims included the deception that he could raise people from the dead.[4] Allen actually launched a "raise the dead"[5] campaign in the midsixties. Thankfully, it died when his disciples refused to bury their departed, and their departed refused to come back from the dead.

Allen's specialty was to heal his disciples from sickness and sin by delivering them from demons. He was especially proud of healing a forty-three-year-old hermaphrodite[6] by casting out the "female spirit." As reported in Allen's *Miracle Magazine,* the hermaphrodite attended an Allen revival and was slain in the spirit. As he lay on the ground, God changed him completely to a male: "I left the other self there. The female spirit left! Even my large breasts had vanished. . . . God removed every trace of the feminine and has healed and strengthened the masculine organs."[7]

Allen's *Miracle Magazine* chronicled not only the casting out of a "female spirit" but also the cure of a "fat sister." Mrs. Alvester Williams, from Las Vegas, Nevada, allegedly "took 200 pounds off instantly using 'God's reducing plan.'"[8] The magazine's editor added a note that read, "This lady's body could be seen shrinking visibly, as she sat in the service."[9]

Financial healings, however, soon outweighed physical healings as Allen's primary claim to fame. The *Dictionary of Pentecostal and Charismatic Movements* notes that he "was one of the first to appeal for support by using the theme of financial blessing for the giver."[10] Allen told adherents that God had given him "a new anointing and a new power to lay hands on the believers who gave $100.00 towards the support of our missionary outreach and bestow upon each of them POWER TO GET WEALTH."[11] Allen said that in 1963 God had revealed to him that he had lots of money. As the Almighty exclaimed, "I am a wealthy God! Yea, I am not poor." God went on to tell Allen that he was planning to "do a new thing in the earth."[12]

Among other "new things," God performed tricks such as changing the one-dollar bills in Allen's pocket into twenty-dollar bills.[13] Recognizing that some devotees might know that this was a common magician's trick, Allen said:

> Of course some of you do not believe this. Listen, you old skeptic, you don't have to believe it, because it doesn't have to happen to you. But it had to happen to me. I'll tell you why. I decreed a thing. . . . God said "Thou shall decree a thing, and it shall be established unto thee. . . ." I believe I can command God to perform a miracle for you financially. When you do, God can turn dollar bills into twenties.[14]

This was not the only trick up Allen's sleeve. He was also adept at creating the illusion that "miracle oil" was flowing from the heads and hands of his followers. He tried to sanitize his sleight of hand by quoting Hebrews 1:9 (KJV): "Thou hast loved righteousness, and hated iniquity; therefore God, even thy God hath anointed thee with the oil of gladness above thy fellows." The fact that the text was taken out of context and used as a pretext did not seem to bother Allen's audiences in the least.

It did, however, bother authorities of the Assemblies of God. Unlike the leaders of today's Counterfeit Revival, they were embarrassed by such outlandish claims and outrageous conduct. Thus, when Allen, who is extolled today by Benny Hinn as "a great man of God,"[15] was arrested for drunk driving during a Tennessee revival in 1955, the first of many alcohol-related experiences for Allen,[16] the leadership of the Assemblies of God had reached its limit. Ralph Riggs, superintendent of the General Council of the Assemblies of God, advised Allen to get out of public ministry.[17] Rather than comply, the outraged Allen concocted an alibi. What really happened, offered an associate, was that Allen was "kidnapped and knocked unconscious. When he awoke, he was in a 'smoke-filled room and somebody was pouring liquor down his throat.'"[18]

When Pentecostal leaders turned against Allen, his wife, Lexie, stood by her man. She blamed the Assemblies of God for doing "everything they could to destroy him."[19] Despite Lexie's loyalty, in the end Allen divorced her. Three years later at the age of fifty-nine, he died in San Francisco from cirrhosis of the liver.[20]

Though he was excommunicated by Pentecostal leaders in his day, he is extolled by endtime restorationists in ours. Rodney Howard-Browne, for one, urges devotees: "Read the life stories of some of the great men of God, men like A. A. Allen."[21]

William Marrion Branham (1909–1965)

One of the most revered leaders of today's Counterfeit Revival is William Branham. Despite the fact that Branham denied such essential Christian doctrines as the Trinity, endtime restorationist Paul Cain calls him "the greatest prophet that ever lived in any of my generations or any of the generations of revival I've lived through."[22] The *Dictionary of Christianity in America* acknowledges that "the post–World War II healing revival in Pentecostalism began in the ministry of William Branham."[23]

On May 7, 1946, while the prophet Branham was still only a humble, if mystical, game warden, a two-hundred-pound angel with shoulder-length hair and a dark complexion appeared to him in a secret cave.[24] The angel spoke, saying:

> Fear not. I am sent from the presence of Almighty God to tell you that your peculiar life and your misunderstood ways have been to indicate that God has sent you to take a gift of divine healing to the people of the world. IF YOU WILL BE SINCERE, AND CAN GET THE PEOPLE TO BELIEVE YOU, NOTHING SHALL STAND BEFORE YOUR PRAYER, NOT EVEN CANCER.[25]

"Vibrations in his left hand," said the angel, would be the sign to Branham that he had, indeed, been chosen as an instrument of healing. Through these vibrations, Branham would be able to detect and diagnose all manner of diseases in his devotees. When the demon of a disease came into contact with his vibrating hand, the "physical commotion" would be so dramatic that it would "stop his wristwatch instantly." As his healing partner Fred Bosworth told the tale, "This feels to Brother Branham like taking hold of a live wire with too much electric current in it. When the oppressing spirit is cast out in Jesus' Name, you can see Brother Branham's red and swollen hand return to its normal condition."[26]

The angel also advised Branham that he would be able to disclose details of the lives of devotees through the word of knowledge.[27] This gift was to make Branham not just a healer but also a "seer as were the Old Testament prophets."[28] Brother Bosworth pointed out that for Branham to exercise his gift, he was dependent on the presence of an angel: "He does not begin to pray for the healing of the afflicted in body in the healing line each night . . . until he is conscious of the presence of the Angel with him on the platform."[29]

As crowds began to dwindle in 1959, Branham announced that he would abandon his "ability to read the very thoughts of men's hearts" and return to a healing ministry.[30] To prepare people for his magical healing powers, he resorted to telling them anecdotal stories of his healing heroics in days gone by.

In 1963 Branham revealed that he had come in the "spirit of Elijah"[31] to warn people to flee their "dead churches and denominations and pledge their loyalty to the prophet of the last days."[32] As Paul was the apostle to the church of Ephesus, Branham had come to fancy himself as the angel to the endtime church of Laodicea.[33] He proclaimed that by "1977 all denominations would be consumed by the World Council of Churches under the control of the Roman Catholics, that the Rapture would take place, and that the world would be destroyed."[34]

Branham's failed prophecies were only exceeded by his false doctrines. His dogmatic "serpent's seed doctrine" held that Eve had sexual intercourse with the serpent and conceived Cain. The *Dictionary of Pentecostal and Charismatic Movements* summarized Branham's new revelation:

> Eve's sin involved sexual relations with the serpent. Some humans are descended from the serpent's seed and are destined for hell, which is not eternal, however. The seed of God, i.e., those who receive Branham's teaching, are predestined to become the bride of Christ. There are still others who possess free will and who may be saved out of the denominational churches, but they must suffer through the Great Tribulation. He considered denominationalism a mark of the Beast (Rev. 13:17).[35]

Branham was adamant in his denial of the biblical doctrine of the Trinity. He firmly believed that the deaths of his wife and baby in 1937 were God's judgment for his failure to conduct revivals in Oneness Pentecostal churches.[36] He began to insist that "believers baptized by a Trinitarian formula must be rebaptized in the name of Jesus only."[37]

Michael Moriarty astutely observed, "Branham's aberrational teachings not only cultivated cultic fringe movements like the Latter Rain movement and the Manifested Sons of God, but they also paved a pathway leading to false predictions, revelatory madness, doctrinal heresies, and a cultic following that treated his sermons as oral Scripture."[38]

On December 18, 1965, Branham was killed in a head-on collision with a drunk driver. Friends who believed him to be "God, born of a virgin" thought he "would rise from the dead."[39] Though he is still in the grave, his message of endtime restorationism lives on. According to the *Dictionary of Christianity in America*, "Branham's followers have partially or totally deified him and have given his sermons scriptural status, the voice of God to this last generation."[40] Counterfeit Revival leaders like Kenneth Hagin[41] and Jack Deere[42] continue to extol the work that God started through the healing revivals of Branham and his imitators.

Jack Coe (1919–1957)

A third pillar of healing restorationism was a man named Jack Coe. An ordained minister in the Assemblies of God, Coe was arguably even more extreme in his preaching and practice than either Allen or Branham. Coe on occasion would actually "pick people up out of the wheelchairs. If they fell, he'd say you didn't have faith."[43]

While Counterfeit Revival leader Oral Roberts considered Jack Coe "a man of great faith,"[44] many other well-known religious leaders considered Coe a master of gimmicks and fabrications. Ministers in the Church of Christ openly challenged him to produce documentation for his boasts of miraculous healing. They caustically characterized Coe as a fake and a fraud. One critic wrote:

> Have you ever noticed that the claim is always made concerning an inward goiter or some trouble that is not outwardly apparent, or some trouble that people usually recover from naturally. *No glass eyes or cork legs are ever replaced!*[45]

Life magazine reported that the American Medical Association believed that the supposed miraculous healings "were the result of either suggestion, spontaneous remission, or wrong diagnosis."[46] Coe responded to the opposition by branding them "Bolsheviks and religious bigots."[47] Like modern faith healers, he suggested that those who opposed him were in danger of being "struck dead by God."[48]

The Assemblies of God were so embarrassed by Coe's exaggerated claims that they finally expelled him in 1953 on the grounds that he was "misleading the public."[49] Coe retaliated by directly attacking the hierarchy of the Assemblies. He lobbied to rid the denomination of the disease of faithlessness and to "remove the men from office who are fighting divine healing and the deliverance ministry."[50] He warned followers "that the day would come when those who consulted physicians would have to take the mark of the beast."[51]

When Coe became critically ill with bulbar polio,[52] however, he himself took the "mark of the beast" and was admitted to the hospital. As his condition worsened, a faithful devotee wrote, "We know that God can and WILL deliver him."[53] Nevertheless, Coe died.

Healing revivalist O. L. Jaggers, who claimed that for the first time in nineteen hundred years "an exact formula has been given as to how to attain physical immortality in this World,"[54] contacted Coe's widow, Juanita, and said "he would come and raise him from the dead if she would only request his assistance."[55] Juanita, however, declined.

Instead, after the death of her husband, she published a devastating series of articles titled *Enemies of the Cross*. The articles, penned by a prominent insider named Granville Montgomery, exposed the fraudulent exaggerations and financial excesses of healing restorationists. Despite being up "against a ruthless group of men who had millions of dollars to fight with,"[56] he exposed the deceptions of healing evangelists who used "great swelling words"[57] to fleece the flock. He documented the deceit of claiming three million converts in Jamaica when the entire population of the island was far less than two million. He bemoaned the manipulation of men who hawked dirt from the Holy Land and pieces of cloth from Jack Coe's revival tent as a means to "make merchandise" of God's people. According to Montgomery, these men were "no better than bank embezzlers or confidence men of any rank."[58]

As a result of his exposé, pastors and parishioners alike were faced with the fact that the power of God had been prostituted through the power of gimmicks. Spiritual manipulation had overpowered spiritual manifestations, money had been exalted over ministry, and scandal was more common than salvation. Healing restorationists retaliated by circulating rumors about Montgomery's alleged personal indiscretions, and they labeled Jack Coe's widow a turncoat.

The wave that had restored the supernatural sign gifts to one segment of the body of Christ had begun to fizzle. Another wave, however, had begun to form. This wave was destined to mainstream Pentecostal distinctives, such as tongues, healing, and deliverance, throughout the entire Christian church. A new and improved Pentecost known as the charismatic renewal was about to emerge.

CHAPTER 13

Endtime Restoration
of Charismatic Unity

A leading facilitator of the charismatic renewal was a South African Pentecostal named David du Plessis. Du Plessis grew up under the influence of a Pentecostal father who was so opposed to using medicine or consulting doctors that it led to his brief imprisonment.[1]

In 1936 du Plessis was given a prophecy that would guide him for the next fifty years of his life. According to the *Dictionary of Pentecostal and Charismatic Movements,* the prophecy came through "an illiterate English evangelist" named Smith Wigglesworth, who was not even able to "read road signs."[2] Although the content of the prophecy has been enhanced and embellished over time, it essentially predicted that du Plessis "was to leave home and take the Pentecostal message to the far corners of the earth, for God was going to perform a work which would dwarf the Pentecostal movement."[3]

Wigglesworth's prophecy so captivated du Plessis that he became obsessed with orchestrating its fulfillment by unifying Christianity. The "intoxicating vision to unite world Pentecostals and ultimately world Christians"[4] eventually led him to enlist as a delegate to the World Council of Churches. It was there that he earned the title "Mr. Pentecost."[5]

While Mr. Pentecost often sparked controversy (for example, by endorsing apartheid in South Africa and extolling Marian apparitions in Yugoslavia), his ecumenical endeavors won him international acclaim. The *Dictionary of Pentecostal and Charismatic Movements* states that the "crown of his ecumenical achievements" was the "development of the Roman Catholic–Pentecostal Dialogue, one of a wide series of discussions with 'separated brethren' begun as a result of Vatican II."[6]

His most long-lasting legacy in terms of charismatic renewal may well have been his impact on the life of Demos Shakarian, whom he encouraged to persevere in developing the Full Gospel Business Men's Fellowship International (FGBMFI). Shakarian saw the counsel of du Plessis as a "life rope dangling over a drowning enterprise."[7] Through the visionary example of du Plessis, Shakarian came to see how he could use the FGBMFI to spread the message of endtime restorationism and denominational unity worldwide.

The FGBMFI provided the charismatic renewal with its first organized expression. Rather than being a conduit into Pentecostal denominations, it became a channel through which supernatural sign gifts were mainlined into the wider body of Christ. As influential business leaders from traditional churches were impacted through FGBMFI, Pentecostal proclivities became more and more accepted and respectable. In time thousands of "traditional" Christians received the Pentecostal experience yet remained in their own local churches. With du Plessis impacting church leadership and Shakarian impacting church laity, it was only a matter of time before the charismatic renewal emerged as a global restoration movement.

The Charismatic Movement

Most historians point to April 3, 1960, as the official birthdate of the charismatic movement. On this Sunday Father Dennis Bennett, an Episcopal priest, publicly announced to his parishioners that he had received the baptism of the Holy Spirit with the evidence of speaking in tongues. Before nightfall, Bennett had resigned his parish. Parishioners were emphatically instructed by the bishop of Los Angeles not to encourage or engage in the tongues experience. Jean Stone, one of the members of St. Mark's Episcopal parish, was determined that Father Bennett's story be told. Thus, she contacted *Newsweek,* which ran an article titled "Rector and Rumpus," and *Time,* which ran an article titled "Speaking in Tongues."[8] The ensuing publicity "generated the sense of a new movement of the Spirit, with the newness being seen in the combination of Pentecostal blessing and historic church attachment."[9]

By 1963 the topic of tongues had become a common subject of conversation in Christian circles. When the venerable Christian publication *Eternity* referred to the "second wave" as "The New Pentecostalism," Jean Stone, along with a Lutheran pastor named Harold Bredesen, took exception. In a published response "they objected to the 'Neo-Pentecostal' label, preferring 'charismatic renewal,' the first time this designation was used in a definitive manner."[10]

This new designation reflected definitive distinctions between the first and second waves of the Spirit. In the first wave, tongues were typically considered *the* evidence of the baptism in the Holy Spirit. In the second, tongues were thought to be *an* evidence. Furthermore, while it had been common for first wave leaders to encourage their devotees to become denominational Pentecostals, prominent second wave leaders urged followers to remain in their denominations and effect change from within. They were convinced that only through the restoration of charismatic gifts would there be hope for global revival.

Losing Steam

Todd Hunter believes that the second wave crested in 1977 at a hugely successful interdenominational charismatic conference in Kansas City. After that the charismatic renewal was "forever divided" and began "to lose its steam." He attributes the decline to a controversy that arose over the shepherding movement: "Agnes Sanford refused to be on a platform with Bob Mumford. They were both very famous charismatics, very famous in the renewal, and it forever split the renewal, and most historians would say that it has never really come back."[11]

Hunter went on to tell his followers that "the division over shepherding" was "one of the saddest things in my life of being a Christian." Nevertheless, he added, we now "get to the fun part." Just as the "charismatic renewal [was] beginning to peter out" something "dramatic happened." Along came a man named John Wimber who, according to such church growth leaders as Peter Wagner, "spawned the third wave—the third wave of the Holy Spirit in this century."[12]

While the first and second waves had restored such supernatural gifts as tongues and healing, the third wave would restore super apostles and prophets. Counterfeit Revival leader Jack Deere says that with the third wave would come endtime apostles and prophets who would "do greater works than the apostles, than Jesus, or any of the Old Testament prophets."[13]

Paul Cain, whom Deere believes to be one of these endtime prophets, says that the emerging third wave will "contain the good of all the previous moves [of God] and much more." When God "releases his mighty wave it's going to engulf everybody from the Baptists to the Episcopalians and from the Episcopalians to the Catholics and every denomination on the face of the earth."[14]

Says Cain, "Something's going to come so strong to you that you won't even know that there *be* any baptism of the Holy Ghost compared to the enormous baptism you're about to receive."[15]

CHAPTER 14

Endtime Restoration
of Super Prophets
and Apostles

Vineyard founder John Wimber believes that Paul Cain is the premier prophet of the third wave.[1] He credits Cain with "saving the Vineyard movement"[2] and calls him "a ten on a scale of ten."[3] Like the apostle Paul, Cain would not "come . . . with great oratory," but "with signs and wonders and power."[4] In Wimber's words, "he's much like Jeremiah, much like John the Baptist, singled out before birth for the ministry that he now has."[5]

The prophetic power resident in Cain is so awesome that Wimber says "he's interacting in two dimensions continually. He's not only seeing you and talking to you, but he's hearing from God constantly. There's a continual flow. I think it's interrupted periodically, but a continual flow of information is coming to him about things." Wimber goes on to say that Cain can actually "be in one room and be listening to the conversation of people in another place at the same time."[6]

Jack Deere alleges that the Creator's communication with Cain even includes disclosing such details as "how many people would die in the earthquake"[7] that hit San Francisco during the 1989 World Series. Cain himself says that the power that rests upon him is, at times, so potent that it "will knock out the cameras and knock out the phone lines and knock out all the power lines and set off the fire alarms like it did in Kansas City."[8]

This kind of power, says Wimber, is not unique: "We are entering a time in history in which the ability to perform mighty deeds is going to become somewhat commonplace." Furthermore, "there are already in Korea and Japan religious groups that do not relate to Christ at all who are healing the sick and casting out demons and performing miracles over nature."[9]

Wimber's awareness of occult power caused him to take a hard look at Cain's background. He made it clear that Cain's prophetic prowess hinged on his personal character, not his prophetic correctness. He assured followers that he had thoroughly checked out Cain, the man who was to discover and disclose the identity of the endtime apostle. In doing so, he had determined that "this man is authentic. He's the most truthful, the most guarded man with his mouth I've ever met."[10]

A Eunuch of the Lord

Wimber claimed that, like the apostle Paul, Cain was "a eunuch of the Lord." Jesus Christ appeared to him on the road to Santa Maria and physically "touched him on the chest," subsequently taking "all sexual desire out of his body. For over forty years he's lived with no cognizant sense of sexuality."[11]

Kansas City prophet Mike Bickle confirmed Wimber's words, adding that when Jesus appeared in the flesh and touched Cain on the chest, "the fire of God went through" him and his "chemistry was changed instantaneously."[12] From that hour on, Cain has not been aware of a single "romantic or sensual thought." Instead, "he was recreated for the Lord's pleasure."[13]

In spite of Cain's transformation into a "eunuch of the Lord," Wimber acknowledged that Cain was accused of being "involved with a woman in Scandinavia."[14] At the time, he was allegedly at the peak of his career. His star had risen to such a height that the angel of the Lord instructed William Branham to let Cain take over some of his largest crusades.[15] Despite Cain's success, however, the accusation of sexual impropriety caused him to abandon his ministry and go into seclusion for twenty-five years.

The New Breed

During these silent years, the Lord promised his beleaguered prophet that "there would be a day that he would stand before a new breed of men" and be "called to initiate the endtime ministry."[16] When the twenty-five years had ended, God sent forth his prophet once again. This time he was called to identify the leader of this new breed of men. Endtime restorationist Mike Bickle characterized him as a "Samuel looking for David." With nothing more than a promise and a pocketful of credit cards, he set out in search of God's chosen instrument.

He went to Seoul, Korea, and met with Paul Yonggi Cho,[17] but "the Spirit of the Lord" said, "No, this is not him." In Baton Rouge, Louisiana, he met with Jimmy Swaggart, but "the Spirit of the Lord said, 'This is not the one.'" He goes "to James Robison, he meets Pat Robertson. He meets leader after leader after leader in other nations, and every time the Lord said, 'This is not the one! This is not the one!'"[18]

By 1988 Cain had traveled to such faraway places as Singapore and Korea. When he was finally invited to meet John Wimber in America, he was "utterly discouraged." He thought to himself, *Well, this is just one more river to cross, one more leader to see.* This was to be his date with destiny.

Shortly after Cain arrived at the Vineyard, God gave him such "an insatiable love" for Wimber that he began to refer to him as "Saint John the beloved." On February 12, 1989, he stood in Wimber's pulpit and poetically proclaimed:

I found that leader that's going, before he dies, to usher in a new move of God, a new wave, and not just a little gathering here and not a few vines out there. But it's going to be more than a cluster. Listen to me, buster, I mean it's going to be more than a cluster. I mean, in spite of all your blunders, God's still going to give you signs and wonders![19]

The Earthquake

The Almighty allegedly announced the day of Cain's coming with "signs and wonders." At 3:38 A.M. on December 3, 1988, an earthquake hit southern California. Even before the full prophetic import of the earthquake struck Wimber, he was shaken. "What kind of man is this?" he exclaimed. "The Lord announces his coming with an earthquake!"[20]

While Counterfeit Revival leader Jack Deere could not recollect the exact day the earthquake had struck (he thought it might have been December 4 or 5), he did recall the sound:

> The noise was frightening. They don't usually occur out here with noise, so I've been told. But this had noise with it. Rumbling, you know, where you thought your bed was just going to fall down in a chasm. . . . Walls were shaking, the bed was shaking, and it just scared us to death.[21]

More foreboding than the earthquake itself was the fact that it portended to be an omen of things to come. As a serious earthquake had shaken California, so too a symbolic earthquake would shake the Vineyard. Wimber found the prophetic significance of the earthquake in the notion that Cain had "come in the spirit of Jeremiah," and the earthquake had "occurred at 3:38 in the morning." Thus, he concluded that the interpretation of this omen would be found in Jeremiah 33:8.

Wimber explained that "near judgment" had "come on the Vineyard as a result of immorality in the ranks." He had "sinned the sin of Eli" and ignored the immorality. But God's promise through Jeremiah 33:8 was "'I will cleanse them'—the Vineyard—'from all the sin they have committed against me and will forgive all their sins of rebellion against me.'"[22]

As Wimber went on to say, God himself appeared to Cain and told him that since the sins of Vineyard leaders had been forgiven:

> I was the man that he had been looking for and . . . we were the people and this is the movement that God wants to endorse and begin this ministry with. And the reason for that is that God says that these people won't be corrupted by the power this time as we were last time.[23]

When corruption struck the Vineyard once again, Wimber acted swiftly. He publicly disciplined a prophet named Bob Jones for using his prophetic powers to "manipulate people for his personal desires, sexual misconduct, rebelling against pastoral authority, slandering leaders and the promotion of bitterness within the body of Christ."[24]

Wimber made it clear, however, that Jones's guilt did not impugn his giftedness. Although Wimber had once informed constituents that he judged Cain on the basis of his personal character, not his prophetic competence, he now instructed them to judge Jones on his prophetic competence, not his personal character. He warns them that judging Jones's sexual sins should not translate into judging Jones's seer status.[25] Counterfeit Revival leader Mike Bickle agreed. While acknowledging that "the pain and trauma" of Jones's victims "was unbearable," he agreed that the anointing on him "was greater than ever."[26]

In fact, according to Bickle, Jones was the very prophet God used to confirm Cain's selection of Wimber as the leader who would usher in a new wave that would "contain the good of all the previous moves and much more to lead the church of Jesus Christ into the greatest season of harvest and manifestation of power and glory and righteousness that the world has ever known."[27] In the words of Jones, Wimber would have "a purpose beyond the Vineyard" and would be led by the Spirit to "introduce to the body of Christ the apostles that were yet to come in the nineties."[28]

The Sands of Time

God revealed the "second purpose" of the Vineyard to Bob Jones by transporting him in the spirit "to a great beach." He stood before "the sands of time" and watched a succession of men put their hands in the sand and pull out empty boxes. Then the Lord came to Jones and said, "Put your hand right here." Jones responded, "Lord, why? All I'm going to do is get an empty box." The Lord said, "Just do it." When he obeyed, he pulled out a massive box. God spoke again, saying, "Now open the box!" As he did, he saw three hundred thousand draft notices that read, "Welcome! You are inducted into the army of the Lord."

The Lord spoke once again, saying, "The men down there were like Martin Luther and then John Wesley and Charles Finney. They were the leaders that thought the appointed generation was theirs. And they all came up empty-handed." However, said God, "out of the sands of time I have preserved the best of all the bloodlines of all the families of the earth for this hour. And this is the generation that will begin the leadership of the endtime army."

God also revealed to Jones that before the "best of all the

bloodlines" would emerge victorious in a great endtime restoration, the body of Christ would be bloodied by a massive civil war.[29]

Civil War in the Church

The prophecy that today is a common refrain among leaders of the Counterfeit Revival was initially given to Jones in 1984. God, in a "voice that sounded like thunder," instructed Mike Bickle to call Jones and tell him that he was about to experience "a full and open visitation" from the Almighty. This was not going to be a thought, an impression, or merely a dream; rather, it would be a vision during which Jones would be lucid and awake.

During his visit, God allegedly took Jones through a panoramic enactment of Genesis 40—the story of Joseph's imprisonment on the false charge that he had attempted to sleep with Potiphar's wife. The Lord then told Bob, "The church is going to go into humiliation. The church is going to go into a time of deprivation."[30]

As the baker whom Joseph met in prison would lose his head, so the church would be pulled down into despair and devastation. The first major ministry to go down was "Jim Bakker—and the baker lost his head."[31] As Joseph experienced deprivation and discomfiture, so too the church would go through a ten-year period of dryness and disillusionment.

After the time of deadness and discouragement, God showed Jones that he would throw a massive party for his church. In evidence he showed Jones a large mansion in the Civil War era. The massive ballroom of the mansion was filled with Christians dressed in colorful clothing. They were laughing, dancing, and having the time of their lives.

Suddenly, however, things began to change. The Christians who were dancing and laughing began to take sides. As they did, their colorful clothing was transformed into either gray or blue. Then a bloody civil war broke out between the blues and the grays. The physical violence that ensued was so horrifying that not a single Christian household escaped unscathed.

Wes Campbell depicts the gray coats from the South as being motivated by greed and characterizes the blue coats from the North as being motivated by God. As he put it, "The North fought the South and the South fought the North, and the South wanted to keep people enslaved. They wanted their money. They wanted their personhood to keep the system going. And the north said NO! Freedom! Freedom! And they went into a terrible fight, and it was father against son and brother against brother, and a man's enemies were in his own house. And the angel said this: There won't be a house that escapes weeping."[32]

According to Campbell, God not only gave Vineyard prophet Bob Jones the "Civil War" vision, but he also gave a similar vision as well as the interpretation to Counterfeit Revival leader James Ryle. As Campbell put it, "The Lord even showed him how the blue coats stand for the revelatory, the revelation, and the gray for gray matter, man's wisdom."[33] Says Ryle, "Blue is the color of the sky, thus blue symbolizes revelation. Gray, conversely, symbolizes the gray matter of the brain and is thus symbolic of man's reason."[34]

In 1996 God allegedly told Counterfeit Revival leader Rick Joyner "to begin preparing for this great war with the resolve to fight until there was a complete victory."[35] In concert with Jones, Campbell, and Ryle, Joyner asserts:

> Like the American Civil War, the coming spiritual civil war will also be between the Blue and the Gray. In dreams and visions blue often represents heavenly-mindedness—the sky is blue—and gray speaks of those who live by the power of their own minds—the brain is often called gray matter—This will be a conflict between those who may be genuine Christians, but who

live mostly according to their natural minds and human wisdom, and those who follow the Holy Spirit.[36]

Joyner is convinced that the grays, whom he characterizes as "spiritually ruthless and cruel,"[37] must be "confronted and exposed and either converted or removed from their place of influence in the church."[38] After the grays, who he says constitute "nearly half of the believers in the world today,"[39] are defeated, there will be "an entirely new definition of Christianity."[40] As Joyner declared, "Believers and unbelievers alike will think that it is the end of Christianity as we know it, and it will be. Through this the very definition of Christianity will be changed, for the better."[41]

CHAPTER 15

Endtime
Restoration Hoaxes

Think back for a moment to the early morning hours of the first day of the twentieth century. Charles Parham laid his hand on a young woman named Agnes Ozman, and she allegedly began to speak Chinese. He was utterly convinced that her experience was a prelude to global revival and a precursor to endtime restorationism. From this day forward, he said, "one need only receive the baptism with the Holy Spirit and he could go to the farthest corners of the world and preach to the natives in languages unknown to the speaker."

Counterfeiting Tongues

As noted in chapter 11, Pentecostal historian Vinson Synan candidly documents that a missionary named A. G. Garr put Parham's theory to the test. He moved to India and attempted to preach to the natives in their own language. The result was a "fiasco." Thankfully, Garr did not give up. After learning Chinese he moved to Hong Kong and began a mission in "the more conventional manner."

Predictably, Rodney Howard-Browne did not learn the

lesson of history. Presumptuously speaking for the Almighty, he said:

> My hand shall be strong upon you, and you shall see wonderful and glorious manifestations of my Spirit, and it shall be heard that even that which transpired in the Book of Acts has happened even in this day, when men and women shall be translated, caught away, and shall be found on the foreign field speaking in a foreign language, and they've had no formal education in that language. But they'll think they're speaking in English, but others will hear them speaking in those foreign tongues, and many shall be added and multitudes shall come into the kingdom.[1]

If Howard-Browne had "tested the spirits" in light of Scripture, he would have immediately realized that his revelation was bogus. The gift of tongues was not poured out so that missionaries could communicate the gospel *to people* but rather as an instrument through which people might better communicate their heartfelt devotion *to God*. As the apostle Paul so aptly put it, "anyone who speaks in a tongue does not speak *to men* but *to God*" (1 Cor. 14:1; emphasis added). Paul goes on to say, "unless you speak intelligible words with your tongue, how will anyone know what you are saying? You will just be speaking into the air" (v. 9). Therefore, when tongues are spoken in public "someone must interpret . . . so that everyone may be instructed and encouraged" (vv. 27, 31).

Likewise, Luke points out that on the day of Pentecost, when Peter was "filled with the Holy Spirit and began to speak in other tongues" (Acts 2:4), he was communicating "the wonders of God" (v. 11). While God miraculously interpreted Peter's praise for the people gathered together in Jerusalem, he did not use tongues as an instrument for communicating the gospel. Instead, when Peter addressed the crowd, he did so in the street language of the day—secular koine Greek.

It should be noted that sincere believers are today divided on the issue of tongues. Some believe that they ceased with the closing of the canon of Scripture or the end of the apostolic age. Others do not see a clear biblical or historical precedent for such a position. While we may vigorously debate the issue of tongues, we must never divide over it. We should, however, strongly resist the prostitution of tongues by today's endtime restorationists. It is, indeed, the height of arrogance for men like Rodney Howard-Browne and Kenneth Copeland to dupe devotees into believing that God has empowered them to speak to one another in "dueling tongues."[2]

Healing Hoaxes

In the mythology of endtime restorationists, another hoax had taken center stage by the middle of the twentieth century. Men like A. A. Allen, William Branham, and Jack Coe perpetrated the myth that the restoration of healing would lead to a final Pentecost greater than the first. While Vineyard leader Todd Hunter claims these men had a "renewing influence in mainline Christianity,"[3] Pentecostal leaders themselves acknowledge that these men were dragging Christ's name through the mud. Rather than commend their healing hoaxes, they condemned them.

Today, Branham protégés such as Paul Cain appear to be taking healing hoaxes to new heights. Cain promises credulous Christians that in the fullness of endtime restorationism, "all the sick are gonna be healed, the dead are gonna be raised, and nations are gonna turn to God in a day."[4] Triumphantly, he proclaimed that one day soon the news media would have "no news to report . . . but good news":

> When you see CBS, NBC, ABC news anchormen come on and say, "Hello there. Ladies and gentlemen, we have no news to report tonight but good news. We don't

even have any sporting events to report. All of the stadiums and all the ballparks are filled with hundreds of
thousands of people. They have hearses lined up, am-
bulances lined up. They have hundreds of stretcher
cases and all that, and there are men standing there
in the pulpit. There are women standing there that
haven't had a change of raiment in three days. They
haven't had a drink of water. They haven't had any
food, and they're preaching under the mighty power.
Why, did you see that last night on ABC? Did you see
that man levitated? Did you see all those preachers
just levitated? Did you see that fixed pose? They stood
there for twenty-four hours in a fixed pose, worshiping
and praising God, and hundreds of thousands came by
and fell on their face, and nobody pushed them, and
nobody shoved them. They fell under the power of God
and everybody, everywhere's crying, "Oh, this is God,
and Jesus is Lord!" It seems like the whole world is
turning to God.[5]

Far from the whole world turning to God, however, critics
are laughing at the credulity of Christians. As one skeptic aptly
put it, "I must confess I share in full the general public's disgust with media preachers, who long since tired of preaching
the Christian gospel, and in its place substituted a *National
Enquirer* style gospel of cheap sensationalism."[6]

Despite the fact that endtime restorationists like John
Wimber are fully aware of their own mortality, they allow
prophets like Cain to parade through their pulpits, duping parishioners into believing that a period of perfect health is just
around the corner. In truth, however, we live in a creation
cursed by sin, in which aging is the primary sickness of humanity. We all get older, we get wrinkles, our eyesight fails,
our muscles contract, and eventually we die.

Unlike such prophets as Cain, the apostle Paul paints a

realistic picture of human frailty. As he warned the Corinthian church in his day, he warns the Christian church today. The hope of Christ's followers is not that their frail and fragile bodies will be fixed in this world but that they will be transformed in the world to come. Since the beginning of time, the righteous and the unrighteous have been subject to disease, decay, and death. And that will not change until the Lord returns.

In the meantime, the creation itself "has been groaning as in the pains of childbirth right up to the present time. Not only so, but we ourselves, who have the firstfruits of the Spirit, groan inwardly as we wait eagerly for our adoption as sons, the redemption of our bodies" (Rom. 8:22–23). For the child of God, confidence and contentment are not found in perfect health and healing here and now but in a resurrected body in the hereafter.

Healing is provided for in the atonement, but it is not guaranteed. We are not saved *from* suffering but rather *in the midst* of suffering. Our earthly bodies have been "sown in weakness," but in eternity they will be "raised in power" (1 Cor. 15:43). In the new heaven and new earth, God himself will wipe every tear from our eyes. There will be no more death or mourning or crying or pain, for the old order of things will have passed away and God will make "everything new" (Rev. 21:4–5). Our hope is not in an endtime restoration but in an eternal resurrection![7]

Super Apostles and Prophets

In 1989 the final pieces of the endtime puzzle finally began to fall into place—the restoration of super apostles and prophets. Endtime prophet Paul Cain stood in John Wimber's pulpit and declared: "I've found that leader that's going, before he dies, to usher in a new move of God." Wimber, in turn, lauded Cain as a prophet who reminded him of the apostle Paul. He told parishioners that, like the apostle Paul, Cain had not come with "great oratory" but with "signs and wonders and power";

like the apostle Paul, Cain was a eunuch of the Lord; and like the apostle Paul, Jesus Christ had appeared to Cain in the flesh.

Unlike the apostle Paul, however, Cain would stand before a new breed of men and be called to initiate the endtime ministry. This "new breed" of people would be the most powerful in the history of humanity. As Cain put it:

> No prophet or apostle who ever lived equaled the power of these individuals in this great army of the Lord in these last days. No one ever had it; not even Elijah or Peter or Paul or anyone else enjoyed the power that is going to rest upon this great army.[8]

Endtime restorationist Rick Joyner claims that God revealed that in the endtime church "the prophetic word will be flowing with purity and accuracy unsurpassed in church history."[9] Bob Jones, who says God spoke to him audibly, saying, "you are a seer-prophet," pushes the envelope even further. He says the new breed will not only have "permission to begin to remit people's sins," but they will also have "permission to remit that which sin has caused in their life, like herpes and AIDS."[10] Jones says that the anointing of the endtime prophets and apostles will be ten times the anointing of Moses.[11]

While Scripture confidently endorses prophets like Peter, Paul, and Moses, Scripture clearly exposes pretenders like Cain, Joyner, and Jones. Not only do they fail the test given by Moses in Deuteronomy 13:1–10 and 18:19–22, but "they mouth empty, boastful words and, by appealing to the lustful desires of sinful human nature, they entice people who are just escaping from those who live in error. They promise them freedom, while they themselves are slaves of depravity" (2 Pet. 2:18–19). More than two millennia ago, a faithful prophet named Jeremiah warned of false prophets like Joyner, Jones, and Cain who presumptuously use God's name to spread their false promises and prophecies. Speaking as the very mouthpiece of God Almighty, he passionately pleaded:

> Do not listen to what the prophets are prophesying to you; they fill you with false hopes.
>
> They speak visions from their own minds, not from the mouth of the LORD.
>
> They keep saying to those who despise me, "The LORD says: You will have peace."
>
> And to all who follow the stubbornness of their hearts they say, "No harm will come to you."
>
> But which of them has stood in the council of the LORD to see and to hear his word?
>
> Who has listened and heard his word?
>
> See, the storm of the LORD will burst out in wrath, a whirlwind swirling down on the heads of the wicked.
>
> The anger of the LORD will not turn back until he fully accomplishes the purposes of his heart.
>
> In days to come you will understand it clearly.
>
> I did not send these prophets, yet they have run with their message; I did not speak to them, yet they have prophesied.
>
> But if they had stood in my council, they would have proclaimed my words to my people and would have turned them from their evil ways and from their evil deeds.
>
> Am I only a God nearby, declares the LORD, and not a God far away?
>
> Can anyone hide in secret places so that I cannot see him? declares the LORD.
>
> Do not I fill heaven and earth? declares the LORD.
>
> I have heard what the prophets say who prophesy lies in my name. They say, "I had a dream! I had a dream!" How long will this continue in the hearts of these lying prophets, who prophesy the delusions of

their own minds? They think the dreams they tell one another will make my people forget my name, just as their fathers forgot my name through Baal worship. Let the prophet who has a dream tell his dream, but let the one who has my word speak it faithfully. For what has straw to do with grain? declares the LORD. Is not my word like fire, declares the LORD, and like a hammer that breaks a rock in pieces?

Therefore, declares the LORD, I am against the prophets who steal from one another words supposedly from me. Yes, declares the LORD, I am against the prophets who wag their own tongues and yet declare, "The LORD declares." Indeed, I am against those who prophesy false dreams, declares the LORD. They tell them and lead my people astray with their reckless lies, yet I did not send or appoint them. They do not benefit these people in the least, declares the LORD. (Jer. 23:16–32)

PART FOUR

Slain in the Spirit

CHAPTER 16

Sisters

Long before Benny Hinn became a household word, he had a vivid dream. In his dream a woman wearing a white dress and no makeup came up to him, handed him a book, and said, "Read." The day after the dream, says Hinn, a man walked up to him and said, "The Lord is telling me to give you this book."[1] On the front page of the book was a picture of the very woman Hinn had encountered in his dream. Her name was Maria Beulah Woodworth-Etter (1844–1924). According to the *Dictionary of Pentecostal and Charismatic Movements,* she is the one person most associated with the "slain in the spirit" phenomenon in early Pentecostalism.[2]

Sister Maria

In 1996 Hinn gave Paul Crouch and his worldwide television audience a dramatic description of the preaching and practice of Maria Beulah Woodworth-Etter. He told them how she had been in the middle of a message when suddenly she "just froze" for twenty-four hours: "Twenty-four hours later she went right back to where she was and continues [*sic*], not knowing she had been frozen for twenty-four hours. In the meantime, thousands of people had come to see her and got saved while she was frozen."[3]

While the *Dictionary of Pentecostal and Charismatic Movements* acknowledges that Woodworth-Etter was dubbed the "trance evangelist," the "priestess of divine healing," and the "voodoo priestess," it does not validate Hinn's wild embellishments. Rather it asserts that Woodworth-Etter often went into trances during services and would stand "like a statue for an hour or more with her hands raised while the service continued."[4]

Kenneth Hagin, like Hinn, attempts to convince devotees that the Holy Spirit would come upon Woodworth-Etter so powerfully that she would go into a trance for days on end. Despite the fact that Hagin provides no documentation for his contention, he confidently claims that Woodworth-Etter's trances would last for three days and three nights:

> She was in her 70's, preaching in a tent which was full, when right in the middle of her sermon, with her hand uplifted to illustrate a point and her mouth open, the power of God came on her. She froze in that position and stood like a statue for three days and three nights. Think about that: All her body had to be under the control of the Spirit of God. She had no bodily functions; for three days and nights she stood there. According to the newspaper account, it was estimated that more than 150,000 people came by to see her in that three-day period.[5]

What neither he nor Hinn divulge to devotees is that Woodworth-Etter was a false prophet who claimed that "the San Francisco Bay area would be destroyed by an earthquake and a tidal wave in 1890."[6] Nor do they disclose that Woodworth-Etter was a false teacher whose "experimental" religion[7] was substantially impacted by Quakerism. Woodworth-Etter was so cavalier about doctrine that she actually accepted "an invitation from Mormons to preach in Nebraska in 1920."[8] Like leaders of today's Counterfeit Revival, she was a master at taking Scripture out of context and using it as a pretext to support endtime restorationism[9] as well as the practice of slaying subjects in the spirit.

The *Dictionary of Pentecostal and Charismatic Movements* correctly notes that, more than anything else, the "slain in the spirit" phenomenon, often referred to as "trances," characterized Woodworth-Etter's ministry even before the rise of Pentecostalism:

> People were experiencing being slain in the Spirit in her evangelistic meetings several years *prior* to her participation in the Pentecostal movement. . . . It seems as if the Pentecostal-charismatic association of slain in the Spirit with particular personalities stems from Woodworth-Etter than any other person.[10]

Woodworth-Etter's book *A Diary of Signs and Wonders* is filled with stories of people being slain in the spirit. On one occasion, she writes, "one of the aged sisters fell prostrate and became cold and rigid, as if dead, with no signs of life excepting the beating of her pulse. We laid her on the pulpit sofa. She remained there the rest of the day and during the evening meeting two other ladies fell over in the same way."[11] On another occasion, Woodworth-Etter merely

> reached over to shake hands with a man who was standing in the aisle. . . . He began to tremble and fell backward. . . . As I stepped back, one of the ministers on the pulpit, the pastor of the church, threw up his hands and fell. The fear of God fell upon the sinners.

They thought if the ministers had to go down, there was no chance for them to escape.[12]

Sister Aimee

The next nationally renowned character to popularize the slain in the spirit phenomenon was another woman evangelist Aimee Semple McPherson. Her succession to Maria Woodworth-Etter is noted by biographer Edith L. Blumhofer, who reflects the common Pentecostal historical assessment by saying, "If there was to be a succession of female evangelists, Aimee clearly stood next in line: she had begun to run with the torch, and she would carry it farther than Etter ever dreamed."[13]

While the *Dictionary of Pentecostal and Charismatic Movements* deals with the controversial aspects of "Sister Aimee's" life—her mysterious disappearances and alleged affairs, multiple marriages (two of which ended in divorce), and death from an apparent drug overdose—it is strangely silent about her theatrical preoccupation with the slain in the spirit phenomenon.

However, Sister[14] herself was not so silent. In vivid detail she described how she personally succumbed to the slaying power of the spirit:

> The Voice of the Lord spoke tenderly: "Now, child, cease your strivings and your begging; just begin to praise Me. . . ." All at once my hands and arms began to tremble gently at first, then more and more, until my whole body was atremble with the power. . . . Almost without my notice my body slipped gently to the floor, and I was lying under the power of God, but felt as though caught up and floating.[15]

Drawing upon her "unerring theatrical instincts, a flair for publicity, and a fertile imagination,"[16] Sister also described subjects slain in the spirit in her services:

What a glorious night it was. . . . Three received the baptisms that night. One lady fell by the organ, another at the other side of the church. . . . Each time someone fell under the power the people would run to that side of the church. . . . Such praying and calling upon the name of the Lord, the minister feared would result in the people's being arrested for disturbing the peace. The third night nineteen received the baptism of the Holy Spirit. Down they went right and left, between the seats, in the aisles, in front of the chancel rail, upon the platform. Oh, Glory![17]

Sister Kathryn

While Sister Aimee died of an apparent drug overdose in 1944,[18] her methods lived on. A young woman had meticulously studied her, "taking in every movement, every song, every dramatic presentation, every altar call,"[19] from the vantage of the Angelus Temple balcony. Biographer Wayne E. Warner suggests that "for much of Kathryn Kuhlman's early ministry, she lived in the shadow of her role model, the most famous woman preacher of all, Aimee Semple McPherson. But when the shadow lifted, Kathryn became the best-known woman preacher in the world, one whose ministry touched lives everywhere."[20] Although she never met Aimee at the Angelus Temple, "enough of the glitter rubbed off to start her toward her own superstar status."[21]

The *Dictionary of Pentecostal and Charismatic Movements* describes Kathryn Kuhlman as "a star, even until her death." As with Sister Aimee, it candidly acknowledges Sister Kathryn's flamboyant lifestyle. Not only does it chronicle her love for "expensive clothes, precious jewels, luxury hotels, and first class travel," but it notes "her marriage to an evangelist, who divorced his wife to marry Kuhlman."[22]

Kuhlman's relationship with evangelist Burroughs A. Waltrip destroyed his family and devastated her followers. One new convert, for example, almost lost his faith when he "got an eyeful" one night as he passed the church office and saw Kuhlman "in the evangelist's arms."[23] Kuhlman candidly referred to her relationship with Waltrip as the "greatest mistake she ever made." She became utterly convinced that only a divorce would bring God's "anointing and blessing" back to her ministry.[24]

While admirers were awe-struck at her renewed anointing to perform miracles, they were even more impressed by her ability to slay people in the spirit. As noted by the *Dictionary of Pentecostal and Charismatic Movements,* "apart from the well-documented healings, the most sensational phenomena associated with Kuhlman was 'going under the power' (sometimes referred to as 'slain in the Spirit') as people fell when she prayed for them."[25] One Kuhlman devotee Agnes Spriggs, when asked about falling in the spirit, said: "That's what sold me—even more than the miracles—that magnificent power."[26]

As it became increasingly "fashionable and spiritual to fall," Kuhlman developed her own explanation for this power: "All I can believe is that our spiritual beings are not wired for God's full power, and when we plug into that power, we just cannot survive it. We are wired for low voltage; God is high voltage through the Holy Spirit."[27]

Among the thousands who tapped into the high voltage flowing through Kuhlman were Oral Roberts University president Richard Roberts, Counterfeit Revivalists Charles and Frances Hunter, ex-priest Francis MacNutt, and a young immigrant named Benedictus ("Benny") Hinn.[28] As Sister Aimee's mantle fell on Sister Kathryn, so Sister Kathryn's mantle fell on Brother Benny.[29]

CHAPTER 17

Suspect Slayings

When Benny Hinn first encountered the raw power coursing through Kathryn, he exclaimed, "I've got to have this. . . . I want what Kathryn Kuhlman's got. I wanted it with every atom and fiber within me."[1] What Hinn wanted, Hinn got. In his book *The Anointing,* he tells the story of how Kathryn's "closest confidante,"[2] Maggie Hartner, personally told him, "You have a lot more than she had when she was your age."[3]

The Power

The power young Hinn got was so enormous that his mere presence often caused people to be slain in the spirit. In *Good Morning, Holy Spirit,* Hinn describes the impact of his power on one of his parents: "My mother was cleaning the hallway while I was in my room talking with the Holy Spirit. When I came out, she was thrown right back. Something had knocked her against the wall."[4]

His power on pastors and parishioners was even more potent than his power on his parent. As Hinn described it, the first time he ever stood in a pulpit, he merely lifted his hands to summon the Holy Spirit when "instantly the power of God hit the place. People began to cry and many fell to the floor."[5]

Hinn was so amazed at the power that he didn't know what to do. Says Hinn, "I turned around to the fellow who was leading the meeting, hoping he would come and take the service out of my hands. But as I turned and pointed toward him, he fell backward several feet. I was trying to get him to come close and suddenly he was farther away."[6] The raw power emanating from Hinn was allegedly so potent that each time the leader would struggle to get near him, he would "hit the wall."[7]

Today the power coursing through Hinn has been passed on to a host of other Counterfeit Revival leaders. As described in chapter 3, John Arnott said that when Hinn got through ministering to his wife backstage, she was so affected that, as he put it, "I'd have to undress her and put her to bed, she was so out of it."[8] Although he too has fallen before Benny, he is not always sure why. As quoted in an earlier chapter: "It's like, I didn't know if he slammed me on the head or if the ushers pulled me back, or if I actually fell down, or if I just cooperated, or if there was so much psychological pressure in front of that many people that I just simply went with it."[9]

The ambivalence articulated by Arnott often arises from the flamboyance of Hinn's performances. In fact, those familiar with Kuhlman's practice of slaying subjects "are not ready to approve what they view as manipulative variations. Those variations include Benny Hinn's blowing on some and throwing his wadded coat at others. 'Kathryn would turn over in her grave,' one Kuhlman admirer told me, 'if she could see what passes today as being slain in the spirit.'"[10] Probably she would not merely turn over in her grave, but she would go into high rotation at hearing Hinn tell devotees that he frequents her gravesite and the gravesite of Sister Aimee and gets the anointing from their bones.[11]

Ironically, one of Kuhlman's biographers Jamie Buckingham

claims that toward the end of her life the anointing was often nonexistent. Here's how Buckingham tells the story:

> Kathryn was moving back and forth across the stage, saying all her favorite phrases. They seemed empty. The singer had climbed to her feet and Kathryn touched her again. Nothing happened this time. In a desperate move I heard her say, "The Spirit is all over you, Jamie." She swept toward me, putting her hands on my jaw as I sang. There had been times in the past when, if she even got close to me, I would go down "under the power." But that day it was just Kathryn—with her hands on my jaw. I loved her too much to disappoint her. With a sigh of resignation, I fell backwards into the arms of the man behind me.[12]

As was the case with so many others, a misplaced sense of loyalty compelled Buckingham to feign being slain. Had he not been confident in the catcher behind him, one wonders whether he would have risked life and limb for love and loyalty. Like other insiders, Buckingham was no doubt aware of the psychological and physical danger inherent in the slain in the spirit phenomenon.

Danger

In Houston, Texas, a woman attending a Hinn crusade crushed a fellow crusader when her fall was not checked by a catcher. The woman she landed on pleaded with her, "Get up, get up," but to no avail. All she could say in response was, "I can't, I can't."[13]

In Oklahoma City a woman attending a Hinn crusade was not merely crushed, she was killed. Ella Peppard died from complications she suffered after someone was slain in the spirit right on top of her. The ensuing lawsuit was settled out of court.[14]

In Maxville, North Carolina, Evelyn Kuykendall fractured her back and spent two months in a hospital as a result of being slain in the spirit at a crusade run by Counterfeit Revival leaders Charles and Frances Hunter. As noted by Father Francis MacNutt in his best-selling book *Overcome by the Spirit,* a federal jury awarded Kuykendall $300,000 in damages. From experiences such as this, MacNutt says, "I learned to be cautious and to ask for catchers to stand by any time I think that people might fall."[15] While catchers may do much to protect practitioners like MacNutt, in the final analysis, they do little to protect parishioners. Only from the perspective of eternity will we have a true valuation of both the physical and the psychological consequences produced by the slain in the spirit phenomenon.[16]

Father Francis MacNutt

Like Hinn and the Hunters, Father Francis MacNutt traces his initiation in the slain in the spirit phenomenon to Kathryn Kuhlman. He heard that a fellow priest had gone to a Kuhlman meeting and was so sensitive to her power "that he couldn't even get near her but repeatedly fell down in the aisle as he tried to approach the platform."[17] MacNutt's curiosity was duly aroused. He traveled to a Kuhlman meeting to experience this power firsthand. Predictably, he was picked out of the crowd and ushered onto the platform:

> As Kathryn approached me I stood determined not to fight it, whatever it was. A "catcher" stood behind me while several thousand people watched. I felt the gentle pressure of Kathryn's hand on my forehead. I had to make a decision; if I didn't take a step backward, her hand's pressure would push me off-balance and I would fall. *But,* I thought to myself, *I don't want to resist in any way if this is from God.*

So I didn't step back and, sure enough, I fell—six feet four inches of me. The crowd made a noise, a combination of surprise and delight at seeing a priest in a Roman collar topple over on the stage.

Then I quickly scrambled to my feet, not sure that I hadn't been pushed. Again Kathryn prayed; again I felt pressure on my forehead that I did not resist. Once more I fell.

It was confusing. Others, I knew, had experienced something remarkable. But if I had only my own experience to go on, I would have judged that nothing in particular had happened—that I might simply have been pushed off-balance. I didn't know what to make of it.[18]

Since that first confusing experience, MacNutt has become one of its most prominent promoters. While Kuhlman called this "spectacular phenomenon being slain in the spirit," MacNutt calls it "resting in the spirit."[19] Since the early seventies, MacNutt has seen it all. He candidly confesses he has "seen people pushed over," slain by the "power of suggestion," and "knocked down by evil spirits." He goes on to point out that the phenomenon is externally similar to "manifestations of voodoo and other magic rites" and is "found today among different sects in the Orient as well as among primitive tribes of Africa and Latin America."[20] In his book *Overcome by the Spirit,* MacNutt demonstrates that the slain in the spirit phenomenon has links not only to heretical pagan rituals but also to historical Protestant revivals.

CHAPTER 10

Shakers and Quakers

The *Dictionary of Pentecostal and Charismatic Movements* points out that among proponents, it is "popular to see the phenomenon of being slain in the Spirit as an accompaniment to great Protestant revivals."[1]

The Methodist circuit rider Peter Cartwright is cited as an illustration of preaching that was "accompanied by listeners falling under the power."[2] What is not mentioned is that Cartwright denounced this phenomenon as a "great evil" that had befallen the revival:

> From these wild exercises, another great evil arose from the heated and wild imaginations of some. They professed to fall into trances and see visions; they would fall at meetings and sometimes at home, and lay apparently powerless and motionless for days, sometimes for a week at a time, without food or drink; and when they came to, they professed to have seen heaven and hell, to have seen God, angels, the devil and the damned; they would prophesy, and, under the pretense of Divine inspiration, predict the time

of the end of the world, and the ushering in of the great millennium.[3]

"Blasphemous Shakers"

Cartwright went on to communicate that even before the Second Great Awakening, the "blasphemous Shakers" had involved themselves in what is today referred to as being slain in the spirit. Like Maria Woodworth-Etter, Shaker founder Ann Lee (1736–1784) was profoundly influenced by the Quakers. Her "message was essentially restorationist." She taught that the "church had lost the gifts" but that "an endtime restoration had been promised."[4]

Unlike Cartwright, MacNutt cites the Shaker movement as an example of authentic "revival." MacNutt quotes from Ronald A. Knox's book *Enthusiasm* to favorably compare the phenomenon that accompanied the Shakers to his own experiences of slaying people in the spirit:

> Later, at the beginning of the nineteenth century, we read about the revival among the Shakers with "trembling, weeping and swooning away, till every appearance of life was gone . . . more than a thousand persons fell to the ground apparently without sense or motion. . . . Towards the close of this commotion, viz. about the year 1803, convulsions became prevalent.
>
> "Men and women fell in such numbers that it became impossible for the multitude to move about without trampling them, and they were hurried to the meeting house. At no time was the floor less than half covered."[5]

MacNutt grossly misrepresents not only the Shakers[6] but also author Ronald Knox. First, MacNutt attributes the preceding words to Knox, even though Knox is clearly quoting *two other* authors. Furthermore, MacNutt uses ellipses to omit statements that are counterproductive to his position. Finally, MacNutt fails to use ellipsis to signal his omission of the following segment from the heart of the preceding quotation:

> The rolling exercise consisted in doubling the head and feet together, and rolling over and over like a hoop. . . . The jerks consisted in violent twitches and contortions of the body in all its parts. . . . When attacked by the jerks, the victims of enthusiasm sometimes leaped like frogs, and exhibited every grotesque and hideous contortion of the face and limbs. The barks consisted in getting down on all fours, growling, snapping the teeth, and barking like dogs. Sometimes numbers of the people squatted down, and looking in the face of the minister, continued demurely barking at him while he preached to them. These last were particularly gifted in prophecies, trances, dreams, rhapsodies, visions of angels, of heaven, and of the holy city.[7]

While MacNutt writes about "revival among the Shakers," he should have written about the need for repentance among the Shakers. Their founder, Ann Lee, not only "denied the Trinity, the Atonement, and the doctrine of grace"[8] but also believed herself to be "a new, female Messiah"[9] and "the second appearing of Christ."[10] In addition, she taught followers that "the source of evil was the sex act."[11] Thus, they worked themselves into altered states of consciousness in order to "shake off sin" and rid themselves of "sexual desire."[12] As some of these Shakers went into a trance state, they "saw visions and received [false] prophecies of Christ's imminent second coming."[13]

John Wesley

MacNutt uses a variety of other historical pretenses to validate the slain in the spirit phenomenon as well. He claims that while John Wesley's "colleagues were split on the issue of these boisterous manifestations," Wesley himself "saw these outbreaks as signs of supernatural power and was worried when they were not present."[14] What he doesn't tell readers is that while Wesley correctly saw physical manifestations as a natural response to an encounter with the gospel, he also attributed enthusiasms such as falling, laughing, and jumping to the "simplicity" of people and to the ploys of Satan.

Wesley recounts the story of a meeting that took place in 1773. A hymn was sung over and over some thirty or forty times, resulting in bodily agitations on the part of some of the people present. In response to this phenomenon he wrote, "Satan serves himself of their simplicity, in order . . . to bring a discredit on the work of God."[15]

In 1740 an epidemic of laughter broke out during a gathering in Bristol. Wesley said, "I was a little surprised at some, who were buffeted of Satan in an unusual manner, by such a spirit of laughter as they could in no wise resist."[16] A short time later the "spirit of laughter" returned. One lady present was "so violently and variously torn of the evil one" that "she laughed till almost strangled; then broke out into cussing and blaspheming; then stamped and struggled with incredible strength, so that four or five could scarcely hold her."[17] Wesley clearly considered these manifestations to be demonic and said that deliverance was subsequently effected through prayer.

Quakers

To further bolster the legitimacy of being slain in the spirit, MacNutt says that similar manifestations "had occurred much earlier (1654) when two Quakers, [John] Audland and [John] Camm, preached conversion in Bristol and some of the congregation fell to the ground and foamed at the mouth."[18] What he doesn't say is that in the same era, Quakers were given to such bizarre practices as "foretelling judgments" by running "through the streets completely naked." Or that Quaker founder George Fox, who "defended this practice,"[19] would also often face his parishioners "for several hours without opening his mouth" because he was allegedly commanded by God to "famish them from words." He considered his parishioners "prophets" who could speak in his place as they were empowered by the "light within."[20] The "inner light" was considered "superior to tradition, Scripture, and reason itself."[21]

Like so many Counterfeit Revival leaders, Father MacNutt alters the historical facts about a broad range of revivalists in an attempt to lend further credence to the slain in the spirit phenomenon. In his words:

> The greatest preachers in the English-speaking world from the mid–eighteenth century to the end of the nineteenth century all regularly saw people fall over in their services. Among Anglicans, John Wesley; among Methodists, George Whitefield and Francis Asbury; among Congregationalists, Jonathan Edwards; among Presbyterians, Charles Finney and Barton Stone—And of course numerous Quakers and Shakers.[22]

CHAPTER 19

Seven Scriptural Pretexts

Ex-Dominican priest Father Francis MacNutt not only creates credibility for the slain in the spirit phenomenon by pointing to Quakers and Shakers in past revivals, but he also points to movers and shakers in the present revival. In *Overcome by the Spirit,* he writes, "in Protestant revivals, as we have seen, many people trembled and shook. So, too, in our day, the shaking phenomenon occurs in John Wimber's conferences." MacNutt points out that at one time Wimber was a Quaker pastor and presumes that the "shaking phenomenon is part of John's spiritual heritage."[1]

Wimber himself, however, focuses on Scripture rather than on his spiritual heritage as a Quaker. In 1981 Wimber (the founder of the international Association of Vineyard Churches) preached a series of sermons titled "Spiritual Phenomena: Slain in the Spirit."

In this series Wimber points out that "the model as we've seen it ministered out in the land" is not found in Scripture:

> There's no place in the Bible where people were
> lined up and Jesus or Paul or anyone else went along

and bapped them on the head and watched them go down, one after another, and somebody else ran along behind. Can you picture Peter and James—"Hold it, hold it, hold it!"—running along behind trying to catch them? And so the model that we're seeing, either on stage or on television, is totally different from anything that's in Scripture.[2]

Wimber's assumption is that while ministry *models* "come and go," *manifestations* such as people being "unceremoniously slammed to the ground . . . and thrown ten, fifteen feet across the floor"[3] have been constant throughout the history of humanity. Says Wimber, when the Holy Spirit "comes on people sometimes it's rather startling the things that he does. Now *that* we have a biblical basis for. In fact, we have a very powerful basis for it."[4] In an attempt to provide this biblical basis, he tries to convince devotees that Adam was the first person in human history to have experienced the slain in the spirit phenomenon.[5]

Adam

So the LORD God caused a deep *sleep* to fall upon the man and he slept; then He took one of his ribs, and closed up the flesh at that place. (Gen. 2:21 NASB; emphasis added)

Wimber uses what appears to be an elaborate deception to fool followers into believing that Bible translators—who have never had the slain in the spirit experience—incorrectly translate the word *sleep* in Genesis 2:21. Says Wimber, "How the interpreter gets 'sleep' out of this, I'll never know. The word is *yashen* and it means to be slack. It means to be languid. . . . It does *not* mean sleep. The Hebrew word for 'sleep' is quite explicit. There are three words that are used commonly. This is not any of those three words."[6]

In truth, however, Wimber has switched terms. The Hebrew word for "sleep" used here is not *yashen* as Wimber asserts; rather, it is *tardemah*. While Wimber seeks to impugn the translators, in reality he should be impugned. Every Hebrew expert I consulted[7] agreed that *sleep* is the correct translation of the Hebrew word used at this point in Genesis 2:21. Only someone with a bias would say otherwise.

It is instructive to note that the word *yashen* is used later in this same verse to reinforce *not* that Adam became *slack* but rather that he did indeed fall into a *deep sleep*. One who claims enough insight into Hebrew to impugn competent translators should be able to isolate the correct word, indicate its customary meaning, and identify other Hebrew words in the same context that reinforce this meaning.[8]

Furthermore, Wimber's interpretation of Genesis 2:21 does not come from an investigation of Hebrew but rather from interviews with "hundreds" of followers who have been slain in the spirit. He takes the description of what they experienced and assumes that Adam experienced the same thing. That is precisely why Wimber says that "the translator today, never having had the experience, doesn't know what is meant by what is said."[9]

Finally, even if Wimber were correct in asserting that Adam was the first person in human history to have been slain in the spirit, that would in no way establish a precedent for people today. If it did, one might well expect to arise after being slain in the spirit lacking a rib and living with a redhead.

Abraham

Abram *fell* on his face, and God talked with him.
(Gen. 17:3 NASB; emphasis added)

The second example Wimber cites in support of the slain in the spirit phenomenon is Abraham's experience in Genesis 17.

As he did with Adam, Wimber again uses his term-switching tactic to fool followers. Says Wimber:

> Now, notice this, "And Abram fell on his face. Abram fell on his face." The word there is *radam*. *Radam*, in the Hebrew, and it means he was stunned, as a blow. He was stupefied, is what the word means. That doesn't mean he voluntarily fell on his face. It means he was knocked flat at the presence of God. Now this is a man that God loves, and yet, in his presence, by the virtue of his presence, he was knocked flat. He didn't just bow down. He was stunned. A blow stupefied him, knocked him senseless, is what the word means.[10]

First, the Hebrew word used for "fell" is not *radam,* as Wimber asserts, it is *naphal*.[11] Furthermore, the Almighty did not cause Abraham to fall through a blow that stupefied and knocked him senseless; rather, Abraham fell of his own accord in response to the majesty of the Almighty. Finally, as he did with Adam, Wimber interprets Scripture in light of experience rather than interpreting experience in light of Scripture.

To explain why his followers fall backward like the foes of God, as opposed to falling forward like the friends of God do in Scripture, Wimber points to his own experience. In a series of messages titled "The Business of Laughing," Wimber said, "I want you to note something too. Abraham fell forward, face down. I've watched it for years now! I've watched it for years now, and most people, when they fall, they fall backwards. But leaders invariably fall forward. I've watched it again and again."[12]

Wimber uses other Old Testament examples in an attempt to justify the slain in the spirit phenomenon. In each case, however, even a cursory examination of relevant Scripture passages demonstrates the absurdity of his argumentation.

In addition it is important to note that God is more concerned with the attitude of our hearts than he is with the position of our bodies. While God most certainly has the power to overwhelm us with his presence, a basic principle communicated in Scripture is that God has created us as volitional beings. We can either fall before him in reverence, or we can fall away in rebellion. The position of our bodies is irrelevant. While today we can still choose,[13] a day is coming when even those who have chosen to rebel will fall at his feet and confess that Jesus Christ is Lord.

Apostle Peter

> Peter went up on the housetop about the sixth hour to pray. And he became hungry, and was desiring to eat; but while they were making preparations, *he fell into a trance*. (Acts 10:9–10 NASB; emphasis added)

Wimber uses the apostle Peter's trance in Acts 10 as proof positive that "God doesn't always use the Book" and "doesn't always color between the lines."[14] God communicated with the apostle Peter about his "rather bigoted condition"[15] via a trance. Thus, according to Wimber, he must also be attempting to communicate with people today via trance states. Wimber uses his experiences while "ministering" to followers as a frame of reference. In his words, "I have seen hundreds and hundreds of you, over the last three years, go into a state similar to that [of Peter]."[16]

First, it should be noted that biblical trance states like that experienced by Peter are sovereignly initiated, not self-induced or induced through human agency. In contrast, unbiblical trance states can be self-induced, induced through sociopsychological manipulation, or initiated by the touch of a shaman/sorcerer.

Furthermore, Peter's trance cannot be used as a precedent

for people today because Peter as an apostle was foundational to the church (Eph. 2:20). Unlike the private revelations received by Wimber's followers while in a trance state, Peter's revelation was the major event that opened the door for the acceptance of the Gentiles into the church. Far from "instructing through means other than Scripture," the revelation God gave to Peter was to become Scripture itself.

Finally, it should be noted once again that Wimber determines truth by the subjective experiences of his subjects rather than by the objective exegesis of Scripture. Says Wimber:

> I'm not going to stop something that seems to be a blessing to you, even though it may be an experience that I can't readily catalog, or easily, you know, as is often said, "Show me that in the Word." I told you already what that means. That means "I haven't had that experience."[17]

Apostle Paul

> And it came about that as he journeyed, he was approaching Damascus, and suddenly a light from heaven flashed around him, and he *fell* to the ground. (Acts 9:3–4 NASB; emphasis added)

As with the apostle Peter, Wimber abuses the biblical account of Christ's appearance to the apostle Paul on the road to Damascus in yet another vain attempt to substantiate the slain in the spirit phenomenon. On the one hand, he alleges that the apostle Paul was in "a supernaturally suspended state" for three days. On the other, he asserts that this condition was far from unique. As he puts it, there are at least "thirty or forty" such events recorded in Scripture, and "many other times it occurred when it wasn't recorded." In addition, says Wimber, "I know in history it's happened many more times than that."[18]

First, it should be pointed out that contrary to Wimber's assertions, Christ's appearance to Paul on the road to Damascus was, indeed, unique. Paul was chosen by God as the apostle to the Gentiles (Acts 9:15), his credentials were confirmed by the other Apostles (Acts 9:27), and his calling was evidenced by the fact that his writing became Scripture (2 Pet. 3:16). In addition, Paul pointed to his Damascus road experience as the basis on which he was counted as an eyewitnesses to the resurrection.

Furthermore, Wimber's claim that the phenomena associated with Christ's appearance to Paul on the road to Damascus are common is patently false. While he attempts to bolster his position through anecdotes—such as his story that Christ appeared to prophet Paul Cain on the road to Santa Maria[19]—there is no evidence to validate his claims.

Finally, one wonders how many of Wimber's devotees would line up to experience the slain in the spirit phenomenon if they truly believed that there were a chance that they, like Paul, would end up blind for three days. The reality is that parallels between what happened to the apostle Paul on the road to Damascus and what happens to Wimber's people in churches around the world are conspicuous by their absence.

Apostle John

And when I saw Him, *I fell at His feet as a dead man.* And He laid His right hand upon me, saying, "Do not be afraid." (Rev. 1:17 NASB; emphasis added)

According to Wimber "the closest thing to the term 'slain in the spirit' in the entire Bible" is found in Revelation 1:17. Wimber suggests that when the apostle John fell at the feet of Jesus, he was "falling in an unconscious state."[20] Again, however, he makes it clear that what happened to John is painfully common. In one church service alone, he says, "probably

150 of you fell as a dead man. Unconscious. Not aware of what was going on. Just, whambo!"[21] While he claims that he would never manipulate anyone's emotions, he confesses that the slain in the spirit phenomenon is commonly manufactured in the church. Says Wimber:

> It's important for you to recognize that when the mani-
> fest presence comes upon believers, there is the possi-
> bility that they will swoon, nod over, fall asleep, and
> in some occasions, their body will fall. Now this can be
> induced . . . in some false way through emotional dis-
> play, through priming people up, and through causing
> them, through manipulation of their emotions, to lit-
> erally "bug out," just pass out. And the horror of it is
> that both are being done in the name of Jesus today in
> the church.[22]

First, as you will read in part 5, it appears that Wimber uses sociopsychological manipulation tactics to work his devo-tees into altered states of consciousness. Not only that, but as we have seen, seekers are seduced through a variety of Scripture-twisting tactics as well.

Furthermore, Wimber again takes the experiences of his subjects and imposes them on Scripture. His notion that 150 followers experienced falling in an unconscious state is no war-rant for suggesting that the apostle John was unconscious during his encounter with Christ. As Robert Mounce commu-nicates in his commentary on the Book of Revelation, the apostle John was "experiencing a supernatural phenomenon of such magnitude that to stand as an equal would be tanta-mount to blasphemy."[23]

Finally, it is crucial to understand that the Almighty ap-peared to the apostle Peter, the apostle Paul, and the apostle John to directly reveal Scripture, which alone is sufficient for faith and practice (2 Tim. 3:15–17). Rather than flocking to conferences to experience new revelations as they are slain in the spirit, Wimber's followers would do well to study the revelation that God has already given through the apostles he has chosen to be the foundation of the church (Eph. 2:20–23).

Arrest of Jesus

When therefore He said to them, "I am He," they drew back, and *fell to the ground.* (John 18:6 NASB; emphasis added)

Wimber claims that as the soldiers fell to the ground in the presence of Jesus, so too scoffers have been flung to the ground in his presence. Says Wimber:

On numerous occasions, on numerous occasions in our ministry in this church, I've seen this very phenomenon, where people who were in some state of unbelief, either outright total or partial, I've watched the Spirit of God work this work. Back 'em down, knock 'em over—I mean, you wouldn't believe that God would be so rough. Gentle Jesus! Wham, you know? Comes on like a sumo wrestler or something, you know? Doing people in, bouncing them on the floor for half an hour to forty-five minutes at a time, you know? They're whamming there. You say, "God, what are you doing?" you know? "Well, I'm working out a little problem that they have," you know? "Working on their theology."[24]

Wimber makes it clear that the soldiers who came to arrest Jesus did not merely fall to the ground. According to Wimber, "the Greek says they were propelled back and were flung, in effect, to the ground."[25] What happened to the soldiers in John 18:6, however, pales by comparison to what

Wimber says he has seen with his own eyes on "numerous occasions." As a case in point, Wimber asserts that "on one occasion a man was lifted and flung thirty feet across the room and slammed against a wall. Now this man had been in the occult most of his adult life and was messing around with evil spirits and when two people turned and raised their hands to pray for him, the man was lifted off the ground and flung thirty feet across the floor, and came up believing, amen!"[26]

Wimber goes on to liken what happens today in his ministry to what happened "in the ministry of Finney, in the ministry of Wesley, under the Moravian explosion, the Anabaptist movement and on and on and on this same kind of phenomena has occurred again and again and again."[27]

First, it should be noted that what Wimber claims happens frequently in his church never once happened in the ministry of the incarnate Christ. Not once in Scripture do we read of either a believer or an unbeliever encountering Christ being "lifted and flung thirty feet across the room and slammed against a wall." Nowhere do we read of Christ coming "on like a sumo wrestler" and "bouncing" unbelievers "on the floor for half an hour to forty-five minutes at a time." Once again, rather than simply reading the text, Wimber takes a text and reads his own "experiences" into it. As noted by the *Dictionary of Pentecostal and Charismatic Movements*:

> There is no mention of the Spirit here [John 18:1–6], and John portrays no relationship between Spirit, power, and Jesus. The text remains enigmatic, especially since John offers neither explanation for, nor effect of, their fall. Obviously they were not converted, because they proceeded to arrest Jesus.[28]

Furthermore, while Wimber constantly wows worshipers with tales of "power encounters," as we have already seen and will see again later on, his stories often do not square with the facts. While

I have personally witnessed the bizarre manifestations that take place in his ministry, I have not seen the kinds of manifestations described above, either in his church or in the cults. Quite frankly, I am convinced that his devotees are being misled.

Finally, to say that the Savior comes on like a sumo wrestler in church services is nothing short of blasphemous. Wimber would do better to attribute the manifestations in his sensational stories to Satan. As Scripture reveals, "the work of Satan" is "displayed in all kinds of counterfeit miracles, signs and wonders, and in every sort of evil that deceives those who are perishing" (2 Thess. 2:9–10).[29]

Angel

And the guards *shook* for fear of him, and *became like dead men*. (Matt. 28:4 NASB; emphasis added)

The last biblical pretext Wimber presents in support of the slain in the spirit phenomenon is found in Matthew 28. He paints a picture in which there were "several hundred [soldiers] in the garden." He goes on to say, "I think when they shook and fell as dead men, that there were bodies littered everywhere." In his opinion the unbelieving soldiers were so afraid "they shook and they died." The believing women, however, "didn't fall down."[30] Again, according to Wimber, this event is not unique. As he puts it:

I have, on numerous occasions, been in places where the Holy Spirit has been released in this kind of power, and I want you to know the first response in my heart has always been fear. "What are you doing, Lord?" Sometimes, "Who is doing this?" I've had to work my way through "Is this God?" because it seems so incredible to me that God would actually work this way, because he didn't fit in a rational Western box that I had been placing him in all these years, and he was operating out of character with what I understood him to be.[31]

First, once again Wimber is reading his own misunderstandings into the Scripture. There is no warrant for suggesting that hundreds of soldiers were literally slain in the spirit at the appearance of the angel. As indicated by the *Dictionary of Pentecostal and Charismatic Movements,* Matthew's statement that the guards "shook and became like dead men" is "simply a figurative way of saying the guards were 'petrified.' Even if the guards were 'slain,' their experience is entirely secondary to the story and did not have any redemptive value as far as the text is concerned."[32]

Furthermore, even Wimber admits that it was the foes rather than the friends of Christ who fell. While Counterfeit Revival leaders like Wimber attribute the slain in the spirit phenomenon to the Holy Spirit, in truth it is better attributed to Hindu gurus, hucksters, and hypnotists. Sadly, even though he admits that he's wondered, "Is this God?" Wimber continues to cultivate constructs that resemble communes and carnivals rather than Christian churches.

Finally, it is revealing that after presenting a plethora of biblical pretexts, Wimber has failed to prove his point. While God can and does overwhelm people by his presence, there is no biblical basis for making this a normative practice in the church. The *Dictionary of Pentecostal and Charismatic Movements* clearly points out:

> An entire battalion of Scripture proof texts is enlisted to support the legitimacy of the phenomenon, although Scripture plainly offers no support for the phenomenon as something to be expected in the normal Christian life. . . . From an experiential standpoint it is unquestionable that through the centuries Chris-

tians have experienced a psycho-physical phenomenon in which people fall down; moreover, they have attributed the experience to God. It is equally unquestionable that there is no biblical evidence for the experience as normative in Christian life.[33]

Wimber ends his series of sermons titled "Spiritual Phenomena: Slain in the Spirit" by recounting the story of how in one of his meetings a man by the name of "Lonnie, was praying on some gals":

> They became so intoxicated—they had their arms around each other—they became so intoxicated they began falling. . . . They began dancing around the room and people were just sort of enjoying them, you know, 'cause they were in a very ethereal state. They were smiling and enjoying themselves and we were all just watching it happen, you know? And one young lady walked up to me and she said, "What's that?" Now I said, "I perceive you disapprove of that?" (I've got discerning of spirits.) And she said, "What rational basis can there be for that kind of behavior?" And I said, "Be not drunk with wine, which is excess, but be filled with the Spirit."[34]

What Wimber did not say is that once again he's taken a text out of context. Paul, in the passage Wimber quoted (Eph. 5:18), is not saying that drunkenness is desirable and has a spiritual counterpart. Rather, in context he is presenting a consistent series of contrasts between cultic and Christian behavior. Inspired by the Holy Spirit, he makes it clear that as Christians we must be "alert and sober" rather than being in an altered state of consciousness or slain in the spirit. Something else Wimber does not divulge is that the guy praying on his "gals" played a prominent role in the development of the Vineyard movement.

CHAPTER 20

Structural Defects

It was Mother's Day 1979, and all hell broke loose. John Wimber had invited a young evangelist to speak during the evening service at his church. He says the "power encounter" that took place that night was "similar to the one described at Pentecost." There was one notable difference. While the Apostles praised God during their Pentecost, Wimber was "extremely irritated and angry at God" during his. Here's Wimber's recollection of that unforgettable evening:

> I had invited a young man to speak at the evening service of the church at which I had only recently become pastor, what would later become the Vineyard Christian Fellowship in Anaheim, California. His background was the California "Jesus People" movement of the late sixties and early seventies and, so I heard, he was unpredictable when he spoke. I was apprehensive about him, but I sensed God wanted him to speak nevertheless. He had been used by God to lead Christians into a refreshing experience of the Holy Spirit, and it was obvious to me that the congregation needed

spiritual renewal. I hasten to point out that asking this young man to speak went contrary to my normal instincts as a pastor. I take seriously the admonition that pastors are to protect their flocks, but in this instance I sensed it was what God wanted. Regardless, I was to stand by the decision, whatever the cost.

When he eagerly agreed to speak, I became even more apprehensive. What will he say? What will he do to my church? The Lord gently reminded me, "Whose church is this?"

That evening he gave his testimony, a powerful story of God's grace. As he spoke, I relaxed. Nothing strange here, I thought. Then he did something that I had never seen done in a church gathering. He finished his talk and said, "Well, that's my testimony. Now the church has been offending the Holy Spirit a long time and it's quenched. So we are going to invite it to come and minister." We all waited. The air became thick with anticipation—and anxiety.

Then he said, "Holy Spirit, come." And it did!

(I must remind you that we were not a "Pentecostal" church with experience or understanding of the sorts of things that began to happen. What happened could not have been learned behavior.)

People fell to the floor. Others, who did not believe in tongues, loudly spoke in tongues. The speaker roamed among the crowd, praying for people, who then immediately fell over with the Holy Spirit resting on them.

I was aghast! All I could think throughout the experience was "Oh, God, get me out of here." In the aftermath, we lost church members and my staff was extremely upset. That night I could not sleep. Instead, I spent the evening reading Scripture, looking for the verse, "Holy Spirit, come." I never found it.

By 4:30 that morning I was more upset than I was earlier at the meeting. Then I remembered that I had read in *The Journal of John Wesley* about something like this happening. I went out to my garage and found a box of books about revivals and revivalists and began to read them. What I discovered was that our experience at the church service was not unique; people like John and Charles Wesley, George Whitefield, Charles Finney, and Jonathan Edwards all had similar experiences in their ministries. By 6:00 I had found at least ten examples of similar phenomena in church history. . . .

Then I asked God for assurance that this was from him, that this was something he—not humans or Satan—was doing. Just after praying this prayer, the phone rang. Tom Stipe, a Denver, Colorado, pastor and good friend, called. I told him what had happened the night before, and he responded that it was from God.[1]

Carol Wimber describes this same event as the "watershed experience that launched us into what today is called power evangelism."[2] No doubt what made the sights and sounds of this service so memorable was that, as Carol put it, "our Quaker background made us more disposed to be quiet."[3] While she disagreed with her husband on the date (John says it was 1979; Carol says it was 1981),[4] she vividly remembers the chaos that ensued:

One fellow, Tim, started bouncing. His arms flung out and he fell over, but one of his hands accidentally hit a mike stand and he took it down with him. He was tangled up in the cord with the mike next to his mouth. Then he began speaking in tongues, so the sound went throughout the gymnasium. . . . The majority of young people were shaking and falling over. At one point it looked like a battlefield scene—bodies everywhere, people weeping, wailing, and speaking in tongues, much shouting and loud behavior. And there was Tim in the middle of it all, babbling into the microphone.

A wide-eyed John sat by softly playing the piano. Some members of our staff were fearful and angry. Several people got up and walked out, never to be seen again—at least they were not seen by us.

But I knew that God was visiting us. I was so thrilled, because I had been praying for power for so long. . . . I got up and started stepping over bodies and putting my hand next to them. I could feel the power, like heat or electricity, radiating off of their bodies.

I asked one boy who was on the floor, "What's happening to you right now?" He said, "It's like electricity. I can't move!" I was amazed by the effect of God's power on the human body. I suppose I thought that it would all be an inward work, such as conviction or repentance. I never imagined there would be strong physical manifestations.

But John wasn't as happy as I. . . . He spent that night reading Scripture and historical accounts of revival from the lives of people like Whitefield and Wesley. . . . But his study did not yield conclusive answers to questions raised from the previous evening's events. By 5 A.M. John was desperate. He cried out to God, "Lord, if this is you, please tell me." A moment later the phone rang and a pastor friend of ours from Denver, Colorado, was on the line. "John," he said, "I'm sorry I'm calling so early, but I have something really strange to tell you. I don't know what it means, but God wants me to say, 'It's me, John.'" That was all John needed. He didn't have to understand the trembling or why everything happened as it did; all he needed to know was the Holy Spirit did it.[5]

While both John and Carol Wimber are convinced that what took place in their church was a work of the Holy Spirit, perhaps what took place might better be described as the work of a hypnotist. Before we unmask this "watershed experience," let's look at yet another version of the same story. This one comes from psychiatrist and Vineyard pastor John White.[6] Contradicting both John and Carol, he says the preacher in question was "self-invited" and the date was "Mother's Day 1978":[7]

What followed was electrifying! To Wimber's intense alarm, the young people fell on the floor, some crying out noisily. One young man seemed to be flung forward in such a way that his mouth was jammed over the microphone. Since he was speaking in tongues, his "gibberish" screeched through the public address system. Pandemonium erupted. The young preacher became agitated, shouting excitedly, "More, Lord. More!" At one point, raising his hand he shouted, "Jesus is Lord." The people his hand faced fell untidily around the bleachers.

Wimber was furious. Unable because of the pile of bodies to reach the glossolalia-broadcasting microphone, he called to some young people to remove the young man. They couldn't. The situation was out of control. Wimber's anger increased at the young people's apparent inability to respond to his instructions and at his own inability to regain control of what was happening. . . .

[Later that night] he gave up on sleep . . . going into his study to search the Scriptures. . . .

After some time he went out under the stars to pray. As the night wore on he remembered some volumes of church history, and soon was reflecting on events described by Jonathan Edwards, John Wesley and

George Whitefield. . . . He prayed for clear guidance, and shortly afterward, about 6:30 A.M., received a long-distance telephone call.

The caller was Tom Stipes [*sic*], a pastor in Denver, who told Wimber he had been awakened early, with the impression that God wanted him to give Wimber a three-word message. Stipes had no idea what the words might mean.

"What is the message?" Wimber asked, wonderingly.

"It is, 'That was me!'"

That was me. At first he was only aware of shock. Yet as the words gripped him, they simultaneously released him from his frustration and fear. . . . A new certainty grew in him that what had seemed at the time to be horrendous and bizarre had actually come from the dear and familiar hand of God.[8]

Irreconcilable Differences

What John Wimber portrayed as a "power encounter similar to the one described at Pentecost" is in fact founded on fantasies and fabrications.

First, even a cursory examination of the three preceding accounts reveals broad-ranging discrepancies. As a case in point, Carol Wimber says, "A wide-eyed John sat by softly playing the piano." John White, however, says that Wimber was "furious" and his anger increased at the young people's apparent inability to respond to his instructions.

Second, John Wimber says he could not find any scriptural basis for what happened Mother's Day 1979. He determined the devastation to be divine rather than demonic on the basis of a phone call that portended to be a message from God. The conditions and content of the call, however, are a matter of serious dispute. The caller, Tom Stipe, says the story that "he had been awakened early, with the impression that God wanted him to give Wimber a three-word message" and that he had "no idea what the words might mean" is patently false. While he felt prompted to encourage Wimber, he did not feel prompted to give him a message of any sort. Only *after* Wimber had told him about the events that had transpired did he offer any encouragement or support. He also made it clear that Wimber did not offer loaded details such as described in the preceding accounts.

Third, after personally spending several years studying historical revivals and revivalists, I find it hard to believe that Wimber could have objectively researched and reviewed "at least ten examples of similar phenomena" in the works of "John and Charles Wesley, George Whitefield, Charles Finney, and Jonathan Edwards"—all between 4:30 and 6:00 A.M.

Fourth, Wimber says what happened Mother's Day 1979 was "something that I had never seen done in a church gathering." He claims he was so "aghast" at seeing people fall to the floor and loudly speak in tongues that he stayed up all night searching for a biblical or historical precedent.

In truth, however, he had seen all this and much, much more before. More to the point, he had done it all before. In 1978, for example, the year before "the evangelist" came to his church,[9] Wimber graphically portrays not only being slain in the spirit but slaying others in the spirit as well:

> One night I walked up to a woman to pray for her and I raised my hand and she went flying, bam. . . . She went over a couch, knocked over a table and lamp, and hit the corner. . . . I thought, *She's crazy,* you know? She's knocked out, she's crazy, and she got up and she was like, kind of like, woozy, you know? I thought, *Well, she's really hurt herself,* you know? And we were all standing in kind of an oval circle, and I turned around to pray for somebody else, and they went like that, and they started to fall down. Another

guy fell against me, and he was a big guy. . . . And then somebody grabbed ahold of me while I was trying to pray for him. They reached out. . . . The moment they touched me, we both went down. And there was this sense of the presence of something in the room—God. And I'd never experienced anything like that before. And I remember sitting down and it was sort of hard to breathe, you know? And I went home, my wife and I went home, and I was sort of drunken. My mouth, I was talking funny. I went home. I remember I was trying to pour a glass of milk and I said, "Carol Kay?" That's what I call her when I've really got something important to say. "Carol Kay, I think we're on to something here." And when I said that I went right to the floor. And so then a few nights later we're at church and we go behind the curtain— we had a curtain then—we went behind the curtain to pray for people, and they're going out like lights. Bam, they're hitting the floor and falling down. . . . Then I heard about catchers, you know, so we got a catcher to go around behind everybody and catch them.[10]

Fifth, Wimber says that what happened Mother's Day 1979 "could not have been learned behavior."[11] The preceding quotation, however, makes it crystal-clear that both he and his congregation had long before experienced the slain in the spirit phenomenon. His wife in fact wrote that in early April of 1978 "John went around the room praying for us, and an incredible power was released from his hands. He touched the people and they fell over. To John it was as though spiritual power came from his hands like electricity."[12]

Sixth, in a 1981 message titled "Spiritual Phenomena: Slain in the Spirit—Part 3," Wimber says, "In my life the Holy Spirit has never knocked me down . . . I'm very open to it, but it's not something God has done for me or to me."[13] Yet, as we have seen, he previously claimed to have been knocked down both publicly and privately.

Seventh, while in one breath Wimber claims he took "seriously the admonition that pastors are to protect their flocks," in the next he conveys that he turned his pulpit over to a man he did not know much about and that what he knew about him was negative. The result was that he turned his church into a laboratory and his church members into guinea pigs.

Tragically, the "lab technician" who experimented on them that night was a hypnotist struggling with homosexuality. In 1993 he died of AIDS.

PART FIVE

Hypnotism

CHAPTER 21

The Arrival
of the Mesmerist

An *exciting event in our village was the arrival of the mesmerizer. I think the year was 1850. As to that I am not sure, but I know the month—it was May; that detail has survived the wear of fifty years. A pair of connected little incidents of that month have served to keep the memory of it green for me all this time. . . .*

So begins a fascinating recollection by humorist Mark Twain of an amazing experience during his teenage years.

The village had heard of mesmerism in a general way but had not encountered it yet. Not many people attended the first night but next day they had so many wonders to tell that everybody's curiosity was fired and after that for a fortnight the magician had prosperous times. I was fourteen or fifteen years old, the age at which a boy is willing to endure all things, suffer all things short of death by fire, if thereby he may be conspicuous and show off before the public; and so, when I saw the "subjects" perform their foolish antics on the platform and make the people laugh and shout and admire I had a burning desire to be a subject myself.

Every night for three nights I sat in the row of candidates on the platform and held the magic disk in the palm of my hand and gazed at it and tried to get sleepy, but it was a failure; I remained wide awake and had to retire defeated, like the majority. Also, I had to sit there and be gnawed with envy of Hicks, our journeyman; I had to sit there and see him scamper and jump when Simmons the enchanter exclaimed, "See the snake! See the snake!" and hear him say, "My, how beautiful!" in response to the suggestion that he was observing a splendid sunset; and so on—the whole insane business. I couldn't laugh, I couldn't applaud; it filled me with bitterness to have others do it and to have people make a hero out of Hicks and crowd around him when the show was over and ask him for more and more particulars of the wonders he had seen in his visions and manifest in many ways that they were proud to be acquainted with him. Hicks—the idea! I couldn't stand it; I was getting boiled to death in my own bile.

On the fourth night temptation came and I was not strong enough to resist. When I had gazed at the disk a while I pretended to be sleepy and began to nod. Straightaway came the professor and made passes over my head and down my body and legs and arms, finishing each pass with a snap of his fingers in the air to discharge the surplus electricity; then he began to "draw" me with the disk, holding it in his fingers and telling me I could not take my eyes off it, try as I might; so I rose slowly, bent and gazing, and followed that disk all over the place, just as I had seen the others do. Then I was put through the other paces. Upon suggestion I fled from snakes, passed buckets at a fire, became excited over hot steamboat-races, made love to imaginary girls and kissed them, fished from the platform and landed mud cats that outweighed me—and so on, all the customary marvels. But not in the customary way. I was cautious at first and watchful, being afraid the professor would discover that I was an impostor and drive me from the platform in disgrace; but as soon as I realized that I was not in danger, I set myself the task of terminating Hicks's usefulness as subject and of usurping his place.

It was a sufficiently easy task. Hicks was born honest, I without that encumbrance—so some people said. Hicks saw what he saw and reported accordingly, I saw more than was visible and added to it such details as could help. Hicks had no imagination; I had a double supply. He was born calm, I was born excited. No vision could start a rapture in him and he was constipated as to language, anyway; but if I saw a vision I emptied the dictionary onto it and lost the remnant of my mind into the bargain.

Then there was another thing: Hicks wasn't worth a tallow dip on mute mental suggestion. Whenever Simmons stood behind him and gazed at the back of his skull and tried to drive a mental suggestion into it, Hicks sat with vacant face and never suspected. If he had been noticing he could have seen by the rapt faces of the audience that something was going on behind his back that required a response. Inasmuch as I was an impostor I dreaded to have this test put upon me, for I knew the professor would be "willing" me to do something, and as I couldn't know what it was, I should be exposed and denounced. However, when my time came, I took my chance. I perceived by the tense and expectant faces of the people that Simmons was behind me willing me with all his might. I tried my best to imagine what he wanted but nothing suggested itself. I felt ashamed and miserable then. I believed that the hour of my disgrace was come and that in another moment I should go out of that place disgraced. I ought to be ashamed to confess it but my next thought was not how I could win the compassion of kindly hearts by going out humbly and in sorrow for my misdoings, but how I could go out most sensationally and spectacularly.

There was a rusty and empty old revolver lying on the table among the "properties" employed in the performances. On May Day two or three weeks before this there had been a celebration by the schools and I had had a quarrel with a big boy who was the school bully and I had not come out of it with credit. That boy was now seated in the middle of the house, halfway down the main aisle. I crept stealthily and impressively toward the table, with a dark and murderous scowl on my face, copied from a popular romance, seized the revolver suddenly, flourished it, shouted the bully's name, jumped off the platform and made a rush for him and chased him out of the house before the paralyzed people could interfere to save him. There was a storm of applause, and the magician, addressing the house, said, most impressively—

"That you may know how really remarkable this is and how wonderfully developed a subject we have in this boy, I assure you that without a single spoken word to guide him he has carried out what I mentally commanded him to do, to the minutest detail. I could have stopped him at a moment in his vengeful career by a mere exertion of my will, therefore the poor fellow who has escaped was at no time in danger."

So I was not in disgrace. I returned to the platform a hero and happier than I have ever been in this world since. As regards mental suggestion, my fears of it were gone. I judged that in case I failed to guess what the professor might be willing me to do, I could count on putting up something that would answer just as well. I was right, and exhibitions of unspoken suggestion became a favorite with the public. Whenever I perceived that I was being willed to do something I got up and did something—anything that occurred to me—and the magician, not being a fool, always ratified it. When people asked me, "How can you tell what he is willing you to do?" I said, "It's just as easy," and they always said admiringly, "Well, it beats me how you can do it."

Hicks was weak in another detail. When the professor made passes over him and said "his whole body is without sensation now—come forward and test him, ladies and gentlemen," the ladies and gentlemen always complied eagerly and stuck pins into Hicks, and if they went deep Hicks was sure to wince, then that poor professor would have to explain that Hicks "wasn't sufficiently under the influence." But I didn't wince; I only suffered and shed tears on the inside. The miseries that a conceited boy will endure to keep up his "reputation"! And so will a conceited man; I know it in my own person and have seen it in a hundred thousand others. That professor ought to have protected me and I often hoped he would, when the tests were unusually severe, but he didn't. It may be that he was deceived as well as the others, though I did not believe it nor think it possible. Those were dear good people but they must have carried simplicity and credulity to the limit. They would stick a pin in my arm and bear on it until they drove it a third of its length in, and then be lost in wonder that by a mere exercise of will power the professor could turn my arm to iron and make it insensible to pain. Whereas it was not insensible at all; I was suffering agonies of pain. . . .

How easy it is to make people believe a lie and how hard it is to undo that work again! Thirty-five years after those evil exploits of mine I visited my old mother, whom I had not seen for ten years; and being moved by what seemed to me a rather noble and perhaps heroic impulse, I thought I would humble myself and confess my ancient fault. It cost me a great effort to make up my mind; I dreaded the sorrow that would rise in her face and the shame that would look out of her eyes; but after long and troubled reflection, the sacrifice seemed due and right and I gathered my resolution together and made the confession.

To my astonishment there were no sentimentalities, no dramatics, no George Washington effects; she was not moved in the least degree; she simply did not believe me and said so![1]

Many years have come and gone since Mark Twain wrote about his firsthand experience with mesmerism. His account, however, is strikingly similar to the story of my encounter with "the world's greatest stage hypnotist" (see pp. 5–8). While the century has changed, the principles used by the mesmerist in Twain's story and the hypnotist in mine are virtually identical.

Mesmerism Today

Today's "mesmerists" operate not only in carnivals but also in churches and communes. Whether they are referred to as hypnotists, Holy Ghost bartenders,[2] or Hindu gurus, the methods they employ have much in common.

First, they all work their subjects into altered states of consciousness. The hypnotist in Twain's story made use of a "magic" medallion, the Holy Ghost bartender uses music, and the Hindu guru utilizes mysterious mantras.

Furthermore, hypnotists, Holy Ghost bartenders, and Hindu gurus use peer pressure to conform followers to predictable patterns. The hypnotist's volunteer goes into a dream state because he "knows" that's what everyone else has done. Patrons of the Holy Ghost bartender see everyone else getting drunk at "Joel's Bar" and become convinced that drunkenness is desirable. Devotees of Hindu gurus conform their dress, decorum, and diet so that they fit in.

Hypnotists, Holy Ghost bartenders, and Hindu gurus also depend heavily on expectations. The hypnotist is well aware of the fact that the best assurance of a successful performance is the enthusiastic embellishment of previous audiences. Twain says that on the day after the mesmerist's first performance, "they had so many wonders to tell that everybody's curiosity was fired and after that for a fortnight the magician had prosperous times."

The Holy Ghost bartender depends on the Christian grapevine to attract the faithful. Pastors from around the world flocked to a small church near a runway in Toronto because they heard that the Holy Spirit had "landed" there. Likewise, people travel across continents with the expectation that communing with Hindu gurus will enable them to achieve enlightenment.

Finally, the power of suggestion is pivotal to the performance of hypnotists, Holy Ghost bartenders, and Hindu gurus. Hypnotists bank on the fact that their subjects have become hyper-suggestible—willing to believe and act upon virtually anything that enters their minds.

Holy Ghost bartenders use the power of suggestion as a "placebo" to "cure" a host of psychosomatic symptoms and sicknesses. They abuse the power of suggestion to seduce subjects and seekers and to provide ammunition for scoffers and skeptics. "George Bernard Shaw once caustically commented that the healings at Lourdes, France, left him unconvinced because he had seen many crutches and wheelchairs on display, but not one glass eye, wooden leg, or toupee."[3]

Like Holy Ghost bartenders, Hindu gurus use the power of suggestion to trap their subjects in a dangerous web of subjectivism. Influenced by the subtle suggestions of gurus, devotees succumb to counterfeit miracles and suppose themselves to be one with the cosmic mind of the universe.

APES

Cynics may write off the use of *altered states of consciousness, peer pressure, expectations,* and the *suggestions* of hypnotists, Holy Ghost bartenders, and Hindu gurus as sociopsychological manipulation. Christians, however, must comprehend an even more significant threat—these manipulation techniques are fertile soil for satanic and spiritual deception.

The threat posed by such manipulation tactics is so significant that I've developed the acronym APES to facilitate remembering and resisting them. The A represents *altered states of consciousness;* the P, *peer pressure;* the E, *expectations;* and the S, *suggestibility.*

As the father of nine children, I have made more than my share of trips to the zoo. It's always humorous to see my kids mimicking the movements of the various mammals they encounter. It really gets hysterical when we get to the apes. They are as likely to mimic my kids as my kids are to mimic them! The apes "ape" the kids, the kids "ape" the apes, and Kathy and I end up breathless with laughter.

What is not particularly funny, however, is that despite the peril, pastors and parishioners worldwide are now "aping" the practices of pagan spirituality. Before looking at the crisis this has caused within Christianity, it is critical that we first gain a perspective on the history of hypnotism.

Franz Anton Mesmer

Back in the eighteenth century Franz Anton Mesmer, from whose name the word *mesmerize* is derived, caused people to laugh, fall into trances, and jerk spasmodically by simply gesturing in their direction. Mesmer was a French physician (1733–1815) who was popularly referred to as "The Wizard from Vienna." His reputation, however, earned him other titles as well:

> He has been called the father of psychotherapy as well as of Christian Science, the discoverer of hypnosis, the progenitor of clairvoyance, telepathy and communication with the beyond; and he has been denigrated as a rogue, a charlatan, an arrogant pursuer of social and monetary favor, a meretricious magician. In his day it was asserted that he had sold his soul to the devil. More subtly, he has been cast as a visionary who unwittingly stumbled upon a discovery the value of which he was not able to see.[4]

He promulgated the principle that a magnetic force emanated from his hands, enabling him to direct the actions and thoughts of his subjects.

Even those who questioned his motives admitted that the impact he had on patients was dramatic. Their convulsions were reported as "extraordinary for their number, their duration, and their force."[5] By simply pointing a finger dramatically in the direction of one patient, "she moved convulsively as if in great pain and arched her body from shoulders to feet into a rigid position until he released her."[6]

Two royal commissions investigating "Mesmerism" in 1784 reported that the convulsions of Mesmer's patients were "marked by violent, involuntary movements of the limbs and the whole body, by constriction of the throat, by throbbing in the chest and nausea in the stomach, by rapid blinking and crossed eyes, by piercing cries, tears, hiccups and uncontrollable laughter."[7]

One of the testimonials sent by Mesmer to the Royal Society of Medicine was that of an army officer named Charles du Hussay who suffered from a number of physical symptoms such as fever, nervous trembling, and partial paralysis. After being treated by Mesmer, he wrote, "I know nothing of the means used by Dr. Mesmer. However I can say in all candor that, without treating me with drugs or any other remedy than what he calls animal magnetism, he caused me to feel powerful sensations from head to foot."[8] Du Hussay went on to testify that after feeling the sensations of intense cold that caused his body to feel like it was turning to ice and heat that caused him to sweat profusely, he was completely healed of his infirmities.

Early in his career, Mesmer maintained that he could heal people by means of metal magnets. By 1775, however, his beliefs had undergone a metamorphosis. He now maintained that his healing prowess was the result of an indwelling force he referred to as "animal magnetism." So convinced was Mesmer of the validity of his method that he wanted to teach it to the clergy of his day. In Germany and other countries, magnetism became so popular that by the early nineteenth century Berlin physicians had erected a monument to Mesmer, and theology students were trained in the treatment of diseases through the use of animal magnetism.[9]

In time the belief that certain men could exercise influence over others by means of the indwelling force of animal magnetism was largely discredited. The manifestations that Mesmer and his successors produced in their subjects could not be dispensed with as easily. The manifestations came to be viewed, not as the result of Mesmer's magnetism, but as the result of mental manipulation.

James Braid

The person most responsible for this shift in perspective was an English doctor named James Braid (1795–1860). The manifestations that Mesmer attributed to the "doctrine of animal magnetism," Braid attributed to the "doctrine of suggestion."

The primary difference between Mesmer and Braid was one of perspective. Mesmerists believed that through an indwelling force called animal magnetism, they could cause their subjects to experience such manifestations as uncontrollable laughter and spasmodic jerking. Hypnotists, on the other hand, believed that the manifestations experienced by their subjects were not the results of a power residing in the hypnotist but rather the result of a heightened state of suggestibility that a subject experienced while in a hypnotic trance.

Braid discovered that through mental manipulation, he could alter a patient's perspective to such an extent that he was able to perform surgical procedures that were virtually painless. By deliberately inducing his subjects to fall into a sleep-like altered state of consciousness, they became extraordinarily responsive to suggestion. Braid termed this sleep state *hypnosis*.[10]

While Braid has been credited with coining the word *hypnosis*, the phenomenon itself can be traced to virtually every culture, every civilization, and every century. As one writer observed, "it is as common in Polynesia today as it was at the fortune-telling shrines of ancient Greece and Rome."[11]

In recent history, pseudo-Christian cults have seized upon the principles of hypnotism to advance their pernicious principles and practices. J. Gordon Melton et al. underscores this reality by correctly associating mesmerism (hypnotism) with the mind science cults:

Mesmerism was developed into a new healing system by Phineas Parkhurst Quimby (1802–1866), a professional mesmerist who felt that many diseases could be cured by suggestion and were therefore essentially illusory. Eventually drawing the conclusion that all diseases are illusory, Quimby in 1859 began teaching the system that he called Science of Christ, Science of Health, and occasionally Christian Science.[12]

What has been commonplace in cultic systems such as Christian Science is today becoming commonplace in the Christian church as well. Like Gnostics in the second and third centuries, many who claim the name of Christ are taking a trip beyond Christianity into the world of the occult. They are being convinced by leaders of the Counterfeit Revival that reality can be reduced to a personal experience of enlightenment—a transformation of consciousness that will initiate them into "true spirituality."

CHAPTER 22

The Altered State
of Consciousness

As we move into an examination of the *A* in the acronym APES, we would do well to note the comments of Dr. Charles Tart, who has been credited with coining the term *altered states of consciousness*. Tart says that during deep hypnosis, "a transition to a new state of consciousness" takes place, a state in which the hypnotized subject's identity "is potentiality, he's aware of everything and nothing, his mind is absolutely quiet, he's out of time, out of space."[1]

As we will see, there are a wide variety of techniques used by leaders of the Counterfeit Revival to work followers into altered states of consciousness. One of the most disarming methods used is to sing one song over and over until participants finally lose touch with reality.

Counterfeit Revival leader Rick Joyner confessed that at one of his conferences participants sang one song "for over three hours."[2] As a result, he said, "the gulf between heaven and earth had somehow been bridged."[3]

Joyner reports that, "when that one song finally ended, some of the musicians were lying on the floor." Says Joyner:

I looked at Christine Potter and Susy Wills, who were dancing near the center of the stage and I have never seen such a look of terror on the faces of anyone. An intense burning, like a nuclear fire that burns from the inside out, seemed to be on the stage. Christine started pulling at her clothes as if she were on fire, and Susy dove behind the drums. Then a cloud appeared in the center of the stage, visible to everyone, and a sweet smell like flowers filled the area.[4]

Likewise, Brownsville Revival evangelist Stephen Hill required worship leaders to play the same music over and over again during the infamous first day of revival Father's Day, June 18, 1995.[5] Leaders like Joyner and Hill see the mind as a lower form of consciousness. Thus, like Eastern gurus, they work their devotees into altered states of consciousness. Joyner, in fact, says that "experience is a much better teacher than words."[6]

In stark contrast, Dr. Elizabeth Hillstrom warns that altered states of consciousness can be an open invitation for demonic deception:

Having largely set aside their ability to think rationally and critically or to exercise their will, they have become hypersuggestible, which means that they are likely to accept any "spiritual truth" that enters their minds. Even more remarkably, they seemed to be primed for mystical experiences and may attach great spiritual significance to virtually any event or thought, no matter how mundane or outlandish. Seeking mystical experiences through altered states, as defined here, looks like an open invitation for deception.[7]

Arnold Ludwig, writing in Tart's *Altered States of Consciousness,* confirms that when "a person enters or is in an ASC, he often experiences fear of losing his grip on reality."[8] A classic illustration is provided by best-selling neopagan author Lynn Andrews. As she progressed into a trance state, she believed she was going insane: "I was terrified. I began to inhale great breaths of air, gasping. I sobbed uncontrollably. I had finally done it—I had lost my mind."[9]

Offending the Mind

Whether in cults or churches, the objective of achieving an altered state of consciousness is always the same: to dull the critical thinking process because the mind is seen as the obstacle to enlightenment. As the worship leader of the Brownsville Assembly of God, Lindell Cooley, has prophesied, "The Lord is saying, 'I'm bypassing your mind and going straight to your heart.'. . . . The heart is what matters to the Lord."[10] John Wimber and John Arnott are explicit and concise: "God offends the mind to reveal the heart."[11]

Counterfeit Revival guru Rodney Howard-Browne explains that "you can't understand what God is doing in these meetings with an analytical mind. The only way you're going to understand what God is doing is with your heart."[12] Thus, while Howard-Browne allows his subjects to make nonsensical sounds, he prohibits them from praying. On one occasion, as a woman was about to lapse into an altered state of consciousness, she became apprehensive and called out to God in prayer. Immediately Howard-Browne commanded her to cease. "Would you listen to me?" he shouted indignantly. "If your praying had helped, it would've helped you; now get laughing."[13]

Even while people are lined up waiting to receive his touch, Howard-Browne commands them not to pray: "Now people in the lines, wait for me to come and lay hands on you, and don't pray, please don't pray." He addresses those who insist on praying as "stubborn people" adding, "People come trying to be all serious and praying. No! This is not the time to pray. This is not a prayer meeting; get in the joy; you can pray on the way home."[14]

Like Howard-Browne and leaders of the Counterfeit Revival, the late Indian guru Baghwan Shree Rajneesh denigrates the mind, going so far as to say that the "goal is to create a new man, one who is happily mindless."[15] Rajneesh's experiences "on the road to enlightenment produced temporary insanity, possession, and almost killed him."[16]

Dynamic Meditation

Rajneesh's prescription for attaining this new consciousness is a process referred to as "dynamic meditation." Dynamic meditation is used to subjugate the critical faculties of idealistic devotees to the will of the "master." Mindlessly they chant in unison until the hushed moaning of their mantras fills the ashram. Sanskrit songs of praise are sung to the accompaniment of rhythmic clapping. At the subtle suggestions of the "master," they engage in repetitive physical motions to complete the process of becoming mindless. Some jump up and down furiously and chop their hands frantically through the air. Others throw their heads backward and forward violently and bend wildly at the waist. Alternately they laugh and sob uncontrollably. Their frenzied behavior produces a mind-altering form of hyperventilation that dulls the critical thinking process and empties the mind of coherent thought. In the end they personify Rajneesh's rendition of the "mindless man."

As shocking as it may seem, what was once relegated to the ashrams of cults is now replicated at the altars of churches. In the ashrams of the cults there is no pretense. Despite such dangers as possession or insanity, Hindu gurus openly encourage trance states through which devotees tap into realms of the demonic and discover their "higher selves." Whether they experience involuntary movements or encounter illusory monsters, all is written off as progress on the road to enlightenment.

When Jack Kornfield, a Western psychologist seeking Eastern enlightenment, suddenly and involuntarily began flapping his arms like chicken's wings for two solid days, he was simply instructed to contemplate his experience.[17] When followers of the Counterfeit Revival have even more bizarre experiences, they are seduced into believing that they have simply overdosed on the Holy Ghost.

What Hindu gurus like Baghwan Shree Rajneesh characterize as a trance state, Holy Ghost bartenders like Rodney Howard-Browne characterize as being "drunk in the spirit." John Arnott is even more crass. He calls it being "marinated in the Holy Spirit."[18]

Southern Baptist pastor Bill Ligon claims that God is directly responsible for this condition of "spiritual drunkenness." According to Ligon, God told him: "I have to get My people drunk in My Spirit because they have been drunk on the world. Their minds have been polluted, they feed their doubts—there is no confidence in Me and My power. I have to get them so drunk that I can change their thoughts and their attitudes."[19]

Striking Parallels

When I first visited the Anaheim Vineyard, the drunken behavior of devotees instantly took me back to Rajneesh's ashram. A member of John Wimber's family stood at the altar, testifying that the power of God was upon her as she jerked spasmodically in what Wimber refers to as a chicken walk. It wasn't long before others had joined her in jerking while rhythmic clapping and repetitive choruses filled the auditorium with sound.

Before the evening had ended, the crowd was engaged in the very practices Rajneesh devotees use to achieve their altered states of consciousness. Some were jumping up and down furiously, chopping their hands frantically through the air. Others were violently throwing their heads backward and forward and bending wildly at the waist. One woman looked as though an invisible hand had grabbed her and was shaking her as if she were little more than a rag doll. All the while, sardonic laughter punctuated by animal noises rose eerily from the bodies writhing on the ground.

Later, when I visited the Airport Vineyard in Toronto, the sights and sounds I experienced were even more shocking. One of the participants was in such a profound altered state of consciousness that even when people tripped over him on the way to the bathroom he remained oblivious.

Counterfeit Revival leader John Arnott says that people are acting "like lions and oxen and eagles and even warriors."[20] Arnott admits that people are deeply frightened by these experiences but maintains they are divine rather than demonic. The problem, according to Arnott, is that we have been conditioned to believe "that the Holy Spirit's a gentleman" who would never do anything "rough or impolite." That, says Arnott, is simply "not true!"[21]

Counterfeit Revival leader Wes Campbell recalls that during a Wimber Vineyard conference, a man named David was merely playing the piano when suddenly:

> He was seized by the spirit like a rag doll and just shaken and bounced like a jackhammer, violently . . . and then he was thrown to the ground, just thrown to the ground. . . . His glasses were knocked off, his nose was pushed to the side, his ears pinned.[22]

Campbell says that this encounter was so violent that David had to be taken to a back room to be checked for demons.[23] During a subsequent meeting, again David was decked by the divine:

Next thing this big—it's like the fist of God just comes right down on his head and goes bang! right on his head. I saw his whole head just snap.[24]

When Campbell's own wife was suddenly seized by the spirit, he was so scared he started screaming. For the first six months, Campbell says, "I was scared to go home with her at night! I'm not kidding. I'm not kidding. . . . The slightest little thing would set her off. The slightest thing. For the first year the slightest thing would set her off."[25] The behavior of the Holy Spirit was so out of control that, as Campbell put it, "we didn't want to let him out of the back room."[26]

Center Stage

Today what was once relegated to the "back room" is center-stage in the Counterfeit Revival. Thousands testify to "getting drunk" and personally experiencing powerful psychological and physical manifestations. These experiences are so "real" that many key evangelical Christian leaders are convinced they cannot be explained apart from the power of the Holy Spirit.

Tragically, many of them are dangerously ignorant of the striking parallels between their experiences and those of Eastern meditators who achieve altered states of consciousness through occult practices. As has been well documented from studies of the world of the occult, the dangerous effects may involve depression, detachment, depersonalization, disillusionment, and many equally serious disorders. Like devotees of the Counterfeit Revival, counterparts in the world of the occult testify to experiencing a variety of troubling physical manifestations in the aftermath of their encounters:

In addition to pain, meditators may sense energy flows coursing through their bodies, or feel tingling, tickling, itching, or vibration on their skin. These sensations usually begin in the feet or pelvic area and move up the back and neck to the crown of the head, then down across the face and abdomen.

Meditators may experience extreme heat or cold, and find their bodies making strange involuntary movements—muscle twitches, prolonged trembling or sinuous writhing. . . . The automatic movements of the body may be accompanied by spontaneous crying, laughing, screaming or whistling. Other common involuntary behaviors include speaking in tongues, chanting unknown songs and making a variety of animal sounds and movements.[27]

In addition to these physical manifestations, Dr. Elizabeth Hillstrom warns of profound psychological disturbances:

Emotions swing wildly from ecstasy, bliss and peace to intense fear, depression, anxiety and anger. Thoughts become strange and irrational, and experiencers may slip into dissociative or prolonged trance states. They may feel very alienated and confused, and often seem to be watching the things that are happening to them as if they were outside observers. Not surprisingly, experiencers often fear that they are losing their minds.[28]

As I have repeatedly warned leaders of the Counterfeit Revival, God is not obligated to protect people from the consequences of unbiblical behavior. Whether one is a Christian or a cultist, the consequences of swallowing cyanide are identical. Likewise, whether people work themselves into an altered state of consciousness in a cult or in the church, the destructive effects are the same. Despite the physical and psychological danger, and my repeated warnings, Counterfeit Revival leaders like John Arnott have been unwilling to reconsider their destructive doctrines and practices. Instead, they have become masters at employing peer pressure to maintain their current following as well as to attract new followers.

CHAPTER 23

The Psychology
of Peer Pressure

Peer pressure is such a powerful force that even the threat of physical or psychological pain does not always prove to be a sufficient deterrent. Think back for a moment to what Mark Twain was willing to endure as the direct result of peer pressure. As Twain recalls, his arm was turned into "iron" by a mere exercise of the hypnotist's will. Thus, it supposedly became insensitive to pain. To prove the point, the hypnotist had audience members drive pins into his arm for a third of their length. While Twain was admittedly in "agonies of pain," he didn't wince. He added, "I only suffered and shed tears on the inside." The acclaim of his peers was worth his private agony; as he put it, "the miseries that a conceited boy will endure to keep up his 'reputation'! And so will a conceited man; I know it in my own person and have seen it in a hundred thousand others."

Peer pressure not only caused Twain to endure physical pain, it caused him to go along with the "professor's" pretenses in other areas as well. As Twain confessed, he was willing to "suffer all things short of death by fire, if thereby he may be conspicuous and show off before the public."

The pressure to be accepted by his peers was so potent that Twain faked a variety of exotic experiences. Says Twain, "on the fourth night temptation came and I was not strong enough to resist. When I had gazed at the disk a while I *pretended* to be sleepy and began to nod" (emphasis added).

From that moment on Twain was like putty in the hands of the "professor." Not only did he succumb to the lure of peer pressure, but with premeditation he also deceived both friends and family.

Predictable Patterns

Tragically, many who fall prey to the Counterfeit Revival are not moved in the least when its deceptions are exposed. The peer pressure that caused them to participate in the first place often keeps them from acknowledging that they were willing participants in a spiritual lie.

A classic case in point involves a well-known charismatic leader who participated in a Benny Hinn television extravaganza. Hinn was "slaying" his subjects "in the spirit" when suddenly he moved in this man's direction. He stretched forth his hand and shouted, "In the mighty name of Jesus!" Immediately the man fell backward into the hands of a designated "catcher."

Later he confessed that his experience had nothing to do with the power of God. Peer pressure had caused him to fake his fall. Ironically, when he asked a cameraman to edit out the faked fall, the cameraman merely chuckled and told him it was common for people to fake it.

Like Hinn, leaders of the Counterfeit Revival use peer pressure to conform their prospects to predictable patterns. They urge them to follow the crowd rather than consider the consequences. John Arnott, for example, tells his prospects that the greatest deception is not false doctrine but being among those who fail to recognize a move of God. In the United Kingdom he told followers:

If you're going to be concerned about deception, then please be concerned about the greatest deception that there is, and the greatest deception of all, in my opinion, is not to fall for teachings of a false prophet or fall for some, you know, wild-goose chase of a rabbit trail out there or whatever and wake up in ten years [*sic*] that you've been deceived. In my opinion the greatest deception of all is to have a move of God come through and you not recognize it.[1]

The Power of Peer Pressure

Arnott and his associates have carefully crafted their services to enhance the likelihood that Christians will cave in to the power of peer pressure. They kick off their meetings with the testimonies of those who allegedly once feared deception but now embrace the exotic experiences of the Counterfeit Revival as a genuine move of God. The "time of testimony" is followed by a "time of teaching" designed to further pressure people to work themselves into an altered state of consciousness. The grand finale is a "time of ministry" in which virtually anything goes. The peer pressure to participate during the ministry time is so potent that even otherwise discerning Christians often end up casting caution to the wind.

During the "time of testimony," pastors and participants routinely testify that once they were blinded by the devil, but now their eyes have been opened. Once they doubted that God could be in such bizarre manifestations as pawing the ground like an angry bull, but now they "know" experientially that God often moves in mysterious ways.

Often, as the initiated give their testimonies, they model the effects of the manifestations. You may recall that while a Wimber family member was testifying to the power of God upon her life, she was bending violently at the waist. It wasn't long before people in the pews were mimicking her strange behavior.

Her testimony gave way to a time of teaching. As she walked back to her seat (still bending at the waist), a Vineyard pastor began reciting his rendition of Paul's experience on the road to Damascus. He hammered home the notion that there were two categories of believers: the initiated and the uninitiated. Before God knocked Paul off his horse, he was an uninitiated Pharisee. Thereafter he joined the ranks of those who had experienced the power of God firsthand.

The pastor's message is cleverly designed to pressure people into becoming initiated like Paul rather than remaining uninitiated like the Pharisees. The "time of testimony" and the "time of teaching" place enormous peer pressure on people to participate during the "time of ministry."

Leaders of the Counterfeit Revival seem well aware that people in crowds are prone to believe that the behavior of their peers is a standard that should not be questioned. They further reinforce this proclivity by intimating that to resist these manifestations is tantamount to resisting the Holy Spirit.

According to Larry Randolph, speaking at the Toronto Airport Vineyard, "the neutral ground is dissipating by the hour. You can't stand in the middle anymore and say, 'Well, I don't know. Maybe it's God; maybe it's not.' You're going to get rolled over."[2] As mentioned previously, in Randolph's estimation the song the Holy Spirit is now singing is "I'm a Steam Roller, Baby, and I'm Going to Roll Right over You."[3]

CHAPTER 24

The Exploitation
of Expectations

As proficient as leaders of the Counterfeit Revival are in using peer pressure as a means of sociopsychological manipulation, they are equally expert in elevating the expectations of followers. Subjects are systematically subjected to the belief that they are poised to take over the sociopolitical systems of society.

According to John Arnott, God is about to exact vengeance upon his adversaries and restore the church to its proper place. As quoted earlier, "Wouldn't it be wonderful," he muses, "if the Lord would start to move in power and restore the church to its proper place and make us the head and not the tail?"[1]

Counterfeit Revival leader Bob Jones suggests that the star status of the leaders of this endtime church will be even greater than that of the apostle Paul. Despite the fact that Paul, under inspiration, penned two-thirds of the New Testament Epistles, Jones tells devotees:

Paul will be more anxious to talk to the endtime apostles and prophets than the endtime apostles and prophets will be to talk to Paul, because what the prophets of this generation will do will be far greater than what he had done. The saints in the New Testament will wait in line to greet the apostles of this generation.[2]

Subjects are led to believe that if they enlist in "Joel's endtime army" these promises will become living reality. Paul Cain claims that this army will be so potent and powerful that "no demon, no man system, no enemy will stop them or hinder or resist them."[3]

Cain elevates expectations to a fever pitch by telling devotees that they will be "invincible"; that God is offering them a "greater privilege than was ever offered to any people of any generation at any time from Adam clear down through the end of the millennium"; and that they are "gonna have more than just a little omnipotent surge—you're gonna behold that glory and become that glory."[4]

What Cain called the "greatest revival of all times,"[5] Randy Clark claims is now reality. He tells credulous Christians that "people are being raised from the dead and temples [are] being hit by lightning or fireballs and knocked off their things [sic]. It's all over. Germany and Africa. It's everywhere. God's doing it."[6]

More Evang-Elastic Stories

Clark and Cain are not alone in circulating evang-elastic stories. Rick Joyner, for example, elevates expectations by telling the faithful that "an eight foot by ten to twelve foot size mist" suddenly appeared in one of their meetings. He claims that this experience was so vivid that one of the women present, Christine Potter, not only saw "this cloud of the Lord" but also felt "an intense heat, as though her clothes were on fire." According to Joyner, Potter was so hot, it "looked like she was trying to remove her clothes in order to escape being burned."[7]

The evang-elastic stories used to enhance the expectations

of believers are now becoming so bizarre that it is a wonder that anyone still takes them seriously. *Charisma* magazine, for example, has circulated a story titled "'Holy Water' Triggers Healing Revival."[8] Followers of the Counterfeit Revival were told that plain old bottled water, when "blessed" by a charismatic bishop, was suddenly transformed into "miracle water."[9] Those who drank this miracle water were not only so mightily touched that they "fell down under the power of God," but were also miraculously healed of such ailments as "cancer, tumors and heart disease." Millions are reportedly hearing about the miracle water from secular sources. Among them are "prominent politicians, celebrities and doctors," all attempting to acquire some of the miracle water for themselves.

Leaders of the Counterfeit Revival seem to bank on the fact that expectations aroused by stories such as *Charisma's* "miracle water" or Clark's "resurrections" can give birth to a broad range of mystical experiences. When they "slay" subjects "in the spirit," they apparently bank on the fact that the expectations of their followers will give birth to the experience itself.

By way of illustration, almost everyone reading these words can successfully navigate the length of a common wooden plank resting on the ground. Suspend that same wooden plank between the twin spires of a cathedral and you have an entirely different proposition. The very fact that you are now suspended hundreds of feet in the air naturally introduces the expectation of a possible fall. The notion of falling inevitably gives birth to the fall itself.

Creating a Miracle

Another classic case of expectations giving birth to experiences can be found in the story of a young Bronx boy named Joseph Vitolo. In his book *The Story of Hypnosis,* Robert W. Marks recounts that in 1945, nine-year-old Joseph was kneeling on a rock in an empty lot when he saw a vision of the Virgin Mary. Mary promised Joseph that she would appear on successive nights and that on the night of her last appearance, a miraculous spring would emerge from the ground.

Following the announcement, crowds trekked to the scene of the alleged vision. On one night twenty-five thousand people surged to the scene with flowers, candles, and statues of saints. It was automatically assumed that Joseph had a special anointing. Thus, a steady stream of cripples were brought to Joseph so that he would lay hands on them.

While Joseph was not able to accomplish anything out of the ordinary, the expectations of the crowd were such that they began to create their own "miracles." On one of the nights, a light rain began to fall, and a woman screamed, "It's pouring, yet Joseph doesn't get wet." Despite the fact that news reporters standing near Joseph observed that he was as soaked as anyone else, the expectations of the miraculous created the illusion.

Another woman claimed she saw an apparition in white materialize behind Joseph. In reality the apparition was nothing more than another woman protectively covered with a white raincoat.

Marks points out that the expectations of the crowd were such that "if imagination and hysterical contagion had been left to do their hallucinatory work, the crowd would have created its own miracle. And it is highly probable that Joseph could have produced some real 'cures' and real 'visions' if the hypnotic effects of the situation could have progressed far enough."[10]

The expectations of the crowd had been heightened to such an extent that, as Marks says, they were "no more capable of resisting the proper hypnotic suggestion than Pavlov's dog was capable of resisting the stimulus to salivate."[11]

CHAPTER 25

The Subtle Power
of Suggestion

The power of suggestion is incredibly potent. In an altered state of consciousness, this power is significantly magnified as people become hypersuggestible. Add to this potion peer pressure plus enhanced expectations, and people become willing to accept virtually anything that enters their minds.

Remember Twain? He was virtually boiled in his own bile as he watched Hicks "scamper and jump when Simmons the enchanter exclaimed, 'See the snake! See the snake!' and hear him say, 'My, how beautiful!' in response to the suggestion that he was observing a splendid sunset." Whether the suggestion came from Simmons or the subject himself ("autosuggestion"), the result powerfully enhanced the performance of the "professor."

Hypersuggestibility

First, it should be noted that some people are far more suggestible than others.[1] Statistically, "one out of twelve Americans is susceptible to creating a memory out of thin air, then believing it."[2] Such fantasy proneness is typically referred to as the "Grade Five Syndrome."[3] While Grade Five personalities are generally very intuitive and intelligent, they also have vivid, visual imaginations. Thus they are highly susceptible to the power of suggestion. To begin with, they are very trusting. Second, they desire to please (particularly an authority figure). Third, they have the capacity to accept contradictory experiences. Fourth, they have a marked propensity for affiliation with new or unusual events. Fifth, they are apt to relate everything they experience to their own self-perception.[4] This complex of characteristics makes Grade Fives particularly susceptible to spiritual fantasies, "psychic and out-of-body experiences, and the occasional difficulty in differentiating fantasized events and persons from nonfantasized ones."[5]

Subtle Suggestions

Furthermore, the subtle power of suggestion can be brought to bear on an individual either directly or indirectly. An example of the direct approach is Rodney Howard-Browne's now famous phrase, "Fill, fill, fill! Let it bubble out your belly!" or John Arnott's mantra, "More, Lord! More, Lord!" (Arnott says, "I know how to say 'More, Lord!' in about fifty languages now."[6])

Indirect suggestions are far more subtle. They can involve "embedded suggestions and commands, paraverbal shifts of tone, voice directionality, enunciation, syntax, and pacing; the use of truisms, binds, double binds, and other semantic variations."[7]

I have attended and analyzed Counterfeit Revival meetings with "performance professionals," including a stage hypnotist and an expert on sleight of hand/sleight of mind. They were readily able to identify numerous instances of these indirect suggestion techniques. They also pointed out that these techniques are not typically learned by formal instruction but rather by frequent imitation. (As noted in my historical analysis of the slain in the spirit phenomenon, Kathryn Kuhlman studied Aimee Semple McPherson, Benny Hinn studied Kathryn Kuhlman, and so on.)

Crowd Dynamics

Finally, as underscored by Robert Marks, "people in crowds are more easily influenced than people taken singly. This fact has been capitalized on by stage hypnotists as well as evangelists, political orators, and dictators."[8] In fact, as Marks points out, "the effect of suggestion on crowds seems virtually without limit. It can make black appear white. It can obscure realities, enshrine absurdities, and impel men pitilessly to cleave the skulls of their brothers."[9]

While epidemics of sardonic laughter, sneezing, and even suicide can appear to be spontaneous, in reality they are often the result of subtle stimuli and suggestions. As noted by Charles Baudouin, "In the sphere of movement, suggestion by imitation is common. Immoderate laughter readily spreads through a crowd; yawning is contagious."[10] Once epidemic suggestion contaminates a movement, human beings can "behave like beasts or idiots and be proud of it."[11] No one "is immune to the force of mass suggestion. Once an epidemic of hysteria is in full force it strikes intellectuals as well as morons, rich and poor alike. Its wellsprings are subconscious and biological, not rational."[12]

When Rick Joyner's devotees sensed "nuclear fire," saw a glorious "cloud," and smelled the "fragrance of flowers,"[13] they may not have been aware that singing one song over and over for three hours had caused them to become hypersuggestible. That, however, does not alter the facts. The three-hour repetition of a spiritual song, being slain in the spirit, or even a spiritualistic seance have at least one thing in common—they all cause subjects to become extremely susceptible to spontaneous suggestions. Charles Baudouin concludes that "in the first place, a condition of mental relaxation is imposed upon the participants. Secondly, an emotional state is invariably aroused by approximation to the mysterious. Thirdly, there exists an expectation that remarkable things will happen."[14]

Leaders of the Counterfeit Revival capitalize on these expectations to create the illusion that they are endowed with supernatural powers. Rodney Howard-Browne dupes devotees into visualizing that his fingertips come off and a full volume of anointing flows from his hands, John Wimber conditions constituents to believe a spiritual power emanates from his hands like electricity, and Franz Anton Mesmer promulgated the principle that a magnetic force pulsated from his hands.

What leaders of the Counterfeit Revival attribute to a dose of the anointing and Mesmer ascribed to the doctrine of animal magnetism, James Braid (the physician who coined the word *hypnotism*) candidly acknowledged to be the dynamic of suggestion. As mentioned previously, he demonstrated that through the power of mental manipulation, he could affect the mind to such an extent that he could perform surgical procedures that were virtually painless.

Pagan religions and pseudo-Christian cults have long capitalized on the power of suggestion to promote their practices. Counterfeit Revival leaders have followed in their train.

Psychosomatic Symptoms and Sickness

Dr. William A. Nolen, chief of surgery at Meeker County Hospital in Minnesota, has spent many years investigating claims of supernatural healing here and abroad. He concludes that

When evangelical healers dramatically call on God to transmit His power through them to cure their patients' diseases, they are using the power of suggestion in the hope that it will so affect the patient's malfunctioning autonomic nervous system (the system that regulates such functions as digestion, heart rate, blood pressure, etc.) that the disease or symptoms caused by the derangement of that system will be cured.[15]

Like hypnotists and Hindu gurus, these "healers" use the power of suggestion to create placebos for psychosomatic symptoms and sickness. In truth, however, there is nothing supernatural about this kind of "healing." Hinn and Howard-Browne can "heal" asthma, allergies, and arthritis, but then, so can mesmerists and medicine men.

The difference between the "magic" of mental manipulations and genuine miracles is dramatic. Christian apologist Dr. Norman L. Geisler has pointed out that, when Jesus and the apostles healed people, the miracles were always 100 percent successful, immediate, and there were no relapses:

> God never performed a miracle "slowly" nor did an "80 percent" healing. Biblical miracles were 100 percent and immediate. In the case of the few immediate cures in the contemporary signs and wonders movement, most are clearly of the psychosomatic type and none are immediate healings of incurable diseases. There is nothing supernatural about these kinds of cures.
>
> Such cures are done regularly by Hindu gurus and by many other false religions and cults. Even non-Christian doctors and counselors witness these kinds of cures in their patients. Both spontaneous remission and psychosomatic cures of the same nature as these "signs and wonders" occur apart from any pretense to the supernatural.[16]

While leaders of the Counterfeit Revival can create the illusion of "lengthening" legs, they can't re-create an amputated limb; while they can create the illusion of slaying subjects in the spirit, they can't resurrect the slain; and while they can create the illusion that someone's vision has been restored, they can't replace a missing orb. In the end they create only disillusionment and self-deception. The power of the Spirit creates life and limb. The power of suggestion only creates a lamentable lie.

As described in chapter 21, thirty-five years after the mesmerist had visited their village, Mark Twain, moved by a "noble" and "heroic impulse," visited his mother and confessed his con:

> It cost me a great effort to make up my mind; I dreaded the sorrow that would rise in her face and the shame that would look out of her eyes; but after long and troubled reflection, the sacrifice seemed due and right and I gathered my resolution together and made the confession.
>
> To my astonishment there were no sentimentalities, no dramatics, no George Washington effects; she was not moved in the least degree; she simply did not believe me and said so!

In the end Twain was left to contemplate how easy it had been to make someone "believe a lie and how hard it is to undo that work again." By God's grace, we will be empowered to undo what Twain could not.

Epilogue

I began this book with the story of how I had traveled to an internationally famous healthcare center in Dallas, Texas. I was absolutely certain that something was desperately wrong. I thought I might even have cancer. After an exhausting day of examination, the doctor looked up from the test results and said he had good news and bad news. The good news was that I had no major health problems. The bad news was that if I did not begin to make major lifestyle changes immediately, I would not live to see my children grow up. He said I needed to stop burning the candle on both ends, switch to the right kinds of food, and start a regular exercise routine.

Rather than feeling elated that my doctor had not discovered any major problems, I immediately began looking for a quick fix—a shot, a megadose of vitamins, anything. Even now his words reverberate through my mind, "Hank, there are no shortcuts. You either get back to the basics of proper rest, proper diet, and proper exercise or you forfeit your health." While I had been looking for some newfangled, faddish formula, he presented me with the facts—I had to get back to basics.

What is true regarding the health of my body is also true regarding the health of the body of Christ. While pastors and parishioners are traveling to "power centers" like Toronto, Canada, and Pensacola, Florida, looking for a quick fix, the solution is found in the fundamentals. While multitudes clamor for a massive revival, what the body of Christ desperately needs is a mighty reformation. Only as the church is reformed can the culture be revived.

The tragedy of modern-day Christianity is that people are looking for experience in all the wrong places. The real experience is not found in the works of the FLESH; rather, it is found in the basic fundamentals. We must rediscover the genuine worship of God, we must rededicate ourselves to the oneness we share in Christ, and we must recommit ourselves to witness by the power of the Holy Spirit.

Worship

First, the body of Christ must rediscover the joy of genuine worship by developing a passion for *prayer*. It is crucial that we become so focused on the purpose, the power, and the provision of prayer that once again prayer becomes our priority. While prayer involves supplication, it is much more than that. Ultimately, prayer is the submission of our will to God. That is precisely why R. A. Torrey said that "to pray the prayer of faith we must, first of all, study the Word of God, especially the promises of God, and find out what the will of God is."[1]

Through prayer we have the privilege of expressing adoration and thanksgiving to the One who saved us, sanctifies us, and one day will glorify us. Through prayer we also confess our sins with the sure knowledge that "he is faithful and just and will forgive us our sins and purify us from all unrighteousness" (1 John 1:9). F. B. Meyer has well said, "The great tragedy of life is not unanswered prayer but unoffered prayer."[2]

Furthermore, we experience genuine worship through a

passion for *praise*. As Matthew Henry so aptly put it, "What we win by prayer we must wear with praise."[3] The apostle Paul urges us to "speak to one another with psalms, hymns and spiritual songs" (Eph. 5:19).[4] Singing psalms is a magnificent means for intercession, instruction, and the internalization of Scripture. In addition the great hymns of the faith have stood the test of time and are rich in theological tradition and truth. Spiritual songs, in turn, communicate the freshness of our faith. It is crucial that we preserve both a respect for our spiritual heritage and a regard for contemporary compositions. We must be wary of excessive repetition or musical mantras that produce hypersuggestibility. In addition, as noted by Dr. Barry Liesch:

> Despite the many benefits of worship choruses, we must acknowledge that they tend to reflect values of popular culture that should not be "bought into" unquestioningly—values that include "instant gratification, intellectual impatience, a-historical immediacy, and incessant novelty." Used exclusively, choruses have real limitations. In general, choruses lack intellectual rigor and fail to offer a mature exposition of biblical doctrines.[5]

The Great Reformation spawned majestic songs of praise such as "A Mighty Fortress Is Our God." By contrast, today's Counterfeit Revival has spawned songs that can only be classified as superficial, shallow, and shameful. Kathryn Riss, wife of Counterfeit Revival historian Richard Riss, says "the Lord" gave her lyrics to be sung to the Shaker[6] tune, "'Tis the Gift to be Simple":

> If you feel too serious and kind of blue,
> I've got a suggestion, just the thing for you!
> It's a little unconventional, but so much fun,

That you won't even mind when people think you're dumb!
Just come to the party God is throwing right now,
We can all lighten up and show the pagans how
Christians have more fun and keep everyone guessing,
Since the Holy Ghost sent us the Toronto Blessing!
I used to think life was serious stuff
I wouldn't dare cry, and I acted kind of tough
Until God's Spirit put laughter in my soul,
Now the Holy Ghost's got me, and I'm out of control!
Now I'm just a party animal grazing at God's trough,
I'm a Jesus Junkie, and I can't get enough!
I'm an alcoholic for that great New Wine,
'Cause the Holy Ghost is pouring, and I'm drinking
    all the time!
I just laugh like an idiot and bark like a dog,
If I don't sober up, I'll likely hop like a frog!
I'll crow like a rooster at the break of day,
'Cause the Holy Ghost is moving, and I can't stay away!
I'll roar like a lioness who's on the prowl,
I'll laugh and shake, maybe hoot like an owl!
Since God's holy river started bubbling in me,
It spills outside, and now it's setting me free!
So, I'll crunch and I'll dip and I'll dance round
    and round,
The pew was fine, but it's more fun on the ground!
So I'll jump like a pogo stick, then fall to the floor,
'Cause the Holy Ghost is moving, and I just want MORE![7]

Finally, the *proclamation of the Word* is axiomatic to experiencing vibrant worship. Paul urged his protégé, Timothy, to "preach the Word; be prepared in season and out of season; correct, rebuke and encourage—with great patience and careful instruction" (2 Tim. 4:2). Through the proclamation of the Word, the body of Christ is edified, educated, and equipped. Today, multitudes march into church sanctuaries color-coordinated with their Bibles, but they are often blithely unaware of the riches encapsulated within its pages. Church leaders must once again produce in their people a holy hunger for the Word of God.

It is crucial for Christians to become so turned on to the treasure of God's Word that Scripture meditation and memorization become part and parcel of their daily lives. Charles Swindoll has said, "I know of no other single practice in the Christian life more rewarding, practically speaking, than memorizing Scripture."[8] From strengthening your prayer life to solidifying your faith, no single exercise pays greater spiritual dividends.

Jesus pointed out in the Sermon on the Mount that wisdom is the application of knowledge: "Therefore everyone who hears these words of mine and puts them into practice [applies them] is like a wise man who built his house on the rock" (Matt. 7:24).

Oneness

As we rediscover the experience of genuine worship, so too we must rededicate ourselves to experiencing oneness as a community of faith. The real experience is not found in focusing in on ourselves but in focusing out on others. We are not to view ourselves in isolation; rather, we are to see ourselves within the context of *community:* "Just as each of us has one body with many members, and these members do not all have the same function, so in Christ we who are many form one body, and each member belongs to all the others" (Rom. 12:4–5). While communism claimed to turn men into comrades, only Christ can turn us into a caring community.

Baptism symbolizes our entrance into a community that is one in Christ. It is a sign and seal that we have been buried to our old life and raised to newness of life through his resurrection power. Likewise, holy communion is an expression of our oneness. As we all partake of the same elements, we partake of what the elements symbolize: Christ, through whom we are one. Our fellowship on earth, celebrated through communion, is a foretaste of the heavenly fellowship we will share when symbol gives way to substance.

Furthermore, we experience oneness through our *confession* of faith. While Counterfeit Revival leaders clamor for unity without regard for truth, genuine oneness can only be experienced in concert with the enduring truths of our Christian confession. In the words of J. I. Packer, "We are not entitled to infer from the fact that a group of people are drawing nearer to each other that any of them is drawing nearer to the truth."[9] We must never forget that it was for these truths that the martyrs spilled their blood. Hugh Latimer, who was burned at the stake for his confession of faith, cried out, "Unity must be ordered according to God's Holy Word, or else it were better war than peace."[10]

We would do well to reignite a passion for such classic confessions of faith as the Athanasian Creed. No statement of the early Christian church sets forth so incisively and with such clarity the profound truths implicit in the scriptural affirmation that God was in Christ reconciling the world to himself. Not only does it codify the truth concerning the Trinity, but it also affirms Christ's incarnation, resurrection, ascension, second coming, and the final judgment. In concert with other classic creeds, the Creed of Athanasius points people back to the essential confessions through which we experience genuine oneness.

Finally, we experience oneness through the contribution of our time, talent, and treasure. Do you want a real experience? Start using your time, talent, and treasure for the edification, exhortation, and encouragement of the body. The question we should be asking is not, "What can the church do for me?" but, "What can I do for the church?" Ah, how our problems would pale if we turned our lives outward rather than inward!

The tragedy of modern Christianity is that when members of the body hurt, too often we relegate them to finding resources outside the walls of the church. That is precisely why the apostle Paul exhorts us to "be devoted to one another in brotherly love. Honor one another above yourselves. Never be lacking in zeal, but keep your spiritual fervor, serving the Lord. Be joyful in hope, patient in affliction, faithful in prayer. Share with God's people who are in need. Practice hospitality" (Rom. 12:10–13).

Witness

If the early Christian church had one distinguishing characteristic, it was their passion to communicate the love, joy, and peace that only Christ can bring to the human heart. As we become entrenched in an era of esotericism, it is essential that Christians rediscover the ultimate experience of being used as a tool in the hands of Almighty God in the process of transforming lives.

First, we must be prepared to communicate *what* we believe. In other words, we must be equipped to communicate the gospel. If Christians do not know how to share their faith, they have never been through basic training. We must make the gospel such a part of our vocabulary that presenting it becomes second nature.

Consider what would happen if every evangelical Christian led one person to faith in Christ each year. If we began with only twelve committed Christians and each of them led one person to Christ and discipled that person, the next year there would be twenty-four believers. If each of them in turn led one person to Christ and discipled that person, the third year there would be forty-eight believers. If this process continued,[11] it would take fewer than thirty years to evangelize the estimated six billion people alive today on Planet Earth. Truly, no experience can compare with that of the Holy Spirit working through you to bring someone to a saving knowledge of the Lord Jesus Christ.

Furthermore, we must be equipped to share *why* we believe what we believe. As Peter put it, we must "always be prepared to give an answer [Greek *apologia*] to everyone who asks you to give the reason for the hope that you have. But do this with gentleness and respect" (1 Pet. 3:15). Too many today believe that the task of apologetics is the exclusive domain of scholars and theologians. Not so! The defense of the faith is not optional; it is basic training for *every Christian*. Thankfully, learning to defend our faith is not nearly as difficult as one might think. Essentially, defending *why* we believe means being able to address three basic issues: (1) that the universe is intelligently designed by the Creator and did not evolve by random chance; (2) that Jesus Christ is God and he demonstrated it through the undeniable fact of his bodily resurrection; and (3) that the Bible is divine rather than human in origin.

Finally, as believers we can experience the joy of communicating not only *what* and *why* we believe but also *who* we believe. Christianity is not a dead religion. Rather, it is a deep relationship with the Redeemer of our souls. Paul Harvey tells the story of a farmer who was a religious skeptic:

> One raw winter night the man heard an irregular thumping sound against the kitchen storm door. He went to a window and watched as tiny, shivering sparrows, attracted to the evident warmth inside, beat in vain against the glass.
>
> Touched, the farmer bundled up and trudged through fresh snow to open the barn door for the struggling birds. He turned on the lights and tossed some hay into the corner. But the sparrows, which had scattered in all directions when he emerged from the house, hid in the darkness, afraid.

The man tried various tactics to get them into the barn. He laid down a trail of Saltine cracker crumbs to direct them. He tried circling behind the birds to drive them toward the barn. Nothing worked. He, a huge, alien creature, had terrified them; the birds couldn't comprehend that he actually desired to help.

The farmer withdrew to his house and watched the doomed sparrows through a window. As he stared, a thought hit him like lightning from a clear blue sky: *If only I could become a bird—one of them—just for a moment. Then I wouldn't frighten them so. I could show them the way to warmth and safety.*

At the same moment, another thought dawned on him. He had grasped the reason Jesus was born.[12]

While the farmer could not become a sparrow, God did become man. The Christ of Christianity is not only the One who spoke and the universe leaped into existence, but he is also the very One who knit us together in our mother's womb. The One who cloaked himself in human flesh can become more real to us than the very flesh upon our bones. While multitudes are looking for God in all the wrong places, you can experience him through genuine worship, oneness, and witness.

Therefore, since we are surrounded by such a great cloud of witnesses, let us throw off everything that hinders and the sin that so easily entangles, and let us run with perseverance the race marked out for us. Let us fix our eyes on Jesus, the author and perfecter of our faith, who for the joy set before him endured the cross, scorning its shame, and sat down on the right hand of the throne of God. Consider him who endured such opposition from sinful men, so that you will not grow weary and lose heart. (Heb. 12:1–3)

APPENDIX A

Counterfeit Critique: A Response to James Beverley[1]

Christianity Today's review of my recent book Counterfeit Revival is, as its title advertises, a "counterfeit critique."[2] When I first read it, Mark Twain's words flashed across my consciousness: "A lie can travel halfway round the world while the truth is putting on its shoes."[3] Since I can expect Christianity Today to allow me only a brief reply to James Beverley, the reviewer, in their letters column, I decided to take advantage of having my own column here in the Christian Research Journal to offer a more substantial response.

James Beverley, the reviewer, begins by mischaracterizing Counterfeit Revival as "misleading" and then proceeds to mislead his readers, using a variety of unprofessional techniques, such as "term switching," "time twisting," and "trashing tactics." Beverley's lack of objectivity is hardly surprising in light of the fact that he self-publishes materials in support of Counterfeit Revivalists. I was disturbed, however, to read about what Beverley refers to as "financial arrangements." In fact, Vineyard pastor and Promise Keepers former director James Ryle and other Vineyard leaders have made payments to Beverley.[4] Tom Stipe, former Vineyard board member and pastor of the

Crossroads Church in Denver, was equally disturbed. In a statement to *Christianity Today*, he wrote:

> [Beverley] represented himself to me as unbiased and neutral. He complained repeatedly about shouldering the cost of the trip himself and appealed to my generosity. I contributed as a friend not knowing that the Vineyard had, in effect, solicited Beverly [sic] to write the anti-Hanegraaff literature under the auspices of "fresh research." Further it is appalling to me to find my financial gift alluded to as proof of my awareness and support of Jim's alleged fairness in approaching the issues. Aside from my concerns about the content, soundness and logic of Jim's writings on this issue, my wife and I feel incredibly manipulated by a "hired gun" sent into the field masquerading as an unbiased researcher.[5]

In divulging what went on "behind the scenes," Stipe stated:

> After some 30 hours of conversation with Jim Beverley over the last few years I believe him to be a consumer of counterfeit revivalist activities, not an unbiased researcher. . . . I am not Jim's doctor or judge. In fact I considered him a friend until observing the obsessive manipulations that lead [sic] to his latest book and the CT review. . . . My church staff, leaders, as well as myself are amazed that *Christianity Today* would print the prejudiced as well as duplicitous views of Jim Beverley as a balanced review of Hank Hanegraaff's *Counterfeit Revival*.[6]

While I do not wish to pass judgment on the motives of a person I hardly know, I would like to take a closer look at the *methods* he employed.

First, let's take a look at his "term-switching" technique. Beverley accuses me of "nasty misrepresentation of key charismatic leaders." To make his point, he writes: "Consider, for example, Hanegraaff's assertion that Howard-Browne *denies* the deity of Christ in order to elevate himself" (emphasis added).[7] What I actually wrote was: "Counterfeit Revival leaders like Howard-Browne *denigrate* the deity of Christ to elevate themselves" (emphasis added).[8] While I provide ample evidence in *Counterfeit Revival* to substantiate that Howard-Browne *denigrates* the deity of Christ, I nowhere attempt to demonstrate that he *denies* the deity of Christ. Once Beverley has successfully completed his term switching, he has little difficulty in destroying a straw man of his own making.

Furthermore, let's briefly examine the "time-switching" tactic that Beverley employs to impugn *Counterfeit Revival*. He writes, "Hanegraaff refers to a 1979 service where Wimber 'turned his church into a laboratory and his church members into guinea pigs.'" Beverley goes on to assert, "The evening service in question was on Mother's Day in 1980, not in 1979."[9] In reality, it is Beverley who should be corrected. Not only does Wimber disagree with the date suggested by Beverley, but also had Beverley objectively looked into the matter, he would have realized that 1979 is the only date that fits with undisputed facts in Vineyard history, as I have carefully documented in *Counterfeit Revival* (pp. 213–20). Because this date is crucial (Carol Wimber refers to what happened that day as the "watershed experience" of the Vineyard), and because other dates have been suggested (Carol Wimber claims it was 1981, John White says it was 1978, and John Wimber agrees with my conclusion that the year was 1979), I meticulously researched this issue. Had Beverley done likewise or even merely read the evidence I provided, he certainly could not have cited this as an example of poor research in *Counterfeit Revival*.

Finally, let's look at the "trashing tactics" employed by Beverley. Not only does he use shrill and sarcastic language, referring to my work with words like "simplistic," but, as previously documented, he also deceptively manufactures straw men and then sets them ablaze. He suggests that *Counterfeit Revival* is based on old and limited research. One need only read *Counterfeit Revival* in context or review the literally hundreds of bibliographic references and endnotes to dispel this outrageous assertion. It is true that I have done (and continue to do) exhaustive research on historical revivals. It is also true that I have gone back and researched the roots of movements like the Vineyard so that I might more accurately analyze their ripened fruit. But as Pastor Tom Stipe wrote in his response to *Christianity Today*, "To dismiss the theological seedlings of Wimber's early teachings, which became the cornerstones of the Toronto and Pensacola movements, as 'outdated' is like relegating E=MC^2 as irrelevant because it's old."[10]

Ironically, while trashing *me*, Beverley self-righteously accuses me of "trashing" Todd Hunter, national coordinator of the Association of Vineyard Churches. Anyone who takes the time to check out Hunter's words in context will agree that, unlike Beverley, I have accurately represented his remarks. The reality is that *Counterfeit Revival* has become the catalyst for open and honest dialogue between Vineyard leaders like Todd Hunter and CRI. One can only pray that men like Beverley will repent of practices like "term switching," "time twisting," and "trashing" and participate in open, honest dialogue.

APPENDIX B

Dr. Michael Brown,
Jonathan Edwards, and
Counterfeit Revival[1]

D r. Michael Brown, president of the Brownsville Revival School of Ministry, has demeaned *Counterfeit Revival*[2] for a lack of serious scholarship regarding Jonathan Edwards. He also charges that I misused Edwards's materials to suit my own purposes. Conversely, he contends that he has consulted scholars working on the Yale University project, *The Works of Jonathan Edwards*, to lend academic credibility to his criticisms.[3]

However, since Brown does not name these Yale scholars, it is impossible to evaluate this claim. Furthermore, Dr. Michael Bowman, the coordinator of another program concerning Edwards's works, STEP: *The Edwards Project* (which is releasing the complete works of Edwards on CD-ROM), was concerned enough about Michael Brown's lack of scholarship and fabrications to release the following statement:

> Having just finished Hanegraaff's *Counterfeit Revival*, I do not see any inaccuracy in his review of Edwards' *Distinguishing Marks* treatise.[4] Overall, I felt that Hanegraaff's analysis was right on. Edwards did not condone excesses, but felt that they could be present

in true revival. Edwards realized that the remorse that the repentant individuals feel, when they realize what they have been saved from, can occasionally lead to emotional outbursts. The bizarre and "drunken" behavior in the "counterfeit revival" movement has nothing to do with repentance. What concerns me the most about this issue is that mainstream Christianity does not seem to seriously and forcefully condemn this movement![5]

Under the guise of academic credibility, Brown not only grossly misrepresents Jonathan Edwards, but he also grossly misrepresents me. While space and time do not permit a complete accounting of his deceptions, let's take a moment to look at how he seduces unsuspecting readers in a book in which he confronts the critics of the Pensacola Outpouring and impugns the research and reasoning of my book *Counterfeit Revival*.[6]

Brown accuses me of committing the logical fallacy of guilt by association, suggesting that I implicate John Arnott as being a prosperity teacher by virtue of his association with Benny Hinn.[7] The reality is in *Counterfeit Revival* I never indict Arnott on those grounds at all, let alone through guilt by association with Hinn. What I actually write is that Hinn "has had a profound impact on such Counterfeit Revival leaders as John Arnott,"[8] which is true since Hinn had been increasingly asked to pray over the Arnotts after John was allegedly told by God to "hang around people that have an anointing."[9] I do, however, expose Hinn's "health and wealth" teaching proclivities, offering substantive quotes by Hinn as evidence.[10] Curiously, Brown then accuses me of indicting Hinn based on an out-of-date quote reflecting a view that Hinn allegedly repented of long ago. Brown fails to acknowledge that I provided a 1996 quote of Hinn in addition to an older quote to substantiate that Hinn has taught and continues to teach a "health and wealth" message.[11] Moreover, Brown ignores the fact that Hinn continues to promote teachers and market books that promote a prosperity gospel.[12]

Brown also accuses me of exhibiting a "lack of serious scholarship." The following is what he refers to as a "representative" example. Brown states, "On page 269, n. 66, Hanegraaff writes that: 'The ruling sect of Jews in Jesus' day, the Pharisees, were empty, unprincipled religionists,' a sweeping statement that is almost unthinkable in Christian scholarship at the end of the twentieth century."[13] Brown fails to acknowledge Jesus' own sweeping statements about Pharisees (e.g., Matt. 23:1–7, 13–36; cf. Luke 7:30). Moreover, Brown quotes only the portion of my endnote that would support his contention, cutting off my statement midsentence and thus midthought. The remainder of the sentence reads, "who, *for the most part*, rejected Christ and attributed Christ's works to Beelzebub, or Satan" (emphasis added).[14] Brown therefore accuses me of making a sweeping statement only by omitting the qualification for the statement.[15]

While much more could be said, unmasking all of the fabrications of Pensacola spin doctors like Michael Brown would be an endless project. As they continue to seduce unsuspecting subjects through fabrications, fantasies, and frauds, Blaise Pascal's poignant words (in *Pensées*) ring down through the ages: "Truth is so obscure in these times and falsehood so established, that unless we love the truth, we cannot know it."

APPENDIX C

John Kilpatrick's Prophetic Pronouncements Regarding the Brownsville Revival

On April 6, 1997, John Kilpatrick, pastor of the Brownsville Assembly of God and promoter of what is variously referred to as the Brownsville Revival or the Pensacola Outpouring, made the following televised prophetic pronouncements:

> I got a word from the Lord last night. . . . The Lord gave me a word last night that I'm going to share with you in a few minutes. . . . It's what he said to me last night. And I heard the Lord, friend. If I didn't hear God I'd tell you, but I heard the Lord. . . .
>
> . . . I want to say something this morning to Hank Hanegraaff. . . . If you want to keep any kind of a semblance of a ministry, you better back off from this revival and what God is doing. You better back off, because I am going to prophesy to you that if you don't, and you continue to put your tongue and your mouth on this move of God, within ninety days the Holy Ghost will bring you down. I said within ninety days the Holy Ghost will bring you down. And I speak that as a man of God. I don't speak that out of vengeance, I don't

speak it out of selfishness, and I don't speak it out of a hurt feeling, because my feelings are not hurt. I feel as normal today as I've ever felt. I don't have a chip on my shoulder, I don't have an ax to grind, but this is a move of God and you better leave it alone.

. . . And I want to tell you something else, if you don't want your head to start shaking—you make fun of someone in the choir shaking—come here a minute, girl. Come down here a minute. Hurry up. Hurry up. If you don't want your head to do like this, you better lay your mouth off of her.

. . . Mr. Hanegraaff, and all other devils, listen up . . . "

On June 18, 1997—*seventy-three days* after the prophecy—Kilpatrick released a public statement in which he acknowledged that the words he had attributed to God were solely his own. While Kilpatrick is to be commended for the following public apology, this episode also highlights the danger of presuming to speak for God:

Hank, I do sincerely humble myself and ask your forgiveness for un-Christlike behavior. I repent before Jesus and I've asked Him to forgive me. I pray you will forgive me and I also ask the body of Christ to forgive me. I was wrong. I take full responsibility for my words and behavior. The statements I made in April were made in an inflammatory way against you and CRI.

. . . When I said, "I'm going to prophesy as a man of God that the Lord bring you down in ninety days," I was not speaking that as a prophet but as a shepherd putting something in the ears of God. I did not say, "Thus saith the Lord"; it was a "Thus saith John Kilpatrick," putting these words into God's ears in the context of the message I was bringing. Let me re-emphasize again, that was me speaking.

Kilpatrick spoke with me by phone June 23, 1997, and made several concessions. First, he apologized for calling me a "devil." Then he acknowledged that he had deceived followers by saying, "I got a word from the Lord last night. . . . The Lord gave me a word last night that I'm going to share with you in a few minutes. . . . It's what he said to me last night. And I heard the Lord, friend. If I didn't hear God I'd tell you, but I heard the Lord. . . ." He confessed that what he had claimed to be a direct communication from God was in reality a fabrication.

Furthermore, he acknowledged that he had been speaking in anger and "in the flesh" rather than from God, but agreed that the context of his April 6 message unmistakably demonstrated that his words were intentionally prophetic in nature. He also agreed that at least some of the bizarre behavior at Pensacola was human and, though I do not see the need to go this far, even demonic in origin. He acknowledged that I had not made fun of the lady in his choir who for one and a half years had been shaking her head wildly from side to side each time she comes into Kilpatrick's church. While he did not apologize for prophesying that my head would start shaking like hers, he did promise me that he would "try to get her some help." Sadly, however, her shaking continued.

Finally, it should be noted that during his April 6, 1997, sermon, Kilpatrick also gave "ten proclamations" for the future of the revival:

> . . . I want to close by giving ten proclamations about how things are going to be. . . . I'm making a proclamation. I'm speaking this not just to you, friends, to impress you, but I'm saying this as a man of God from behind this holy desk in this holy environment of a great outpouring of the Holy Spirit. And I'm not saying this to you, but I'm saying this for the ears of God. Y'all just forget this for a minute. I'm saying this in the ears of God. And here's what I'm saying. This

revival shall not diminish and this revival shall turn into a national awakening.

. . . That all misunderstandings and rumors and calculated error shall turn from being a snake into hot bread, that an evil report shall actually be the forerunner for curiosity and repentance and conviction to follow millions in America and come to Christ.

. . . That the numbers that's [sic] presently out there on our marquee by the road of over 100,000 people that have made decisions for Christ shall in a short period of time to come, because of the great awakening and because of God's power about to fall in an unprecedented way from the White House to Pensacola, from Maine to California, and from Washington to Florida, that the numbers shall change in the near future from over 100,000 to millions before all is said and done. I said millions, millions, millions, millions, millions!

. . . Father, let some heathen, let some devil-possessed person load up a truck full of explosives or put a bomb in a bag. Let 'em do it. Father, I say in your ears, you're great. You sent angels to take the wheels off the chariots in the Bible. You told men to blow a trumpet and walls fell down on the ground as the people shouted. Lord, there's so much glory and praise in this place that even if a bomb is brought on this campus, I make a proclamation, Lord, it shall never, ever go off, in the Name of Jesus.

. . . I make a proclamation in the ears of the Lord that supernatural, divine, Holy Ghost healings and deliverances and signs and wonders begin to drastically increase so as to leave no doubt that God is still in the miracle-working business.

. . . I make this proclamation and we close. That all of the above nine things happen expeditiously as possible, for the hour is drawing nigh of the soon coming of our Lord Jesus.

As for the possible prescience of these declarations, let me briefly summarize the current state of affairs. It has now been almost six years since the "revival" broke out. According to religion pollster George Barna, as of the year 2000, general church attendance in America has dropped 10 percent since the early nineties and was unchanged since 1994, one year before the Pensacola Revival. Barna also reports that the number of Christians claiming to be born again has not changed since 1995, calling the notion that revival is taking place in America a myth.[1] I imagine we must now relegate Kilpatrick's emphatic "millions, millions, millions, millions, millions" to hyperbole.

Thankfully, no one has taken up Kilpatrick's unfathomably irresponsible and presumptuous "invitation" to demolish his church. As for a drastic increase in truly miraculous healings, deliverances, signs, and wonders, the evidence says otherwise. It is not only clear that Kilpatrick's prophetic proclamations have not come to pass, but the catalyst for the revival, Stephen Hill, has now moved on to pursue his own ministry objectives, and a widely publicized split has occurred between Brownsville apologist Michael Brown and the Brownsville Assembly of God.

CRI Statement on December 1997 Meetings Between Hank Hanegraaff and Brownsville Revival Leaders[1]

In November 1997, Dr. Michael Brown, president of the Brownsville Revival School of Ministry, and I were invited to communicate our respective views on revival before a gathering of radio broadcasters in Dallas, Texas. As a result, a renewed dialogue developed between the Christian Research Institute and leaders of the "Brownsville Revival." In December, I participated in a series of private meetings, which included an impromptu address to their School of Ministry students. According to a Brownsville press release posted shortly after these meetings, "The visit was historic because Mr. Hanegraaff has been the most visible and prominent critic of the renewal/ revival movement in North America." Said Michael Brown, " I don't know that people of this public prominence and this pronounced difference have gotten together on this level—I'm sure it must have happened, but I'm not aware of it. I don't want to exaggerate this, but it seems historic."

Unfortunately, what I had envisioned as a series of private meetings has become grist for the rumor mill. Within days of my visit, people reported hearing that I had been "slain in the spirit" and had succumbed to sensational manifestations such as spasmodic jerking. Faxes and phone calls flooded the Christian Research Institute's international offices ranging from pleas "to say it isn't so" to chastisements for "selling out to the enemy."

In light of the confusion and controversy surrounding my visit to Pensacola, allow me to set the record straight.

First and foremost, let me emphasize that my meetings with John Kilpatrick, Stephen Hill, Michael Brown, et al., should not be interpreted as an endorsement of the "Pensacola Outpouring." Not only I, but Pensacola leaders have underscored this fact. In the words of Michael Brown, "Hank Hanegraaff is not now saying that he endorses the revival." Rather than an endorsement, my meetings with Pensacola leaders should be viewed as an encouragement to carry on dialogue with those with whom you disagree, in a manner that reaches rather than repels. Years ago I began meeting with leaders of the Worldwide Church of God as they were transitioning from cultism to Christianity. Not only did these meetings result in meaningful dialogue, but they produced lasting friendships as well.

Furthermore, let me underscore the fact that I continue to be gravely concerned about the spiritual and physical consequences of unbiblical manifestations such as spasmodic jerking and being "slain in the spirit." As I communicated on *Larry King Live,* I am particularly concerned for people like the Brownsville . . . Finally, I remain concerned that the Brownsville Revival is indicative of a paradigm shift taking place within Christianity—a shift from faith to feelings, from fact to fantasy, and from reason to esoteric revelation. This shift is what I call the Counterfeit Revival. While Brownsville leaders strongly emphasize holiness and repentance in their preaching, they also emphasize that "God will choose to offend our minds in order to reveal what is in our hearts" (John Kilpatrick) or "The Lord is saying, 'I'm bypassing your mind and going straight to your heart. . . . The heart is what mat-

ters to the Lord'" (Lindell Cooley). As I point out in my book
Counterfeit Revival, this notion is in reality a fictional antago-
nism or a false dichotomy. Not only is the mind of tremendous
importance in successful Christian living, but from the perspective of Scripture, the heart is more a matter of understanding than of sentiment. As John Wesley, founder of the Methodist Church, correctly stated, "It is a fundamental principle that
to renounce reason is to renounce religion, that religion and
reason go hand in hand; all irrational religion is false religion." While Wesley recognized heartfelt emotions as a natural response to an encounter with the gospel, he attributed
enthusiasms such as falling, jumping, and jerking to the "simplicity" of people and to the ploys of Satan. In response to such
exotic manifestations, he wrote, "Satan serves himself of the
simplicity of people in order to bring a discredit on the work of
God."

The tragedy of modern-day Christianity is that people all
too often look for experience in all the wrong places. The real
experience is not found in self-indulgent manifestations but
rather in using one's time, talent, and treasure for the glory of
God and the edification of others. Jonathan Edwards, the leading figure of the first Great Awakening, was utterly convinced
that in genuine revival the Spirit of God is at work "to lessen
men's esteem of the pleasures, profits, and honors of the world,
and to take off their hearts from an eager pursuit after these
things; and to engage them in a deep concern about a future
state and eternal happiness which the gospel reveals—and puts
them upon earnestly seeking the kingdom of God and His righteousness."

Like leaders of the Brownsville revival, I am thrilled by
the dialogue that is taking place. To quote Michael Brown,
"Let us see if we can model our dialogue as an example to the
body of Christ to show how leaders can have strong disagree-
ments, and yet dialogue in a way that is gracious and
Christlike, and learn from each other in doing so."

Notes

Preface

1. Some material in this preface appeared in my article "The Counterfeit Revival Revisited," *Christian Research Journal* 21, no. 4 (1999): 54–55.

2. John Kilpatrick, "Declarations on How Things Are Going to Be," Brownsville Assembly of God, 6 April 1997, videotape. Kilpatrick proclaimed, "This revival shall not diminish and this revival shall turn into a national awakening. . . . The numbers that's *[sic]* presently out there on our marquee by the road of over 100,000 people that have made decisions for Christ shall in a short period of time to come, because of the great awakening and because of God's power about to fall in an unprecedented way from the White House to Pensacola, from Maine to California, and from Washington to Florida, that the numbers shall change in the near future from over 100,000 to millions before all is said and done. I said millions, millions, millions, millions, millions!"

3. As Counterfeit Revival fires go out in one "hot spot," they are inflamed in another. Obviously, there are too many revival locations to trace and document in detail. However, I wrote *Counterfeit Revival* to equip believers with all the essential

principles for discerning and dealing with these various permutations of devastating "wildfire," which now includes the Smithton Outpouring in Missouri and a plethora of other contemporaneous "hot spots" around the world.

4.   7 March 1999 e-mail from a devoted observer named Kathy to multiple recipients of the NEW-WINE list (posted at www.grmi.org/renewal/new-wine/list/archives/1339.html).

5.   Ibid. See the TACF Web site for some "incredible" photographs of gold fillings (www.tacf.org).

6.   17 March 1999, TACF Web site at www.tacf.org/confs/archives/intercession99/pressrelease.html.

7.   Elizabeth Moll Stalcup, "It Happened before Our Eyes," *Charisma,* November 1999, 80.

8.   The Canadian Press, "TV Evangelists Forced to Recant Claims of God's Divine Dentistry: An Honest Mistake," 12 May 1999, in National Post Online at www.nationalpost.com.

9.   Ibid.

10. Teresa Watanabe, "Struck by 'Golden Miracles,'" *Los Angeles Times,* 25 January 2000, in on-line archives at www.latimes.com.

11. Elizabeth Moll Stalcup, "When the Glory Comes Down," *Charisma,* November 1999, 77.

12. Elizabeth Moll Stalcup, "Glory Dust from Heaven?" *Charisma,* November 1999, 78.

13. Ibid., 79.

14. "Praise the Lord," Trinity Broadcasting Network, 10 September 1999.

15. "This Is Your Day," Trinity Broadcasting Network, 29 March 2000.

16. "PTL Praise-a-Thon," Trinity Broadcasting Network, 2 April 2000.

17. Personal conversation with Michael Brown; as well, Brown wrote in a 17 June 1997 Reapernet chat session (chat.reapernet.com): "David Hogan is a dear friend of mine. He has been shot, stoned, cut with machetes; 12 of his men have been martyred; he often fasts every other day. He's the real thing! He has personally raised more than 10 people from the dead among the Mexican Indians. The workers themselves (native and American) have seen more than 200

raised through the years. Incredible but true. (Enjoy this one, dear critical friend!)"

Additionally, Phill Gammill, a ministry associate of David Hogan, iterated in a CRI phone conversation (7 October 1998) the claim that churches under Hogan's ministry leadership have witnessed 200 people raised from the dead.

18. John W. Allman, "Revival Prays to Raise an Infant from the Dead," *The Pensacola News Journal,* 20 September 1998, Web site at www.pensacolanewsjournal.com/brownsville/september%2098/pray.htm.

19. See John Kilpatrick's sermon of 6 April 1997 at Brownsville Assembly of God, Brownsville, Fla.

20. J. Lee Grady, "When God Interrupts Your Agenda: An Interview with the Leaders of Brownsville Assembly of God," *Ministries Today,* November–December 1996, 20.

21. Advertisement for "Good News New York" crusade with Rodney Howard-Browne in *Charisma,* April 1999, 81.

22. Ibid.

23. Ibid.

24. There is increasing controversy within the professional dental community over adverse side effects of placing foreign metals in the mouth, which include such potential problems as creating over time an electromagnetic interference field that negatively affects the innumerable nerves traveling through the jaw area from the brain to various parts of the body; and the battery effect of mixed metals in the mouth causing outgassing of toxic components within the metals.

25. For frank and unashamed accounts of these prayer meetings see the Brownsville Assembly of God official Web site (www.brownsville-revival.org; retrieved February 1997).

26. Another significant problem with the Brownsville Revival is the lack of accountability offered for new converts. The Brownsville Assembly of God acknowledges that they do not know whether the vast majority of the thousands upon thousands of recorded conversions have been baptized, enrolled in a discipleship program, or regularly attend church. (Fax response from Rose Compton of the Brownsville Assembly of God, Pensacola, Fla., 13 December 1996.)

27. Figure as of 7 September 1997 posted at the official Brownsville Web site (www.brownsville-revival.org). The Web site no longer posts the alleged number of visitors to the revival, apparently due to controversy surrounding the posts.

28. 2–4 May 1997.

29. E. G. and Joseph R. Chambers, "False Brags and Real Facts," *The End Times and Victorious Living,* March–April 1997, 7. See also the report offered during the 10 June 1997 Internet Reapernet chat session (chat.reapernet.com).

Before You Begin

1. John Arnott, Toronto Airport Vineyard, 16 December 1994, audiotape.

2. Mike Bickle, as quoted in Stephen F. Cannon, "Old Wine in Old Wineskins, a Look at Kansas City Fellowship," *Personal Freedom Outreach, The Quarterly Journal,* no. 4 (October– December 1990): 10. Bickle and other Counterfeit Revival leaders, such as Bob Jones, were disciplined without lasting effect under Vineyard founder John Wimber in the early 1990s for this kind of false and damaging prophecy. This situation highlights the fact that relying on special, direct revelation apart from Scripture is unbiblical, irresponsible, leads to double-mindedness in those who offer such prophecies, and in the end severely damages the credibility of both Christian leadership within the church and the church's witness in the world.

3. Figures given by news sources and leaders of the Counterfeit Revival are not always consistent.

4. Richard Ostling, "Laughing for the Lord," *Time,* 15 August 1994, 38.

5. Kenneth L. Woodward, Jeanne Gordon, Carol Hall, and Barry Brown, "The Giggles Are for God," *Newsweek,* 20 February 1995, 54.

6. Walter Goodman, "About Churches, Souls, and Show-Biz Methods," *New York Times,* 16 March 1995, B4.

7. *The Phil Donahue Show,* 19 September 1995, videotape.

8. *60 Minutes,* 18 June 1995, videotape.

9. Peter Jennings, *Peter Jennings Reporting: In the Name of God,* New York: An MPI Home Video Presentation of an ABC News Production, 1995, videotape.
10. Abraham Kuyper, as quoted in Charles Colson, *Against the Night, Living in the New Dark Ages* (Ann Arbor, Mich.: Servant Books, 1989), 163.

Charting the Course

1. George C. Bedell, Leo Sandon Jr., and Charles T. Wellborn, *Religion in America* (New York: Macmillan, 1975), 159–60.
2. Bob Jones and Paul Cain, "Selections from the Kansas City Prophets," audiotape (tape 155C). See comment in endnote 2 under Before You Begin, above.
3. John Wimber, "Spiritual Phenomena: Slain in the Spirit—Part 2" (Anaheim, Calif.: Association of Vineyard Churches, 1981), audiotape.
4. Stanley M. Burgess and Gary B. McGee, eds., *Dictionary of Pentecostal and Charismatic Movements* (Grand Rapids, Mich.: Zondervan, 1988), 790–91.

Chapter 1 ✦ The Holy Ghost Bartender

1. Rodney Howard-Browne, Melodyland Christian Center, Anaheim, Calif., 17 January 1995.
2. Ibid.
3. Ibid., 16 and 17 January 1995.
4. Rodney Howard-Browne, *Fresh Oil from Heaven* (Louisville, Ky.: RHBEA Publications, 1992), 28; *The Touch of God* (Louisville, Ky.: RHBEA Publications, 1992), 73; *Manifesting the Holy Ghost* (Louisville, Ky.: RHBEA Publications, 1992), 14; and related in *Charisma* magazine, August 1994, 22–23.
5. Rodney Howard-Browne, *Flowing in the Holy Ghost* (Louisville, Ky.: RHBEA Publications, 1991), 15. In other booklets, such as *Manifesting the Holy Ghost* (p. 14), Howard-Browne says he shouted, "God, I want your fire! Let the fire fall here tonight like it did at Pentecost!"
6. Howard-Browne, *Fresh Oil from Heaven,* 27–28. In some renditions of this story (such as in his *The Touch of God,* 74),

Howard-Browne says the fire burned in his body for three
rather than for four days.

7. Howard-Browne, *Manifesting the Holy Ghost,* 16.
8. Howard-Browne, *Fresh Oil from Heaven,* 28.
9. Ibid.
10. Ibid.
11. Howard-Browne, *Touch of God,* 74.
12. Richard M. Riss, *A History of the Worldwide Awakening of 1992–1995* (e-mail source address: self-published, eleventh edition, October 1995), 7–8.
13. Howard-Browne, *Touch of God,* 76.
14. Ibid.
15. Riss, *Worldwide Awakening of 1992–1995,* 6.
16. Howard-Browne, *Touch of God,* 77.
17. Ibid., 79.
18. Ibid.
19. Riss, *Worldwide Awakening of 1992–1995,* 7.
20. Howard-Browne, *Manifesting the Holy Ghost,* 29.
21. Ibid.
22. Howard-Browne, *Touch of God,* 100.
23. Howard-Browne, *Manifesting the Holy Ghost,* 22.
24. Ibid., 25.
25. Ibid.
26. Howard-Browne, *Touch of God,* 133–34.
27. Ibid., 134.
28. Howard-Browne, *Manifesting the Holy Ghost,* 25.
29. Ibid., 26–27.
30. Ibid.
31. Rodney Howard-Browne, Orlando Christian Center, 1990, videotape.
32. Benny Hinn originally told me this during a private dinner conversation in 1994 and then reaffirmed the details publicly in a conversation during the 1995 National Religious Broadcasters convention in Nashville, Tenn.
33. Riss, *Worldwide Awakening of 1992–1995,* 10.
34. Ibid., 8–9.
35. Julia Duin, "Praise the Lord and Pass the New Wine," *Charisma,* August 1994, 23.
36. Ibid., 21.

37. Ibid.
38. Dave Roberts, *The Toronto Blessing* (England: Kingsway, 1994), 87.
39. "News Briefs," *Charisma*, August 1994, 62.
40. Charles and Frances Hunter, *Holy Laughter* (Kingwood, Tex.: Hunter Books, 1994), 35.
41. Howard-Browne, *Manifesting the Holy Ghost*, 22, 25; *Touch of God*, 134.
42. Julia Duin, "An Evening with Rodney Howard-Browne," *Christian Research Journal*, Winter 1995, 44.
43. Duin, "Praise the Lord and Pass the New Wine," 24.
44. Riss, *Worldwide Awakening of 1992–1995*, 10, says it was thirteen weeks.

Chapter 2 ✦ The Party

1. J. Lee Grady, "Laughter in Lakeland," *Charisma*, August 1995, 61–62. *Bizarre* and other pejorative adjectives are employed by Counterfeit Revival leaders. See for example: John Arnott, "Understanding and Responding to Movers of God Conference," 25 April 1996; Jerry Steingard, "Catch the Fire 1994: Handling Objections to Manifestations," 13 October 1994; Gail Reid, "Joy on the Other Side of Offense," (Sidebar) *Spread the Fire*, March–April 1995; Mike Bickle and Michael Sullivant, "Understanding the Phenomena That Accompany the Spirit's Ministry"; Richard M. Riss, *A History of the Worldwide Awakening of 1992–1995, 11th ed.* (e-mail source address: self-published, October 1995).
2. Julia Duin, "Praise the Lord and Pass the New Wine," *Charisma*, August 1994, 24.
3. Riss, *Worldwide Awakening of 1992–1995*, 12.
4. *Rumors of Revival*, dir. and prod. Alan Matthews (Milton Keynes, England: Nelson Word, 1995), videotape.
5. Riss, *Worldwide Awakening of 1992–1995*, 12.
6. Duin, "Praise the Lord and Pass the New Wine," 24.
7. Riss, *Worldwide Awakening of 1992–1995*, 12.
8. Oral Roberts's message on Daniel at Melodyland Christian Center, Anaheim, Calif., 8 January 1995, audiotape.
9. Ibid.

10. Julia Duin, "An Evening with Rodney Howard-Browne," *Christian Research Journal,* Winter 1995, 44.

11. Hank Hanegraaff, *Christianity in Crisis* (Eugene, Ore.: Harvest House, 1993), 351–52.

12. Charles and Frances Hunter, *Holy Laughter* (Kingwood, Tex.: Hunter Books, 1994), 36. As Charles and Frances Hunter put it, they "had never heard Marilyn so excited."

13. Ibid.

14. Ibid., 35.

15. Ibid.

16. Ibid., 48.

17. Ibid., 39.

18. Ibid., front cover copy.

19. Ibid., 5.

20. Dave Roberts, *The Toronto Blessing* (England: Kingsway, 1994), 33–34. The claim that Holy Trinity Brompton understands its parishioners "are safe to have in the taxi" is made by Roberts, an ardent supporter of the Counterfeit Revival in general, and in this context, specifically, of the Holy Trinity Brompton revival, as indicated in his book, *The Toronto Blessing.* While Roberts differentiates the taxi story from "other stories circulating that would seem to have little basis in truth" (34), Sandy Millar, Vicar of Holy Trinity Brompton, disputed Roberts in a personal letter he sent to me. Thus, presumably, if Millar is to be believed, the spiritually inebriated travel home on their own without the aid of a sober taxicab driver.

21. For an interesting rendition of this story, see Roberts, *Toronto Blessing,* 33.

22. Ibid.

23. Hunter, *Holy Laughter,* 121.

24. Ibid., 95.

25. Ibid., 151.

26. Ibid., 159.

27. Ibid., 97.

28. Ibid., 98.

29. Ibid., 99.

30. Ibid.

31. Ibid., 18.
32. Ibid., 23.
33. Ibid., 27.
34. Ibid.
35. On 8 May 1995 my office contacted Hunter Ministries seeking documentation and spoke with someone who identified herself as Barbara. After checking with Frances Hunter, Barbara related that they had no documentation of the story, not even the woman's name. She relayed Frances's recollection that the incident had happened more than twenty-three years earlier and that the woman had volunteered her story when she walked up to the Hunters' book table at one of their meetings. The Hunters never did any follow-up on the story, such as requesting a doctor's report, and consequently had never substantiated the story.
36. Hunter, *Holy Laughter,* 27.
37. Ibid., 60.
38. Ibid., 52. Dye is pastor of Kensington Temple, which is one of the largest British churches.
39. Ibid., 53.
40. Ibid., 56.
41. Ibid.
42. Ibid., 55.
43. Ibid.
44. Ibid. As in the case of the miracle breast, the Hunters admit that they do not have evidence to document this story.
45. Ibid., 54.
46. Ibid., 55.
47. Ibid., 57.
48. Ibid., 58–59 (emphasis added).
49. Ibid., 59.
50. Kenneth E. Hagin, *I Believe in Visions,* 2nd ed. (Tulsa, Okla.: Rhema Bible Church, 1989), 122.
51. Rodney Howard-Browne, *Flowing in the Holy Ghost* (Louisville, Ky.: RHBEA Publications, 1991), 53. Wigglesworth (1859–1947) was an English Pentecostal healing evangelist.
52. Ibid., 53–54.
53. Ibid., 54.

Chapter 3 ✦ The Vineyard Connection

1. Randy Clark, "Catch the Fire '94, Test Me Now . . . I Will Back You Up," Toronto Airport Vineyard, 13 October 1994, audiotape.
2. Ibid.
3. Ibid.
4. Ibid.
5. Ibid.
6. Ibid.
7. Richard M. Riss, *A History of the Worldwide Awakening of 1992–1995* (e-mail source address: self-published, *11th ed.,* October 1995), 22.
8. Clark, "Test Me Now . . . I Will Back You Up," audiotape.
9. Ibid.
10. Ibid.
11. Ibid.; Riss, *Worldwide Awakening of 1992–1995*, 22.
12. Riss, *Worldwide Awakening of 1992–1995*, 22.
13. Ibid.; Clark, "Test Me Now . . . I Will Back You Up," audiotape.
14. Riss, *Worldwide Awakening of 1992–1995*, 22; Clark, "Test Me Now . . . I Will Back You Up," audiotape.
15. Clark, "Test Me Now . . . I Will Back You Up," audiotape, 6. Although this is the consistent story found in most of Clark's messages and recounted in Riss as well (p. 22), Dr. Chevreau tells a different story, perhaps about a subsequent event, or perhaps he is confused about when the revival began in Clark's church. Chevreau says, "Five months later, at a Browne meeting Randy attended in Lakeland, Florida, Rodney discerned a powerful anointing being released in Randy's life—he came over to him and said, 'This is the fire of God in your hands; go home and pray for everyone in your church.' The first Sunday of Randy's return, he did as instructed, and saw a similar outbreak of the Spirit as he ministered" (Guy Chevreau, *Catch the Fire: The Toronto Blessing—An Experience of Renewal and Revival* [London: Marshall Pickering, 1994], 24–25).
16. Riss, *Worldwide Awakening of 1992–1995*.

17. Clark, "Test Me Now . . . I Will Back You Up," audiotape.
18. At the beginning of 1996, the Toronto Airport Vineyard changed its name to the Toronto Airport Christian Fellowship after the church was "disengaged" from the Association of Vineyard Churches. Since in this book most of the comments quoted from Toronto leaders were said before the name change, in most instances I have retained the name Toronto Airport Vineyard.
19. Clark, "Test Me Now . . . I Will Back You Up," audiotape.
20. Ibid.
21. Ibid. There is a slightly different version of this message recounted by Guy Chevreau, *Catch the Fire*, 25.
22. Clark, "Test Me Now . . . I Will Back You Up," audiotape.
23. Ibid.
24. Richard M. Riss, *A History of the Revival of 1993–1995, 7th ed.* January 1995, 14. Interestingly, in a more recent edition (Riss, *A History of the Worldwide Awakening of 1992–1995 11th ed.,* October 1995,), this statement has been changed to read: "Randy would probably never have had a central role in the Toronto Revival" (p. 23).
25. John Arnott, "The Love of God," Mission Viejo Vineyard, Mission Viejo, Calif., 17 July 1995, audiotape.
26. Ibid.
27. John Arnott, Discovery Church, Orlando, Fla., 29 January 1995, audiotape.
28. John Arnott and Guy Chevreau, Pastors' Meeting, Toronto Airport Vineyard, 19 October 1994, audiotape.
29. Arnott, Discovery Church, Orlando, Fla., 29 January 1995, audiotape.
30. Ibid.
31. Dave Roberts, *The Toronto Blessing* (England: Kingsway, 1994), 64.
32. Ibid.
33. Ibid., 15.
34. Ibid., 18.
35. Guy Chevreau, *Catch the Fire: The Toronto Blessing—An Experience of Renewal and Revival* (London: Marshall Pickering, 1994), 23.

36. Ibid.
37. Ibid., 24.
38. Ibid.
39. Arnott, Discovery Church, Orlando, Fla., 29 January 1995, audiotape.
40. John Arnott, *The Father's Blessing* (Orlando, Fla.: Creation House, 1995), 20.
41. Ibid., 71–72.
42. Quoted in Riss, *Worldwide Awakening of 1992–1995,* 26.
43. Ibid.
44. Arnott, Discovery Church, Orlando, Fla., 29 January 1995, audiotape.
45. Ibid.
46. Ibid.
47. Ibid.
48. Ibid.
49. Ibid.
50. Ibid.
51. Ibid.
52. Ibid.
53. Arnott, Toronto Airport Vineyard, 16 December 1994, audiotape.
54. John Arnott, "Dynamics of Receiving Spiritual Experiences," Toronto Airport Vineyard, 18 November 1994, audiotape.
55. Ibid.
56. Arnott, Toronto Airport Vineyard, 16 December 1994, audiotape.
57. Arnott, Discovery Church, Orlando, Fla., 29 January 1995, audiotape.
58. Ibid.
59. Ibid.
60. Ibid.
61. John Arnott, Pastors' Meeting, Toronto Airport Vineyard, 19 October 1994, audiotape.
62. Arnott, *Father's Blessing,* 210.
63. Ibid., 206.
64. Ibid., 224, 209–10.
65. Ibid., 167.

66. Ibid., 183.
67. Ibid.
68. Riss, *Worldwide Awakening of 1992–1995,* 22.
69. John Arnott and Guy Chevreau, Pastors' Meeting, Toronto Airport Vineyard, 19 October 1994, audiotape.
70. Randy Clark, "Catch the Fire," Questions and Answers, Toronto Airport Vineyard, 14 October 1994, audiotape.
71. Ibid.
72. Ibid.
73. *The Phil Donahue Show,* 19 September 1995.
74. Ibid.
75. Chevreau, *Catch the Fire,* 13.
76. Ibid.
77. Ibid., 14. Emphasis in original.
78. Wes Campbell, Toronto Airport Vineyard, 14 October 1994, audiotape.
79. Ibid.
80. Ibid.
81. Ibid.
82. Ibid.
83. Arnott, *Father's Blessing,* 204.
84. Ibid., 205.

Chapter 4 ✦ The Pensacola Outpouring

1. Portions of this chapter appeared previously in my article "The Counterfeit Revival (Part Three): Separating Fact from Fiction on the Pensacola Outpouring," *Christian Research Journal* (November–December 1997): 10–20, 42.
2. Speaking of the Brownsville Revival, Kilpatrick later said, "Right now, Brownsville Assembly of God is still in the middle of an opportunity of a lifetime . . ." (John W. Allman, "Revival Revises Routine," *Pensacola News Journal,* 7 March 1999).
3. Personal interviews with former members of Brownsville Assembly of God church. See also the interview with Lindell Cooley, Minister of Music, Brownsville Assembly of God, by Dr. Larry H. Walker, Managing editor, *Destiny Image Digest*

at www.reapernet.com/did/winter97_supp_cooley.html
(retrieved 16 Mary 2000); and Alice Crann, "Pastors Orchestrated First Revival," *Pensacola News Journal,* 19 November
1997, front page.

4. Personal interviews with former members of Brownsville
   Assembly of God church.

5. See "The Hunger Before revival" at www.theremnant.com/
   june4.html (retrieved 7 December 2000).

6. John Kilpatrick, Brownsville Assembly of God, 18 June 1995;
   videotape. Unless otherwise noted, this videotape comprises
   the principal source of documentation for the events and
   teachings of that first day of the revival, 18 June, 1995.

7. As quoted in "The Hunger Before Revival" at
   www.theremnant.com/june4.html (retrieved 7 December
   2000).

8. Here is Hill's statement in context with emphasis added:

> And I also remember, friends, on October 28,
> 1975, at 11:00 in the morning when Jesus Christ got
> ahold of me. I will never forget the day a Lutheran
> vicar came into my room. I was going through with-
> drawal. He came into my room and grabbed my hand
> and he said this, he said,
>
> "Steve, I can't help you, but I know Somebody
> who can. His name is Jesus and He can heal you. He
> can set you free, Steve."
>
> I remember looking up at that man like he was
> crazy.
>
> "You got to be crazy. Look at me, man, I've been
> on drugs for twelve years. I'm a junkie. I'm a main-
> liner. I'm a thief."
>
> He said, "God can deliver you, son." He said,
> "Pray with me."
>
> And I said, "I don't know how to pray and I don't
> believe in God."
>
> He said, "That's okay. Say this name." He said,
> "Say the name Jesus."
>
> Friend, how many know that there's power in

the name of Jesus? You can talk all day about religion, friends, but when you say the name Jesus, the
demons tremble. The devil trembles. He knows that
name. And I remember laying on my bed and I looked
up at the sky and that man put—I call that—on
moron status, okay? The moron level—when he said,
"Just say the name Jesus." Anybody can say the name
Jesus. *He didn't say, "Here are the four spiritual laws.
You need to understand them, Steve, and then I'll lead
you to Christ." No, he said, "Say the name Jesus."*

And I'll never forget squeezing his hand. I
remember the wonders of the Lord, friends. I looked
up at the ceiling of the room and in unbelief I said
"Jesus, Jesus, Jesus, Jesus, Jesus, Jesus, Jesus," and
I began saying that louder and louder and with more
conviction and the more I said His name the more
powers went through my body and I went "Jesus,
Jesus, Jesus, Jesus, Jesus," and in thirty seconds,
friends, I was a brand-new person.

9. Maul Ely, Brownsville Assembly of God, 16 March 1997;
    audiotape.
10. John Kilpatrick, *In Times Like These* (Fla., Brownsville
    Assembly of God, 30 May 1996, videotape.
11. Stephen Hill, Brownsville Assembly of God, 30 May 1996,
    videotape.
12. Michael Brown, *From Holy Laughter to Holy Fire*
    (Shippensburg, Pa.: Destiny Image, 1996), back page promotion.
13. Brownsville Revival Testimonies Web page at
    www.brownsville-revival.org/testimon.html. This testimonial
    remained on the official Brownsville Revival Web site for at
    least nine months in 1997. We first noticed it in March, and I
    confronted Michael Brown with it when he was a guest on
    the *Bible Answer Man* broadcast March 23; I confronted him
    again concerning it in November of 1997.
14. Stephen Hill, Brownsville Assembly of God, 6 April 1997,
    videotape.
15. Dr. Carl Sightler, "Revival Results," on the offical
    Brownsville Revival Testimonies Web pages at

www.brownsville-revival.org/revival/revival–info/results.htm
(retrieved 6 March 2001).

16. Dr. Michael L. Brown, "Pensacola: God or Not?" *Destiny Image Digest* (winter 1997): 39. However, Stephen Hill confessed within the same publication, "We've received a lot from the Toronto church on how to pray with people and care for folks. We model a lot of what is going on here from them" (Steve Hill, "Heart to Heart, with Evangelist Steve Hill," *Destiny Image Digest* [winter 1997]: 14).

17. "Honey, Where Are We From?" *In Times Like These,* Brownsville Assembly of God, 8 June 1996, videotape.

18. Larry Walker, "Sisters in the Fire: Alison and Elisabeth Ward," *Destiny Image Digest* (winter 1997): 27.

19. "Amy Elizabeth Ward, 'Mercy Seat,' Alison Ward," *In Times Like These,* Brownsville Assembly of God, n.d., videotape.

20. "The Voice of Many Waters," *In Times Like These,* Brownsville Assembly of God, n.d., videotape (testimonies from baptismal services).

21. Michael Brown, "Revival in Brownsville?" *Destiny Image Digest* (winter 1997): 36.

22. For example, Brownsville Assembly of God, Sunday evening service, 16 March 1997, my personal eyewitness testimony.

23. CRI's research included interviews with eyewitnesses to this case. See also Greg Stone, "Prayer Service Shakes Maranatha Teens; Pastor Maintains God is at Work; Parents Left Searching for Answers," *The Charleston Gazette,* 15 November 1997, 1A.

Chapter 5 ✦ The Fatal Fruit

1. Portions of this chapter appeared previously in my article "The Counterfeit Revival (Part Three): Separating Fact from Fiction on the Pensacola Outpouring." *Christian Research Journal* (November–December 1997): 20–20, 42.

2. See *Charisma,* July 1997, 36–41, 60–62.

3. Jon Ruthven, "They Called Jesus a Counterfeit, Too," *Charisma,* July 1997, 61.

4. Franz Delitzsch, *Isaiah,* vol. 7 of *Commentary on the Old*

Testament in Ten Volumes, by C. F. Keil and F. Delitzsch (Grand Rapids, Mich.: William B. Eerdmans, 1976), 372.

5. Dr. Oliver Wilder-Smith, *Bible Answer Man* radio broadcast, 15 May 1997.

6. John Kilpatrick, "God's Ears," Brownsville Assembly of God Revival service, 6 April 1997, videotape. The violent shaking that Kilpatrick deemed to be a mark of revival would for me become the mark of God's wrath. Kilpatrick went on to prophesy, had minutes earlier prophesied judgment upon me: "I want to say something this morning to Hank Hanegraaff. . . . If you want to keep any kind of a semblance of a ministry, you better back off from this revival and what God is doing. You better back off, because I am going to prophesy to you that if you don't, and you continue to put your tongue in your mouth on this move of God, within ninety days the Holy Ghost will bring you down. I said within ninety days the Holy Ghost will bring you down."

Upon recognizing his presumption, however, Kilpatrick repented. Here is a portion of his public apology: "Hank, I do sincerely humble myself and ask your forgiveness for un-Christlike behavior. I repent before Jesus and I've asked him to forgive me. I pray you will forgive me and I also ask the body of Christ to forgive me. I was wrong. I take full responsibility for my words and behavior. The statements I made in April were made in an inflammatory way against you and CRI." (From "Public Statement Issued by Pastor John Kilpatrick at the Brownsville Revival, June 18, 1997"). See also appendix C.

7. Brownsville Revival Testimonies Web page at www.brownsville-revival.org/testimon.html.

8. The Brownsville Assembly of God reports as of 10 August 1997, over 115,000 have responded to the altar calls since the revival began 18 June 1995 (www.brownsville-revival.org). Dale Schlafer, *Becoming an Agent of Revival: Revival Primer* (Denver: Promise Keepers, 1997), 21, reports 102,000 converts. A publisher's blurb on the last page of Dr. Michael Brown's book, *From Holy Laughter to Holy Fire: America on the Edge of Revival* (Shippensburg, Pa.: Destiny

Image, 1996), says, "In less than two years, Evangelist Steve
Hill has won hundreds of thousands to Christ. . . ." A widely
distributed promotional flyer for Awake America at Anaheim, Calif., 28–29 September 1997 with Pastor John
Kilpatrick and Evangelist Steve Hill states: "In Pensacola
hundreds of thousands of people have come to Jesus." In an
Internet Reapernet Chat session, 6 May 1997
(chat.reapernet.com), Dr. Michael Brown wrote: "As for the
question of why we are now speaking about numbers of
people responding to the altar calls as opposed to numbers of
people being 'saved,' the reasoning is simple. In point of fact,
all of us HATE exaggeration and hype, and from the start,
conservative figures were being used. Actually between
250,000–300,000 people have responded to the altar calls,
not the 103,000 figure you may see. But we know that not all
of these people were actually being saved or coming back to
the Lord, therefore we used a very low number for people
'saved.' However, since we cannot follow-up on every individual, and since we don't want to exaggerate anything in
the slightest, we speak now of those coming to the Lord or
responding to the altar calls, also avoiding unnecessary
controversy. Of course—and this is the good news!—we can
point to multiplied thousands of radical converts, and really,
hundreds of thousands around the country through the
revival." In *Good News* (July–August 1996 n.p.), Steve Hill is
quoted as saying: "We're seeing a thousand people saved a
week, but we are very conservative with the figures"
(www.goshen.net/gnm/hill.htm).

9. To the extend that true conversions have taken place as a
result of the Pensacola Outpouring, I rejoice (see Phil. 1:18).
Of course, what I am concerned about is the *kind* of Christianity these converts are being led into and the *kind* of
Christianity this movement is depicting to the world. Conversions do not relieve teachers of responsibility and accountability for their unbiblical teachings and practices.

10. My office contacted the Pensacola Sheriff's Department on
20 March 1997 and spoke with Sheriff Loman and Sergeant
Spears—Brownsville is in their district. Not only were we

told that this did not happen, but also that the only possible reason for suspected drug dealers to be taken to a revival would be if it were part of a parole stipulation ordered by a parole judge.

11. See *Bible Answer Man* broadcast interview with Michael Brown, 20 March 1997.

12. This fabrication remained on the Brownsville Assembly of God Web site for at least nine months after they were confronted with their error.

13. Stephen Hill, Brownsville Assembly of God, 6 April 1997, videotape.

14. As Christians, we should not make public claims without verifiable evidence to back up those claims (e.g., 1 Thess. 5:21; 2 Cor. 13:1; Heb. 10:28).

15. Dr. Carl Sightler, "Results from the Revival," "Revival Results," on the official Brownsville Revival Testimonies Web page at www.brownsville-revival.org/revival/revival–info/results.htm (retrieved 6 March 2001).

16. Statistics available through the Pensacola Police Department.

17. Steve Rabey, "Pensacola Outpouring Keeps Gushing," *Christianity Today,* 3 March 1997, 57.

18. *Orange County Register,* 13 March 1997, Metro 1. Of course, CRI does not claim responsibility for the drop in Orange County's crime rate.

19. Dr. Michael L. Brown, "Pensacola: God or Not?" *Destiny Image Digest* (winter 1997): 39. However, Stephen Hill confessed within the same publication, "We've received a lot from the Toronto church on how to pray with people and care for folks . . . we model a lot of what is going on here from them" (Steve Hill, "Heart to Heart, with Evangelist Steve Hill" *Destiny Image Digest* [winter 1997]): 14).

20. Steve Hill, "Heart to Heart, with Evangelist Steve Hill," *Destiny Image Digest* (winter 1997): 14.

21. Ibid.

22. John Arnott, "Valuing the Anointing," Toronto Airport Vineyard, 15 October 1994, audiotape.

23. James A. Beverley, *Holy Laughter and the Toronto Blessing* (Grand Rapids, Mich.: Zondervan, 1995), 117–19. Even

Arnott has admitted that early accounts of Sarah's story were in error (see James A. Beverley, *Revival Wars* [Toronto: Evangelical Research Ministries, 1997], 23.

24. Guy Chevreau, *Catch the Fire: The Toronto Blessing—An Experience of Renewal and Revival* (London: Marshall Pickering, 1994), 148.

25. Beverley, *Holy Laughter and the Toronto Blessing,* 117–20.

Chapter 6 ✦ Animals, Animation, Advertisements, and Athletics

1. James Ryle is a key player in the popularization of the Counterfeit Revival. He is pastor to Bill McCartney, founder of the national Christian men's movement, Promise Keepers, and is also a member of the Promise Keepers board of directors.

2. James Ryle, *A Dream Come True* (Orlando, Fla.: Creation House, 1995), 218.

3. Ibid., 218–19, 224–25.

4. Ibid., 229.

5. James Ryle, *Hippo in the Garden* (Orlando, Fla.: Creation House, 1993), 13.

6. This story should not be confused with Ryle's dream about the rhino in the field (*Hippo in the Garden,* 143–45), about which Ryle was told, "What you are seeing is a religious spirit." Ryle came to understand that what the "voice" that spoke to him was helping him to see was that like the rhino, religious people "cannot see past their own noses!"; "intimidate others with critical words"; "are very temperamental" and "subject to violent fits of unprovoked anger"; but that "a small dagger in the hands of a skilled hunter can pierce the armor-skin of the rhino."

7. Ryle, *Hippo in the Garden,* 268.

8. Ibid., 263.

9. Ibid., 277–78.

10. Ibid., 263.

11. Ibid., 108–9.

12. Ibid., 108–10.

13. Ibid., 128.

14. Ibid., 130.

15. James Ryle, "The Beatles' Anointing Story: The Sons of Thunder (A New Generation of Worshipping Warriors)," 21 June 1990, audiotape.

16. Ibid. Much ado has been made about Ryle's public recanting of this very peculiar prophecy, which recanting he was happy to relate to me during a phone conversation 5 June 1995. However, Ryle obviously did not learn his lesson since he went on to offer equally bizarre and obviously false prophetic revelations, as I point out in the text of this chapter. Ryle's situation further highlights the dangerous disregard so many Counterfeit Revivalists demonstrate for the sanctity of the Word of God. (See also comment in endnote 2 under Before You Begin, p. 292).

17. Ryle, *Hippo in the Garden,* 46–47.

18. Ibid,. 181.

19. Ibid.

20. Ibid., 182.

21. The word *omen* is defined as "an occurrence or phenomenon believed to portend a future event" (*Merriam Webster's Collegiate Dictionary,* 10th ed. [Springfield, Mass.: Merriam-Webster, 1994]).

22. Ryle, *Hippo in the Garden,* 182–83.

23. Ryle didn't worry about taking the verse in its historical context because he believes that while "the verse may, in fact, be taken completely out of its historical context, it nevertheless has direct bearing on some immediate situation we're facing" (Ryle, *Hippo in the Garden,* 77).

24. Ryle, *Hippo in the Garden,* 182.

25. Ibid., 183.

26. Ibid.

27. Ibid., 12–24.

28. Ibid., back cover copy.

29. In Acts 16:16–19, the slave girl, whose occult abilities were exploited by her owners, declared of Paul and Silas, "These men are servants of the Most High God, who are telling you the way to be saved" (v. 17).

30. Transcript of conversation, 15 August 1996.
31. The pastor in question, whose name I shall not mention, denies ever bringing a prophet into his church before this incident and also denies providing insider information to be passed off as revelation. What is curious, however, is that the pastor apparently does not consider Ryle to be a prophet, even though he certainly offered his pulpit to someone claiming prophetic prowess. The pastor explains, "On Friday, August 24, 1990, James Ryle came and ministered for the first time, by my invitation. . . . Quoting from the book *[Counterfeit Revival]*, Sal said, 'she was well aware of her pastor's usual "preparation" for a visiting prophet.' As she put it, 'I worked closely with the pastor, so I knew precisely how the manipulation worked in that church.' This was disturbing to me. We had never had a prophet come to our church before. In my eight-and-one-half-year relationship with James Ryle, I have never heard him call himself a prophet. Sal's implication that I prepared visiting prophets is absurd. . . . I have not, nor would I ever, manipulate the people of God to make my ministry or another ministry look other than what the Lord had given them. I know that God holds me accountable for the church he has given me. I fear the Lord too much to do such an abominable thing." (As quoted in James A. Beverley, *Revival Wars* [Toronto: Evangelical Research Ministries, 1997], 68–69).
32. Transcript of conversation, 15 August 1996.

Chapter 7 ✦ A Jack with a Lantern

1. An examination of the prophetic ministry in the New Testament demonstrates it to be completely consistent with Old Testament prophecy with respect to the standard of accuracy by which it is judged. Like their counterparts in the Old Testament, New Testament prophets such as John the Revelator, Simeon, Agabus, and others both proclaimed God's Word and predicted with precision what was to come. For a concise overview on this subject see *New Bible Dictionary* (Wheaton, Ill.: Tyndale House Publishers, 1983), 985.

2. David Ravenhill, "Understanding Prophecy and Its Fulfillment: Introduction to the Prophetic," tape 90917, 17 September 1989, audiotape. On one reading of Ravenhill's statement
   one could argue that he intended merely to emphasize the
   value of a prophet's character over prophetic accuracy
   without eliminating the necessity of prophetic accuracy.
   However, this interpretation requires a generous and, I
   believe, unwarranted benefit of the doubt. Here is
   Ravenhill's passage within its surrounding context:

   > Finally, the last thing, the testing of the vessel. I
   > think it's important that we test the vessel through
   > which the word comes. Now, this may sound contra-
   > dictory, but in Deuteronomy chapter 18 and verse 18,
   > it says there that God will speak through his prophet
   > and he'll put his word in his mouth and the test of a
   > prophet is whether that word comes to pass. I believe
   > that that is sort of overridden, if you like, and there's
   > another way of looking at that, if you look at that
   > portion of Scripture. But I believe the test of a
   > prophet is not whether his word comes to pass; it's his
   > lifestyle. It's the character of the individual. That is
   > how you test a prophet. You don't test him by his
   > prophetic word you test him according to the quality
   > or the character of his life. I say that for this reason;
   > because in Deuteronomy chapter 13, a few chapters
   > prior to that, Moses writes this: "If a prophet or a
   > dreamer of dreams arises among you and gives you a
   > sign or a wonder and that sign or wonder comes true
   > concerning which he has spoken to you, saying, 'Let
   > us go after the other gods (whom you have not known)
   > and let us serve them.'"
   > Now notice, here is a prophet or a dreamer, he
   > gives you a sign and a wonder, and there is a fulfill-
   > ment. That sign and wonder comes true. The Bible
   > says that what he's trying to do is deceive you. So it's
   > not a matter of whether the word comes to pass or
   > not; it's the nature of that person's life.

In Matthew chapter 7, and I'll close with this, but Jesus warns there about false prophets and of course we've got another warning there in Matthew chapter 24. But in Matthew 7 verse 15: "Beware of false prophets, who come to you in sheep's clothing." Now notice they come to you appearing like sheep, and it says "but inwardly they are ravenous wolves." Now notice there is something about their makeup, about their nature, their character. Not inwardly, sorry, not outwardly they are giving false prophecies, but inwardly they are corrupt in their nature, their character. And he says "You shall know them by their fruit. Grapes are not gathered from thorn bushes, or figs from thistles, are they? Even so, every good tree bears good fruit; but the bad tree bears bad fruit. A good tree cannot produce bad fruit, nor can a bad tree produce good fruit."

And then he goes on to say, verse 20, "So you will know them by their fruits. Many will say unto Me in that day, 'Lord, Lord, did we not prophesy in Your name, in Your name cast out demons, and in Your name perform many miracles?' And I will declare, 'I never knew you. Depart from Me, you who practice iniquity, a lawlessness.'" Notice their lifestyle did not back up what they were saying with their mouth. These were not backslidden prophets. The Greek word that is used there "depart from Me, I never knew you" means "never, at any time, have I never known you." It wasn't that there was a deterioration in their relationship with the Lord. He says, "I've never known you. Not even at any time have I ever known you." And the test, again, was the fact that they did not have any sort of character.

Furthermore, in response to the first edition of *Counterfeit Revival,* in which I quote Ravenhill precisely as in this revised edition page 89, Ravenhill writes:

What Hank H[anegraaff] printed in his book was
taken out of the context of which I spoke it. I was
seeking to emphasize the importance of character
over gifting and was making reference to
Deuteronomy 13, where is *[sic]* says, "If a prophet or a
dreamer of dreams arises among you and gives you a
sign or a wonder and the sign or wonder comes true . . .
you shall not listen to the words of that prophet or
dreamer of dreams. For the Lord your God is testing
you to find out if you love the Lord your God with all
you heart and all your soul." What I was saying was
that it was possible for a false prophet to give a word
that comes to pass. Therefore the accuracy of the
prophetic word is not always as important as the
character of the one giving it. Hank believes that New
Testament prophecy is to be held to the same scrutiny
as that of the Old Testament prophet. I do not believe
that the Bible teaches that. I believe that it is possible for a New Testament believer to prophecy *[sic]*
and the prophecy be that of mixture, otherwise we
would be exhorted to judge prophecy. This is a *[sic]*
issue that needs much more elaboration than I could
give it at this time. (Scott Volk and David Ravenhill
[IP: 153.34.207.206], ReaperChat, 3 February 1998.)

3. Bob Jones, "The Shepherd's Rod," October 1989, audiotape
   (tape 160).
4. Jack Deere, Toronto Airport Vineyard, 20 November 1994,
   audiotape.
5. Ibid.
6. James Ryle, *Hippo in the Garden* (Orlando, Fla.: Creation
   House, 1993), 96–98.
7. See Jeremiah 18:2; 19:1–11; cf. Zechariah 11:12–13.
8. See Zechariah 12:10; John 19:34.
9. The phrase "the Holy Spirit says" in the New Testament is
   equivalent to statements such as "thus says the Lord" in the
   Old Testament. In both cases, the standards of Deuteronomy
   13 and 18 apply. To assert fallibility at one point is tanta-

mount to accepting fallibility at any point. Both the Old and the New Testaments are perfect representations of what God wanted to say. Fallibility is not an option. (It should go without saying that infallibility refers to God's perfect protection of the autographa. While God's Word does not endorse the lies and mistakes of sinful men and angels, when they are recorded in Scripture, they are recorded accurately.)

10. Ryle wrongly says that the Holy Spirit, through the Christians at Tyre, was telling Paul not to go to Jerusalem. Instead, it is much more contextual to the other related passages in the immediately preceding and succeeding chapters to say that *by the Spirit* the Christians were told that he would be bound if he went to Jerusalem, and so they (on their own) urged him not to go. The parallel to this is Matthew 16:21–22, where Peter learns *by Jesus* that Jesus would die in Jerusalem, and so Peter (on his own) urged Jesus not to go. Just as Peter's sentiment was wrong, even though his information from Jesus was true, so the Tyre Christians' sentiment was wrong, even though their information from the Spirit was true. In fact, in the final analysis, they recognized this, which is why, when Paul persisted, they gave up and said, "Let the will of God be done!"

11. Jonathan Edwards, *The Works of Jonathan Edwards,* ed. Edward Hickman (Carlisle, Pa.: Banner of Truth Trust, 1992; reprint of 1974 edition, first published in 1834), vol. 1, 404.

12. Ibid.

13. Ibid., vol. 2, 260.

14. Ibid., vol. 1, 404 and vol. 2, 275.

Chapter 8 ✦ A Great Apostasy

1. John Arnott, Pastors' Meeting, Toronto Airport Vineyard, 19 October 1994, audiotape.

2. William DeArteaga, *Quenching the Spirit* (Altamonte Springs, Fla.: Creation House, 1992), 52.

3. J. D. Douglas, Philip W. Comfort, and Donald Mitchell, eds., *Who's Who in Christian History* (Wheaton, Ill.: Tyndale House, 1992), 156.

4. William DeArteaga, "What Is Heresy?" Toronto Airport Vineyard, 13 October 1994, audiotape.

5. Nick Needham, *Was Jonathan Edwards the Founding Father of the Toronto Blessing?* (Welling, Kent, England: Nick Needham [self-published], 1995), 20.

6. Jonathan Edwards, *The Works of Jonathan Edwards,* ed. Edward Hickman (Carlisle, Pa.: Banner of Truth Trust, 1834 [1974 edition]), vol. 2, 257–77.

7. My thanks to Dr. Nick Needham for sharing with me his comparison of the Edwards essay with the Counterfeit Revival. Although our analyses are substantially different, they are complementary, and it is to him that I owe the inspiration for making my own comparison.

8. Edwards, *Works of Jonathan Edwards,* vol. 2, 261.

9. Guy Chevreau, *Catch the Fire: The Toronto Blessing—An Experience of Renewal and Revival* (London: Marshall Pickering, 1994), 12–13.

10. Ibid., 13.

11. Ibid.

12. Needham, *Was Jonathan Edwards the Founding Father?* 50.

13. Chevreau, *Catch the Fire,* 12.

14. Edwards described his wife's experience in this way: "Transporting views and rapturous affections were not attended with any enthusiastic disposition to follow impulses, or any supposed prophetical revelations; nor have they been observed to be attended with any appearance of spiritual pride, but very much of a contrary disposition, an increase of humility and meekness, and a disposition of honor to prefer others" (Edwards, *Works of Jonathan Edwards,* vol. 1, 376).

15. Needham, *Was Jonathan Edwards the Founding Father?* 20.

16. Mick Brown, "Unzipper Heaven, Lord," *Telegraph Magazine,* 3 December 1994, 30.

17. Ibid.

18. Mike Taylor, "What Happened Next?" *Evangelicals Now,* February 1995 (transcript), 1.

19. Ibid.

20. Ibid., 8.

21. Ibid.

22. Needham, *Was Jonathan Edwards the Founding Father?* 20.
23. Edwards, *Works of Jonathan Edwards,* vol. 2, 261.
24. Julia Duin, "Praise the Lord and Pass the New Wine," *Charisma,* August 1994, 24.
25. Julia Duin, "An Evening with Rodney Howard-Browne," *Christian Research Journal,* Winter 1995, 44.
26. Edwards, *Works of Jonathan Edwards,* vol. 2, 261.
27. Ibid.
28. Duin, "An Evening with Rodney Howard-Browne," 44; and John Arnott, Discovery Church, Orlando, Fla., evening service 29 January 1995, audiotape.
29. Needham, *Was Jonathan Edwards the Founding Father?* 11.
30. Edwards, *Works of Jonathan Edwards,* vol. 2, 262.
31. John Arnott, *The Father's Blessing* (Orlando, Fla.: Creation House, 1995), 230.
32. John Arnott, "Moving into Increasing Anointing," *Spread the Fire* 1, no. 3 (May–June 1995).
33. Arnott, *Father's Blessing,* 220.
34. Arnott, "Moving into Increasing Anointing." Arnott goes so far as to claim that this is a prophetic word received by Lois Gott. In *Father's Blessing* (p. 224) Arnott says Gott came to Toronto from an Assembly of God church in Sunderland, England, and got "thoroughly blasted."
35. Rick Joyner, *The Harvest* (Pineville, N.C.: MorningStar, 1990), 9.
36. Arius was a presbyter to Bishop Alexander of Alexandria and the founder of the heresy commonly referred to as Arianism. Arius taught that (1) the Father existed before the Son; (2) there was a time when the Son did not exist; (3) the Son was created by the Father and as such was the highest of all creatures but did not have the same nature or essence as the Creator.
37. Edwards, *Works of Jonathan Edwards,* vol. 2, 263.
38. James Ryle, *A Dream Come True* (Orlando, Fla.: Creation House, 1995), 15.
39. Ibid.
40. Ibid. Ryle has gone so far as to brand those who, like me, would criticize his position as the "very kind of people who crucified Christ. They are scribes and Pharisees, religious

and angry, attacking and persecuting anyone who dares to differ from their exclusive views." For Ryle to quote approvingly from Kelsey is at best irresponsible, and at worst it is tacit agreement with the unbiblical views that permeate Kelsey's writings.

41. Morton Kelsey, *The Christian and the Supernatural* (Minneapolis, Minn.: Augsburg, 1976), 92–95, as quoted in John Ankerberg and John Weldon, *Encyclopedia of New Age Beliefs* (Eugene, Ore.: Harvest House, 1996), 200.

42. Ibid.

43. Carlos Castaneda became a wildly popular author during the late 1960s and early 1970s for his fanciful recountings of his supposed apprenticeship to a Native American shaman or sorcerer named Don Juan. Although his story was exposed as completely untrue, he remains a popular author today among New Agers and occultists. Further information on his historical revisionism is available in Bob Passantino, *Fantasies, Legends, and Heroes* (Costa Mesa, Calif.: Answers in Action, 1990).

44. As quoted in John Ankerberg and John Weldon, *Encyclopedia of New Age Beliefs* (Eugene, Ore.: Harvest House, 1996), 206.

45. Carlos Castaneda, *The Art of Dreaming* (New York: HarperCollins, 1993), 125.

46. Ibid., 110.

47. Edwards, *Works of Jonathan Edwards,* vol. 2, 263.

48. Ibid.

49. Ibid.

50. Ibid.

51. John Arnott, "The Love of God," Vineyard Christian Fellowship, Mission Viejo, Calif., 17 July 1995, audiotape (tape 621).

52. Edwards, *Works of Jonathan Edwards,* vol. 2, 264.

53. Ibid.

54. Larry Randolph, "Renewal and Revival Today," Toronto Airport Vineyard, 18 November 1994, audiotape.

55. Ibid.

56. *Morning Star Prophetic Bulletin,* May 1996.

57. Ibid.
58. Ibid.
59. Ibid.
60. Edwards, *Works of Jonathan Edwards,* vol. 2, 265.
61. Ibid.
62. Joyner, *The Harvest,* 96.
63. Ibid., 133.
64. Ibid., 134.
65. Ibid., 15–16.
66. William DeArteaga, Toronto Airport Vineyard, 13 October 1994, audiotape. See also William DeArteaga, *Quenching the Spirit,* 2nd ed. (Orlando, Fla.: Creation House, 1996), 16–26. DeArteaga explains his pejorative use of the terms *Pharisee* and *orthodoxy:* "A Pharisee is a deeply religious person who, among other things, staunchly asserts and defends the status quo with regard to tradition, order and *consensus orthodoxy.* I use the term consensus orthodoxy . . . to refer to the theological interpretations accepted by most people of the day. . . . The Pharisee exaggerates the traditions and truths of consensus orthodoxy in order to oppose any new work of the Holy Spirit" (italics in original; *Quenching the Spirit,* 16).

    Historically, the Pharisees were a significant religious and political party in Jesus' day who, for the most part, rejected Christ and attributed Christ's works to Beelzebub, or Satan. Orthodoxy (with a small *o)* in reality simply means "right teaching" and is used in general by evangelicals to refer to that body of beliefs which forms the core of our Christian confession or the essence of the Christian world-view without which there would be no Christian faith.

67. Ibid. It is not as though all biblically sound doctrine is irrelevant to DeArteaga. I doubt that he would include within his view of Christian unity those who reject, for example, Jesus' deity, incarnation, atoning death, or resurrection. The problem, ironically, is that he is unbalanced in the other extreme. He holds to a "consensus orthodoxy" or "consensus interpretation" of his own, which dictates that belief in the working of the Holy Spirit in believers today as

broadly understood by Counterfeit Revivalists is essential to genuine faith.

68. Edwards, *Works of Jonathan Edwards,* vol. 2, 265.
69. Ibid.
70. Comments made by James Ryle subsequent to his appearance on John Leoffler's radio program "Steel on Steel" in February 1995, e-mail transcript.
71. Paul Crouch, "Praise-a-Thon" program on TBN, 2 April 1991.
72. Marc Dupont, "The Father's Heart and the Prophetic," Toronto Airport Vineyard, 16 November 1994, audiotape; and "Prophetic School, Part 3," Pastors' Meeting, Toronto Airport Vineyard, 16 November 1994, audiotape.
73. Edwards, *Works of Jonathan Edwards,* vol. 2, 265.
74. Ibid.
75. Ibid., 266.
76. Randy Clark, "Catch the Fire," Toronto Airport Vineyard, 14 October 1994, audiotape.
77. J. I. Packer popularized the word *eudaemonism* in his magnificent little book *Hot Tub Religion* (Wheaton, Ill.: Tyndale House, 1987), 75.
78. Ibid.
79. Arnott, *Father's Blessing,* 175.
80. Mark Noll, *The Scandal of the Evangelical Mind* (Grand Rapids, Mich.: Eerdmans, 1994), 77.
81. Clyde E. Fant Jr. and William M. Pinson Jr., *A Treasury of Great Preaching* (Dallas, Tex.: Word, 1995), vol. 3, 101.
82. Ibid., 102.
83. Edwards, *Works of Jonathan Edwards,* vol. 2, 265.
84. Ibid., 265–66.

Chapter 9 ✦ A Great Awakening

1. Rodney Howard-Browne, *The Coming Revival* (Louisville, Ky.: RHBEA Publications, 1991), 24.
2. Bill Bright, *The Coming Revival* (Orlando, Fla.: New Life Publications, 1995), 155.
3. Robert Coleman, *The Coming World Revival* (Wheaton, Ill.: Crossway Books, 1995), 160.

4. Jonathan Edwards, *The Works of Jonathan Edwards,* ed. Edward Hickman (Carlisle, Pa.: Banner of Truth Trust, 1992; reprint of 1974 edition, first published in 1834), vol. 2, 266.

5. John Arnott, *The Father's Blessing* (Orlando, Fla.: Creation House, 1995), 28.

6. Jonathan Edwards, "Christian Love," in Clyde E. Fant Jr. and William M. Pinson Jr., *A Treasury of Great Preaching* (Dallas, Tex.: Word, 1995), vol. 3, 93.

7. Rodney Howard-Browne, *The Touch of God* (Louisville, Ky.: RHBEA Publications, 1992), 13–14.

8. Edwards, *Works of Jonathan Edwards,* vol. 2, 277–78.

9. Ibid., 267.

10. Benny Hinn, "Praise the Lord," 8 November 1990, audiotape. Despite alleged repentances in the early 1990s Hinn continues to promote a prosperity message. For example, Hinn states, "When Israel begins to prosper, the church will prosper . . . and the church then will see the wealth of the sinner dropped in our lap to preach the gospel, to get it to the ends of the earth" (*Praise the Lord,* Trinity Broadcasting Network, 20 December 2000). See also the many evidences presented in G. Richard Fisher and M. Kurt Goedelman, *The Confusing World of Benny Hinn,* rev. ed. (St. Louis: Personal Freedom Outreach, 1996), 93–159.

11. Benny Hinn, "Praise the Lord," 8 July 1996, audiotape.

12. Bob Jones and Paul Cain, "Selections of the Kansas City Prophets" (tape 155C).

13. Ibid.

14. Ibid.

15. Rick Joyner, *The Harvest* (Pineville, N.C.: MorningStar, 1990), 128–29.

16. Ibid.

17. Howard-Browne, *Coming Revival,* 24–28.

18. Kenneth Hagin, "Rejoice! This Is the Day Which the Lord Hath Made!" *The Word of Faith,* July 1996, 16.

19. Edwards, *Works of Jonathan Edwards,* vol. 2, 267.

20. Edythe Draper, *Edythe Draper's Book of Quotations* (Wheaton, Ill.: Tyndale House, 1992), 305.

21. Edwards, *Works of Jonathan Edwards,* vol. 2, 267.
22. John Wimber, "Healing: An Introduction" (audiotape no. 5), as quoted in Stephen F. Cannon, "Kansas City Fellowship Revisited: The Controversy Continues," *Personal Freedom Outreach* 11, no. 1 (1991).
23. John Wimber, "Healing: An Introduction" (audiotape no. 5) and "Church Planting Seminar," as quoted in Stephen F. Cannon, "Kansas City Fellowship Revisited."
24. Edwards, *Works of Jonathan Edwards,* vol. 2, 267.
25. Ibid., 266.
26. Walter A. Elwell, ed., *Evangelical Dictionary of Theology* (Grand Rapids, Mich.: Baker Book House, 1984), 431.
27. Stanley M. Burgess and Gary B. McGee, eds., *Dictionary of Pentecostal and Charismatic Movements* (Grand Rapids, Mich.: Zondervan, 1988), 889. In the early nineteenth century, Quakerism underwent a split between those who sought a more biblically rooted faith, which included a commitment to the final authority of Scripture, and those who retained the views of George Fox, especially his teachings regarding "inner light." While Wimber was involved with the more evangelical branch of Quakerism, one could only wish he had adhered to his expressed commitment to the final authority of Scripture. As I demonstrate in this volume (see esp. chap. 19), Wimber in practice did manifest significant Quakerisms of Fox.
28. Todd Hunter, "Revival in Focus," Mission Viejo Vineyard, Mission Viejo, Calif., 23 October 1994, audiotape.
29. Edwards, *Works of Jonathan Edwards,* vol. 2, 267–68.
30. Ibid., 268.
31. Carol Arnott, "Receiving the Spirit's Power," *Together for the Kingdom '95,* Thursday afternoon, audiotape (tape 793C). James Beverley writes that Carol Arnott has "admitted that her statement (about the Holy Spirit missing Jesus) was expressed carelessly" (James A. Beverley, *Revival Wars* [Toronto: Evangelical Research Ministries, 1997], 34).
32. Edwards, *Works of Jonathan Edwards,* vol. 2, 260.
33. John Arnott, Toronto Airport Vineyard, 16 December 1994, audiotape.

34. Jesse Duplantis, "Close Encounters of the God Kind" (New Orleans, La.: Jesse Duplantis Ministries), audiotape.

35. Edwards, *Works of Jonathan Edwards,* vol. 2, 268.

36. Ibid., 260.

37. Ibid., 268.

38. Arnott, *Father's Blessing,* 20.

39. John Arnott, Discovery Church, Orlando, Fla., 29 January 1995, audiotape.

40. Arnott, *Father's Blessing,* 26.

41. Ibid., 163–65.

42. Edwards, *Works of Jonathan Edwards,* vol. 2, 268.

43. Ibid.

44. Iain H. Murray, *Jonathan Edwards: A New Biography* (Carlisle, Pa.: Banner of Truth Trust, 1987), 216. Indeed, Edwards warned that such "wildfire" has commonly halted genuine revival throughout church history:

> If we look back into the history of the church of God in past ages, we may observe that it has been a common device of the devil, to overset a revival of religion; when he finds he can keep men quiet and secure no longer, then he drives them to excesses and extravagances. He holds them back as long as he can; but when he can do it no longer, then he will push them on, and, if possible, run them upon their heads. And it has been by this means chiefly that he has been successful, in several instances, to overthrow most hopeful and promising beginnings. Yea, the principal means by which the devil was successful, by degrees, to overset the grand religious revival of the world, in the primitive ages of Christianity, and in a manner to overthrow the Christian church through the earth, and to make way for the great Anti-Christian apostasy, that master-piece of all the devil's works, was to improve the indiscreet zeal of Christians, to drive them into those three extremes of *enthusiasm, superstition,* and *severity towards opposers;* which should be enough for an everlasting warning to the Christian church (Edwards, *Works of Jonathan Edwards,* vol. 1, 397–98, emphasis in original.)

45. H. S. Stout, "Great Awakening," in Daniel G. Reid, Robert D. Linder, Bruce L. Shelley, and Harry S. Stout, eds., *Dictionary of Christianity in America* (Downers Grove, Ill.: InterVarsity Press, 1990), 495.

46. Os Guinness, *Fit Bodies, Fat Minds* (Grand Rapids, Mich.: Baker Book House, 1994), 47.

47. George C. Bedell, Leo Sandon, Jr., and Charles T. Wellborn, *Religion in America* (New York: Macmillan, 1975), 153.

Chapter 10 ✦ A Muddy Mixture

1. Keith J. Hardman, *Seasons of Refreshing* (Grand Rapids, Mich.: Baker Book House, 1994), 128.

2. Ibid., 129.

3. Ibid.

4. Ibid., 130.

5. Mark Galli, "Revival at Cane Ridge," *Christian History,* issue 45, XIV, 1 (1995): 10.

6. Ibid.

7. Stone "was sharply criticized for his unorthodox views, which included a denial of the Trinity. 'The word *Trinity*,' he said, 'is not found in the Bible.' So he refused to accept 'that the Son of God was very and eternal God and yet eternally begotten.' Stone's view became the stated cause of his later disassociation with the Trinitarian Presbyterians." David L. Goetz, "Trendsetters in the Religious Wilderness," *Christian History,* issue 45, XIV, 1 (1995): 27.

8. Vinson Synan, *The Holiness-Pentecostal Movement in the United States* (Grand Rapids, Mich.: Eerdmans, 1971), 24.

9. Hardman, *Seasons of Refreshing,* 134–35.

10. "Did You Know," *Christian History,* issue 45, XIV, 1 (1995): 2.

11. Ibid.

12. George C. Bedell, Leo Sandon Jr., and Charles T. Wellborn, *Religion in America* (New York: Macmillan, 1975), 159–60.

Chapter 11 ✦ Endtime Restoration of Tongues

1. Vinson Synan, *The Holiness-Pentecostal Movement in the United States* (Grand Rapids, Mich.: Eerdmans, 1971), 101.
2. Ibid.
3. Sincere Christian believers are divided on this theological issue. Some believe that the "gifts of the Spirit" ceased at the close of the apostolic age or with the closing of the canon of Scripture. Others do not believe there is clear biblical evidence that they ever ceased. In any case, the "prostitution" of the gift of tongues only serves to bring unnecessary division. This is an issue we may vigorously debate, but over which we should never divide.
4. Synan, *Holiness-Pentecostal Movement,* 102.
5. Ibid., 102–3.
6. Ibid., 111.
7. Ibid., 103.
8. Stanley M. Burgess and Gary B. McGee, eds., *Dictionary of Pentecostal and Charismatic Movements* (Grand Rapids, Mich.: Zondervan, 1988), 778.
9. Synan, *Holiness-Pentecostal Movement,* 103.
10. Ibid.
11. Daniel G. Reid, Robert D. Linder, Bruce L. Shelley, and Harry S. Stout, *Dictionary of Christianity in America* (Downers Grove, Ill.: InterVarsity Press, 1990), 865.
12. Synan, *Holiness-Pentecostal Movement,* 106.
13. Ibid.
14. Ibid., 95.
15. Ibid., 110.
16. Ibid., 112.
17. Ibid.
18. Ibid.
19. Ibid., 180.
20. Ibid., 109.
21. Rick Joyner, "Azusa Street, the Fire That Could Not Die," *Morning Star Journal* 6, no. 4 (1996): 63.
22. Ibid., 69.
23. Ibid.
24. Ibid., 62.

Chapter 12 ✦ Endtime Restoration of Healing

1. Todd Hunter, "Revival in Focus," Mission Viejo Vineyard, Mission Viejo, Calif., 23 October 1994, audiotape.
2. Ibid.
3. Ibid. I received a letter from Todd Hunter 15 February, 1997 in which Hunter indicated that his intent was not to extol the virtues of Azusa Street nor to lift up Allen, Branham, or Coe as models to emulate. Hunter went on to write, "I would be horrified for Vineyard pastors to in any way follow their models."

   In truth, however, Hunter did extol Azusa Street during his sermon, going so far as to say, "Well, from Azusa Street to today the Pentecostals have been *the* largest, most dynamic force of Christians on the earth. And one of the things that I've been saying to my friends is I'm sick and tired of being impugned about being a Pentecostal. You know, they like, spit when they say it. *You guys are just Ppppentecostals.* And I'm starting to say, 'Well, heck, there's a whole lot worse things to be called than Pentecostal.' I mean, they really have shook the earth. Pentecostals are now *the* largest group of Christians on the face of the earth. They have been responsible for literally hundreds of millions of conversions in our century. In the first three years of Azusa Street it is estimated that 1.8 million people were touched and converted to Christ. Reconverted, converted, whatever, but they've got on fire for Christ. 1.8 million people in 3 years." (emphasis in original)

   Here is what Hunter originally said about Allen, Branham, and Coe: "Well, now you come down to about 1940 and the Healing Revival. And you have people like William Branham and Jack Coe and A. A. Allen and others who were—they thought of themselves as evangelists because so much healing happened in their meetings that they started being known as healing evangelists. Well, they're also thought of as Pentecostals, right? When I mention those names, don't you think of Pentecostals? Well, but they had some renewing influences in mainline Christianity at that time. But they didn't really have a vision for renewing the church. They were just Pentecostal evangelists out doing their thing. But occasionally they would touch a Presbyterian, a Lutheran, a Methodist, somebody like that, and they would get, quote, 'renewed.'"

4. Michael Moriarty, *The New Charismatics* (Grand Rapids, Mich.: Zondervan, 1992), 35.

5. David Edwin Harrell Jr., *All Things Are Possible: The Healing and Charismatic Revivals in Modern America* (Bloomington: Indiana University Press, 1975), 199.

6. A hermaphrodite has physiological characteristics of both genders.

7. Harrell, *All Things Are Possible,* 198–99.

8. Ibid., 198.

9. Ibid.

10. Stanley M. Burgess and Gary B. McGee, eds., *Dictionary of Pentecostal and Charismatic Movements* (Grand Rapids, Mich.: Zondervan, 1988), 8.

11. Harrell, *All Things Are Possible,* 200.

12. Ibid., 201.

13. Moriarty, *New Charismatics,* 38.

14. Harrell, *All Things Are Possible,* 75.

15. Benny Hinn, *Praise the Lord,* telecast by Trinity Broadcasting Network, 12 April 1991, audiotape.

16. Moriarty, *New Charismatics,* 35.

17. Harrell, *All Things Are Possible,* 71.

18. Ibid., 70.

19. Ibid., 72.

20. Burgess and McGee, *Pentecostal and Charismatic Movements,* 8.

21. Rodney Howard-Browne, *Fresh Oil from Heaven* (Louisville, Ky.: RHBEA Publications, 1992), 23.

22. Bob Jones and Paul Cain, "Selections from the Kansas City Prophets," audiotape (tape 155C). Benny Hinn includes Branham and A. A. Allen among his list of great men and women of God: "God uses normal individuals, whether it's Smith-Wigglesworth or Katherine Kuhlman or Aimee [Semple McPherson], or A. A. Allen or William Branham. Great men of God!" (*Praise the Lord,* Trinity Broadcasting

Network, 19 June 1989). James Beverley acknowledges that Jack Deere, too, cites Branham approvingly (James A. Beverley, *Revival Wars* [Toronto: Evangelical Research Ministries, 1997], 22).

23. Daniel G. Reid, Robert D. Linder, Bruce L. Shelley, and Harry S. Stout, *Dictionary of Christianity in America* (Downers Grove, Ill.: InterVarsity Press, 1990), 182. This is confirmed in Burgess and McGee, *Pentecostal and Charismatic Movements,* 95.

24. According to Harrell (*All Things Are Possible,* 27), Gordon Lindsay reported that the angelic visitation was in a furnished room while Burgess and McGee (*Pentecostal and Charismatic Movements,* 95) report that the angelic visitation was in a cave.

25. Harrell, *All Things Are Possible,* 28, emphasis in original.

26. Ibid., 37.

27. Reid et al., *Dictionary of Christianity in America,* 182.

28. Harrell, *All Things Are Possible,* 38.

29. Ibid., 37.

30. Ibid., 160.

31. Ibid., 163.

32. Moriarty, *New Charismatics,* 55–56.

33. Michael Moriarty provides an excellent overview on the impact of Branham's endtime restorationism as well as his beliefs concerning the messengers of the churches of the Book of Revelation. See Moriarty, *New Charismatics,* 47–56.

34. Burgess and McGee, *Pentecostal and Charismatic Movements,* 96.

35. Ibid.

36. Ibid., 95. The Oneness Pentecostals deny the biblical doctrine of the Trinity, confusing the persons of the Trinity so that they teach only the Father is God. This heresy, modalism, has been condemned throughout church history.

37. Ibid., 95–96.

38. Moriarty, *New Charismatics,* 55.

39. Harrell, *All Things Are Possible,* 164.

40. Reid et al., *Dictionary of Christianity in America,* 182.

41. Burgess and McGee, *Pentecostal and Charismatic Movements,* 96.

42. Jack Deere, "Intimacy with God and the End Time Church," Vineyard Fellowship, Denver, Colo., 1989, audiotape (session 2B, side 1).
43. Harrell, *All Things Are Possible,* 59.
44. Ibid.
45. Ibid., 91.
46. Ibid., 101.
47. Ibid., 100.
48. Ibid., 59.
49. Ibid., 111.
50. Ibid., 112.
51. Ibid., 101.
52. Reid et al., *Dictionary of Christianity in America,* 295; and Burgess and McGee, *Pentecostal and Charismatic Movements,* 223.
53. Harrell, *All Things Are Possible,* 62.
54. Ibid., 79.
55. Ibid., 63.
56. Ibid., 140–41.
57. Ibid., 142.
58. Ibid., 143.

Chapter 13 ✦ Endtime Restoration of Charismatic Unity

1. Stanley M. Burgess and Gary B. McGee, eds., *Dictionary of Pentecostal and Charismatic Movements* (Grand Rapids, Mich.: Zondervan, 1988), 250.
2. Ibid., 251.
3. David L. Smith, *A Handbook of Contemporary Theology* (Wheaton, Ill.: Victor Books, 1992), 119.
4. Michael Moriarty, *The New Charismatics* (Grand Rapids, Mich.: Zondervan, 1992), 68.
5. Burgess and McGee, *Pentecostal and Charismatic Movements,* 252.
6. Ibid., 253.
7. Moriarty, *New Charismatics,* 68.

8. Burgess and McGee, *Pentecostal and Charismatic Movements,* 132.

9. Ibid.

10. Ibid., 133.

11. Todd Hunter, "Revival in Focus," Mission Viejo Vineyard, Mission Viejo, Calif., 23 October 1994, audiotape. Agnes Sanford popularized "inner healing" and "healing of the memories" in charismatic circles. Her controversial blending of Jungian psychology and mystical Christianity created a heretical pantheistic concept of God. Bob Mumford is distinguished among charismatics as a strong proponent of church authoritarianism. While he renounced his more obviously unbiblical "shepherding" teachings from the late 1970s and early 1980s, his persistent advocacy of personal accountability in every area of life for each Christian to a more mature Christian has remained problematic.

12. Ibid.

13. Jack Deere, "Intimacy with God and the End Time Church," Vineyard Christian Fellowship, Denver, Colo., 1989, audiotape (session 2A).

14. Paul Cain, "God Speaking the Second Time," Leadership Conference, General Session, Grace Ministries, Grandview, Mo., 1990, audiotape.

15. Paul Cain, "Prophecy for the Vineyard," Vineyard Christian Fellowship, Anaheim, Calif., February 1989, audiotape (tape 3).

Chapter 14 ✦ Endtime Restoration of Super Prophets and Apostles

1. Fuller Seminary's C. Peter Wagner coined this term in an interview in *Pastoral Renewal* (July–August 1983, 1–5) to refer to "a new stage . . . of the Holy Spirit's work in this century. The first, Dr. Wagner noted, was the Pentecostal movement at the turn of the century. The second, popularly known as the charismatic renewal, began in the sixties and touched mainline Protestants and Catholics. He predicted a third wave affecting evangelical Protestants" (John Wimber with Kevin Springer, *Power Evangelism* [San Francisco: Harper & Row, 1986], 122).

2. Michael Maudlin, "Seers in the Heartland," *Christianity Today,* 14 January 1991, 21.
3. Ibid., 18.
4. John Wimber, "Speaking on Paul Cain and the Office of the Prophet," Vineyard Christian Fellowship, Anaheim, Calif., 19 February 1989, audiotape.
5. Ibid.
6. Ibid.
7. Jack Deere, "Intimacy with God and the End Time Church," Vineyard Christian Fellowship, Denver, Colo., 1989, audiotape (session 2A).
8. Paul Cain, "Prophecy for the Vineyard," Vineyard Christian Fellowship, Anaheim, Calif., February 1989, audiotape (tape 3).
9. Wimber, "Speaking on Paul Cain," audiotape.
10. Ibid.
11. Ibid.
12. Mike Bickle, Regional Pastors' Conference, Vineyard Christian Fellowship, Newport Beach, Calif., 1989, audiotape (session 2G). While Mike Bickle claims Cain's "chemistry was changed *instantaneously,*" Wimber claims that God "took all sexual desire out of his body" during a *subsequent* meeting."
13. Ibid.
14. Wimber, "Speaking on Paul Cain," audiotape.
15. Paul Cain, "Selections from the Kansas City Prophets," audiotape (tape 155C).
16. John Wimber, "Speaking on Paul Cain," audiotape.
17. In April 1992, Cho rejected the name Paul and changed it to David. See "People & Events: Yonggi Cho Changes His Name," *Charisma,* November 1992, 80.
18. Mike Bickle, Regional Pastors' Conference, Vineyard Christian Fellowship, Newport Beach, Calif., 1989, audiotape (session 2G).
19. Paul Cain, "Prophecy for the Vineyard," audiotape (tape 3); and Mike Bickle, Regional Pastors' Conference, Vineyard Christian Fellowship, Newport Beach, Calif., 1989, audiotape (session 2G).

20. Deere, "Intimacy with God and the End Time Church," audiotape (session 2A).
21. Ibid.
22. Wimber, "Speaking on Paul Cain," audiotape.
23. Ibid.
24. Public statement from John Wimber, 12 November 1991, Association of Vineyard Churches.
25. John Wimber, "A Biblical Approach to Fallen Leaders," Vineyard Ministries International, Anaheim, Calif., 10 November 1991, audiotape.
26. Mike Bickle, "Public Disciplining of Bob Jones," Metro Vineyard Fellowship, Grandview, Mo., 1990, audiotape.
27. Paul Cain, "God Speaking the Second Time," Leadership Conference, General Session, Grace Ministries, Grandview, Mo., 1990, audiotape.
28. Bickle, Regional Pastors' Conference, Vineyard Christian Fellowship, Newport Beach, Calif., 1989, audiotape (session 2G).
29. Ibid.
30. Wes Campbell, Toronto Airport Vineyard, 14 October 1994, audiotape.
31. Ibid.
32. Ibid.
33. Ibid. It should be noted that in a phone conversation I had with James Ryle on 5 June 1995, Ryle further clarified "blue stands for revelatory" in that blue represents the sky from which God's revelations come and gray represents the reasoning of men with their heads. He also pointed out that he does not hold to the sharp dichotomy of head versus heart that is being proclaimed by the leaders of the Toronto Blessing.
34. Conversation with James Ryle, 5 June 1995.
35. Rick Joyner, *The Morning Star Prophetic Bulletin,* May 1996, 2.
36. Ibid., 5.
37. Ibid., 3.
38. Ibid., 7.
39. Ibid., 3.
40. Ibid., 6.
41. Ibid., 2.

Chapter 15 ✦ Endtime Restoration Hoaxes

1. Rodney Howard-Browne, New Life Christian Fellowship, Jacksonville, Fla., 10 November 1994, audiotape.
2. Kenneth Copeland and Rodney Howard-Browne, Southwest Believers' Convention, Kenneth Copeland Ministries, Ft. Worth, Tex., 5 August 1993, videotape.
3. Todd Hunter, "Revival in Focus," Mission Viejo Vineyard, Mission Viejo, Calif., 23 October 1994, audiotape.
4. Bob Jones and Paul Cain, "Selections from the Kansas City Prophets," audiotape.
5. Ibid.
6. Cited in Hank Hanegraaff, "Frauds, Fictions, Fantasies, and Fabrications," *Christian Research Journal* (Winter 1996): 55.
7. For a comprehensive biblical analysis of "healing in the atonement," see Hank Hanegraaff, *Christianity in Crisis* (Eugene, Ore.: Harvest House, 1993), 235–37.
8. Paul Cain, "Selections from the Kansas City Prophets," audiotape (tape 155C). For reference to the "new breed of men," see John Wimber, "Speaking on Paul Cain and the Office of the Prophet," Vineyard Christian Fellowship, 19 February 1989, audiotape.
9. Rick Joyner, *The Harvest* (Pineville, N.C.: MorningStar, 1989), 26.
10. Jones and Cain, "Selections from the Kansas City Prophets," audiotape.
11. Bob Jones, "An Interview with Bob Jones by Mike Bickle," Kansas City Prophets, Kansas City, Mo., 1989, audiotape.

Chapter 16 ✦ Sisters

1. Benny Hinn, *Praise the Lord* program, Trinity Broadcasting Network, 12 June 1996, audiotape.
2. Stanley M. Burgess and Gary B. McGee, eds., *Dictionary of Pentecostal and Charismatic Movements* (Grand Rapids, Mich.: Zondervan, 1988), 900.
3. Benny Hinn, *Praise the Lord*, 12 June 1996.
4. Burgess and McGee, *Pentecostal and Charismatic Movements*, 901.

5. Kenneth Hagin, *Why Do People Fall under the Power?* (Tulsa, Okla.: Kenneth Hagin Ministries, 1981), 4–5.

6. Burgess and McGee, *Pentecostal and Charismatic Movements*, 901.

7. Maria Woodworth-Etter, *A Diary of Signs and Wonders* (Tulsa, Okla.: Harrison House, 1916), 48.

8. Burgess and McGee, *Pentecostal and Charismatic Movements*, 900.

9. Long before Counterfeit Revivalists like Paul Cain and Bob Jones "revealed" Joel's endtime army, Maria Woodworth-Etter preached the same ideas using the same terminology. (See, for example, her sermon titled "The Outpouring of the Holy Spirit in the Last Days—according to Joel's Prophecy," *Diary of Signs and Wonders,* 528–36.)

10. Burgess and McGee, *Pentecostal and Charismatic Movements*, 789–90.

11. Woodworth-Etter, *Diary of Signs and Wonders,* 48.

12. Ibid., 66.

13. Edith L. Blumhofer, *Aimee Semple McPherson: Everybody's Sister* (Grand Rapids, Mich.: Eerdmans, 1993), 140.

14. She preferred being called simply "Sister" (Blumhofer, *Aimee Semple McPherson,* 2).

15. Aimee Semple McPherson, *This Is That* (Los Angeles: Echo Park Evangelistic Association, 1923), 90–91.

16. Blumhofer, *Aimee Semple McPherson,* 3.

17. McPherson, *This Is That,* 91.

18. Daniel Mark Epstein, *Sister Aimee: The Life of Aimee Semple McPherson* (New York: Harcourt Brace Jovanovich, 1993), 437–38.

19. Wayne E. Warner, *Kathryn Kuhlman* (Ann Arbor, Mich.: Servant Books, 1993), 205.

20. Ibid., 203.

21. Ibid., 205.

22. Burgess and McGee, *Pentecostal and Charismatic Movements*, 529–30.

23. Warner, *Kathryn Kuhlman,* 81.

24. Information on this period of Kathryn's life is in Warner, *Kathryn Kuhlman,* 79–111.

25. Burgess and McGee, *Pentecostal and Charismatic Movements*, 529.
26. Warner, *Kathryn Kuhlman*, 215.
27. Ibid., 220.
28. Ibid., 214–15.
29. Ibid., 214.

Chapter 17 ✦ Suspect Slayings

1. Benny Hinn, *Good Morning, Holy Spirit* (Nashville, Tenn.: Thomas Nelson, 1990), 9, 11–12.
2. Benny Hinn, *The Anointing* (Nashville, Tenn.: Thomas Nelson, 1992), 57.
3. Ibid., 59.
4. Hinn, *Good Morning, Holy Spirit,* 42.
5. Hinn, *The Anointing,* 25.
6. Ibid., 26.
7. Ibid.
8. John Arnott and Guy Chevreau, Pastors' Meeting, Toronto Airport Vineyard, 19 October 1994, audiotape.
9. John Arnott, Discovery Church, Orlando, Fla., 29 January 1995, audiotape.
10. Wayne E. Warner, *Kathryn Kuhlman* (Ann Arbor, Mich.: Servant Books, 1993), 220.
11. Benny Hinn, "Double Portion Anointing, Part 3," Orlando Christian Center, Orlando, Fla., audiotape (A031791-3, sides 1–2, aired on TBN, 7 April 1991).
12. Jamie Buckingham, *Daughter of Destiny* (Plainfield, N.J.: Logos, 1976), 281.
13. Hinn, *The Anointing*, 98.
14. G. Richard Fisher, Stephen F. Cannon, and M. Kurt Goedelman, "Benny Hinn's Anointing: Heaven Sent or Borrowed?" *The Quarterly Journal, Personal Freedom Outreach* 12, no. 3 (July–September 1992): 12.
15. Francis MacNutt, *Overcome by the Spirit* (Grand Rapids, Mich.: Chosen Books, 1990), 171.
16. Physical or psychological carnage is not limited to people being crushed or killed when they fall. Rather, it extends to

those who erroneously believe they have been healed of
cancer, heart disease, diabetes, or other diseases and to
those who become spiritually vulnerable because they trust
their experience of being slain in the Spirit. (See chapter 22
for an extensive treatment of the psychological dangers of
altered states of consciousness.)

17. MacNutt, *Overcome by the Spirit,* 18.
18. Ibid., 19–20.
19. Ibid., 27.
20. Ibid., 25–26.

Chapter 18 ✦ Shakers and Quakers

1. Stanley M. Burgess and Gary B. McGee, eds., *Dictionary of Pentecostal and Charismatic Movements* (Grand Rapids, Mich.: Zondervan, 1988), 789.
2. Ibid.
3. Peter Cartwright, *Autobiography of Peter Cartwright,* as quoted in George C. Bedell, Leo Sandon Jr., and Charles T. Wellborn, *Religion in America* (New York: Macmillan, 1975), 159–60.
4. Burgess and McGee, *Pentecostal and Charismatic Movements,* 783.
5. Francis MacNutt, *Overcome by the Spirit* (Grand Rapids, Mich.: Chosen Books, 1990), 105–06.
6. Although the Shakers were notable for their "bodily enthusiasms," in this particular passage Knox is not even referring to the antics of the Shakers. He is quoting remarks on the Cane Ridge Revival enthusiasts, some of whom *later* became Shakers.
7. H. Caswell, as quoted in Ronald A. Knox, *Enthusiasm: A Chapter in the History of Religion* (Notre Dame, Ind.: University of Notre Dame Press, 1950), 560–61.
8. Knox, *Enthusiasm,* 559.
9. Ibid.
10. Burgess and McGee, *Pentecostal and Charismatic Movements,* 782.
11. Ibid.

12. Ibid., 783.
13. Knox, *Enthusiasm,* 560.
14. MacNutt, *Overcome by the Spirit,* 100.
15. John Wesley's *Journal,* as quoted in Knox, *Enthusiasm,* 533.
16. Ibid., 525.
17. John Wesley's *Journal,* as quoted in Nick Needham, "Appendix: Holy Laughter—The Experience of John Wesley," in *Was Jonathan Edwards the Founding Father of the Toronto Blessing?* (Welling, Kent, England: self-published, 1995), 39.
18. MacNutt, *Overcome by the Spirit,* 99.
19. Knox, *Enthusiasm,* 151.
20. Ibid., 157–59.
21. Ibid., 156.
22. MacNutt, *Overcome by the Spirit,* 112.

Chapter 19 ✦ Seven Scriptural Pretexts

1. Francis MacNutt, *Overcome by the Spirit* (Grand Rapids, Mich.: Chosen Books, 1990), 160.
2. John Wimber, "Spiritual Phenomena: Slain in the Spirit— Part 1," Vineyard Christian Fellowship, Anaheim, Calif., 1981, audiotape.
3. Ibid.
4. Ibid.
5. John Wimber says he prefers the phrase "resting in the Spirit."
6. Wimber, "Spiritual Phenomena: Slain in the Spirit—Part 1," audiotape.
7. In addition to consulting commonly cited Hebrew scholarship, I also interviewed a Jewish rabbi who is well known for his skill in biblical Hebrew. Rabbi Yisroel Kelemer of Temple Mogen David in Los Angeles confirmed the other scholarship. I asked him whether the physical phenomena associated with the Counterfeit Revival would have any biblical foundation from his perspective as a Jewish rabbi. His response was immediate and telling: "If this were a biblical example of what you describe, why have there never been any practices like

this at any time in Jewish history?" When I asked him why two different words for *sleep* were used in Genesis 2:21, his response was humorous. "My, my," he said, "you don't think an inspired Jewish writer would be so dull and redundant as to use the same word twice in the same phrase, do you?"

8. Perhaps Wimber did less academic study of this passage than he implies. Perhaps he merely looked up the passage in James Strong's popular *Concordance/Dictionary* and embellished what he read, unaware that this century-old lay resource makes a citation mistake at this point, misidentifying the word and confabulating its meaning with the meaning of a related Greek word. Regardless, Wimber's "expertise" is contradicted by a plain reading of the Hebrew text and by all available Hebrew scholarship. For example, the great Old Testament scholars Keil and Delitzsch note that *tardemah* (which is used with similar meaning in Genesis 15:12 and 1 Samuel 26:12) is the word used at this point in Genesis 2:21, and it means "a deep sleep, in which all consciousness of the outer world and of one's own existence vanishes" (C. F. Keil and F. Delitzsch, *Commentary on the Old Testament, Volume I: The Pentateuch* [Grand Rapids, Mich.: Eerdmans, 1976], 88–89). Hebrew scholar William L. Holladay's Hebrew lexicon gives synonymous definitions for both words, also noting that *yashen* ("he slept") is sometimes even used to mean "the sleep of the dead," as in Job 3:13 (William L. Holladay, *A Concise Hebrew and Aramaic Lexicon of the Old Testament Based upon the Lexical Work of Ludwig Koehler and Walter Baumgartner* [Grand Rapids, Mich.: Eerdmans, 1988], 147).

9. Wimber, "Spiritual Phenomena: Slain in the Spirit—Part 1," audiotape.

10. Ibid.

11. Jay P. Green Sr., *The Interlinear Hebrew-Aramaic Old Testament* (Peabody, Mass.: William Hendrickson, 1985), 36; A. Alt, O. Eissfeldt, P. Kahle, and R. Kittel, eds., *Biblia Hebraica Stuttgartensia* (Stuttgart, Germany: Deutsche Bibelgesellschaft, 1984), 22.

12. John Wimber, "The Business of Laughing: What the Spirit Is Saying—Volume 1," Anaheim Vineyard, Anaheim, Calif., 1 May 1994, audiotape.

13. See John 3:18, 36; Deuteronomy 30:15–19; Ezekiel 18:1–32.
14. Wimber, "Spiritual Phenomena: Slain in the Spirit—Part 2," audiotape.
15. Ibid.
16. Ibid.
17. Ibid.
18. Ibid.
19. See John Wimber, "Speaking on Paul Cain and the Office of the Prophet," Vineyard Christian Fellowship, Anaheim, Calif., 19 February 1989, audiotape. (Also see chapter 14, "Endtime Restoration of Super Prophets and Apostles," for a complete accounting of this story.)
20. Wimber, "Spiritual Phenomena: Slain in the Spirit—Part 2," audiotape.
21. Ibid.
22. Ibid.
23. Robert H. Mounce, *The Book of Revelation* (Grand Rapids, Mich.: Eerdmans, 1977), 80.
24. Wimber, "Spiritual Phenomena: Slain in the Spirit—Part 2," audiotape.
25. Ibid.
26. Ibid.
27. Ibid.
28. Stanley M. Burgess and Gary B. McGee, eds., *Dictionary of Pentecostal and Charismatic Movements* (Grand Rapids, Mich.: Zondervan, 1988), 790.
29. It is interesting to note that critics of *Counterfeit Revival* have seized upon this paragraph to suggest that I may have committed the unpardonable sin and blasphemed the Holy Spirit. If so, in their view I would be eternally damned. A careful reading of this paragraph, however, makes it clear that I am not attributing the manifestations in Wimber's stories to Satan. I'm simply suggesting that Wimber would do better to attribute the manifestations in his stories to Satan rather than to the Savior since it is less of an error to falsely accuse Satan than to falsely impugn the Sovereign of the universe. In my view, Wimber's "manifestations" are nothing more than the product of his sensationalistic storytelling.

30. Wimber, "Spiritual Phenomena: Slain in the Spirit—Part 2," audiotape.
31. Ibid.
32. Burgess and McGee, *Pentecostal and Charismatic Movements,* 790.
33. Ibid., 790–91.
34. Wimber, "Spiritual Phenomena: Slain in the Spirit—Part 3," audiotape.

Chapter 20 ✦ Structural Defects

1. John Wimber with Kevin Springer, *Power Evangelism* (San Francisco: Harper & Row, 1986), 24–25.
2. Carol Wimber, "A Hunger for God," in Kevin Springer, *Power Encounters* (San Francisco: Harper & Row, 1988), 12.
3. Ibid.
4. Ibid.
5. Ibid., 12–13.
6. John White was a missionary in Latin America. He also copastored the Vineyard Christian Fellowship of North Delta, British Columbia.
7. The actual date of this experience was Mother's Day 1979. This is the date John Wimber gives repeatedly, and it is the only date that fits with other known and undisputed dates in Wimber/Vineyard history.
8. John White, *When the Spirit Comes with Power* (Downers Grove, Ill.: InterVarsity Press, 1988), 158–60.
9. John Wimber, "History and Vision of Vineyard Christian Fellowship," Vineyard Christian Fellowship, Anaheim, Calif., 18 May 1980, audiotape. The events recounted occurred in 1978, the year *before* the Mother's Day 1979 "watershed experience." In the full transcript of this message, John Wimber identifies "Mother's Day 1977" as his first Sunday as pastor, followed by "months" of teaching on and praying for healings before the first person is healed, and "1978" as the time period for the events that are recounted in this excerpt. We know from other corroborating chronologies that Wimber assumed the pulpit on Mother's Day 1977, his

first healing was at least "ten months later," or in February or March of 1978, and that the "watershed experience" with the evangelist was on Mother's Day 1979. Therefore, it is indisputable that all of the events recorded in this excerpt took place the year *before* the "watershed experience." (The chronology was confirmed by this transcript, Wimber and Springer, *Power Evangelism,* 23–25; Carol Wimber, "A Hunger for God," in Springer, *Power Encounters,* 8–13; Tom Stipe, "Recovering the Ministry I Left Behind," in Springer, *Power Encounters,* 166–68; telephone interviews with Tom Stipe on 15 and 17 October 1996; John Wimber's message, "Spiritual Phenomena: Slain in the Spirit—Parts 1 and 3," audiotape; and John White, *When the Spirit Comes with Power,* 158–71.)

10. Wimber, "History and Vision of Vineyard Christian Fellowship," audiotape.

11. Carol Wimber even asserts, "There was no way we could have been preprogrammed to fall over" (Wimber, "A Hunger for God," in Springer, *Power Encounters,* 10).

12. Ibid.

13. Wimber, "Spiritual Phenomena: Slain in the Spirit—Part 3," audiotape.

Chapter 21 ✦ The Arrival of the Mesmerist

1. Abridged from Bernard DeVoto, ed., *Mark Twain in Euroption* (New York: Harper & Row, 1922), 118–29.

2. Rodney Howard-Browne and others claim to be dispensing the "new wine" of the Spirit.

3. Norman Geisler, *Signs and Wonders* (Wheaton, Ill.: Tyndale House, 1988), 92.

4. James Wyckoff, *Franz Anton Mesmer* (Englewood Cliffs, N.J.: Prentice-Hall, 1975), vii.

5. Vincent Buranelli, *The Wizard from Vienna* (New York: Coward, McCann & Geoghegan, 1975), 110.

6. Ibid., 65.

7. Ibid., 110.

8. Ibid., 110–11.

9. Albert Moll, *Hypnotism* (New York: DaCapo Press, 1982), 11.
10. Ibid., 14–15.
11. Robert W. Marks, *The Story of Hypnotism* (New York: Prentice-Hall, 1947), 152.
12. J. Gordon Melton, Jerome Clark, and Aidan A. Kelly, as quoted in John Ankerberg and John Weldon, *Encyclopedia of New Age Beliefs* (Eugene, Ore.: Harvest House, 1996), 322. Mary Baker Eddy, once a patient of Quimby, took his system, modified it with her own theology, and developed the Church of Christ, Scientist, commonly known as the Christian Science church, one of the best known of the mind science cults.

Chapter 22 ✦ The Altered State of Consciousness

1. Charles T. Tart, "Transpersonal Potentialities of Deep Hypnosis," *Journal of Transpersonal Psychology,* no. 1 (1970): 37.
2. Rick Joyner, "The Heart of David: Worship and Warfare," Conference Report, April 1996, audiotape.
3. Ibid.
4. Ibid.
5. See Brownsville Assembly of God, 18 June 1995, videotape.
6. Joyner, "The Heart of David."
7. Elizabeth L. Hillstrom, *Testing the Spirits* (Downers Grove, Ill.: InterVarsity Press, 1995), 79.
8. Arnold M. Ludwig, "Altered States of Consciousness," in *Altered States of Consciousness,* Charles Tart, ed., (Garden City, N.Y.: Doubleday/Anchor, 1972), 16.
9. Lynn Andrews, as quoted in John Ankerberg and John Weldon, *Encyclopedia of New Age Beliefs* (Eugene, Ore.: Harvest House, 1996), 23.
10. Lindell Cooley, "1997 Conference on the Ministry," Grand Rapids, 7 January 1997, as cited in G. Richard Fisher and M. Kurt Goedelman, "The Murky River of Brownsville: The Strange Doctrine and Practice of the Pensacola Revival," *The Quarterly Journal,* April–June 1997, 17.
11. John Arnott, *The Father's Blessing* (Orlando, Fla.: Creation House, 1995), 182; also John Arnott, "Go for the Kingdom,"

Toronto Airport Vineyard, audiotape; John Arnott, "Understanding and Responding to Moves of God Conference," Calgary Family Church and Downtown Full Gospel Church, 25 April 1996, audiotape.

12. Larry Thomas, *No Laughing Matter* (Excelsior Springs, Mo.: Double Crown, 1995), 48.

13. Rodney Howard-Browne, Carpenter's Home Church, 9 March 1993, audiotape.

14. Ibid.

15. Baghwan Shree Rajneesh, in *Fear Is the Master,* Jeremiah Films, 1986, videotape.

16. Ankerberg and Weldon, *Encyclopedia of New Age Beliefs,* 21.

17. Hillstrom, *Testing the Spirits,* 120–21.

18. Arnott, *Father's Blessing,* 96, 167.

19. Mona Johnian, *The Fresh Anointing* (South Plainfield, N.J.: Bridge, 1994), 129–30.

20. John Arnott and Guy Chevreau, Pastors' Meeting, Toronto Airport Vineyard, 19 October 1994, audiotape.

21. John Arnott, Discovery Church, Orlando, Fla., 29 January 1995, audiotape.

22. Wes Campbell, "Spiritual and Physical Manifestations of the Holy Spirit," Toronto Airport Vineyard, 15 October 1994, audiotape.

23. Ibid.

24. Ibid.

25. Ibid.

26. Ibid.

27. Hillstrom, *Testing the Spirits,* 122.

28. Ibid.

Chapter 23 ✦ The Psychology of Peer Pressure

1. John Arnott, "Catch the Fire," Midland and Wales, U.K., 2 February 1996, audiotape.

2. Larry Randolph, "Renewal and Revival Today," Toronto Airport Vineyard, 18 November 1994, audiotape.

3. Ibid.

NOTES

Chapter 24 ✦ The Exploitation of Expectations

1. John Arnott and Guy Chevreau, Pastors' Meeting, Toronto Airport Vineyard, 19 October 1994, audiotape.
2. Mike Bickle and Bob Jones, "An Interview with Bob Jones," Kansas City Prophets, 1989, audiotape.
3. Bob Jones and Paul Cain, "Selections from the Kansas City Prophets," audiotape.
4. Ibid.
5. Ibid.
6. Randy Clark, "Catch the Fire: Questions and Answers," Toronto Airport Vineyard, 14 October 1994, audiotape.
7. Quoted by Richard M. Riss in "Impression of Morningstar Conference from Kent McKuen," 24 April 1996, e-mail communication.
8. Cincilla Grant, "'Holy Water' Triggers Healing Revival," *Charisma,* June 1996, 21–23.
9. Ibid., 21.
10. Robert W. Marks, *The Story of Hypnotism* (New York: Prentice-Hall, 1947), 150.
11. Ibid.

Chapter 25 ✦ The Subtle Power of Suggestion

1. Different terms are used in different spheres of psychological study.
2. Jon Trott, "The Grade Five Syndrome," *Cornerstone,* vol. 20, no. 96, 16.
3. Gradations of hypnotizability range from zero (almost no hypnotizability) to five (extremely hypnotizable).
4. This information was summarized from a variety of sources, including Dr. George Ganaway, "Historical versus Narrative Truth," *Journal of Dissociation* 2, no. 4 (December 1989): 205–20; and Steven Jay Lynn and Judith W. Rhue, "Fantasy Proneness," *American Psychologist,* January 1988, 35–44.
5. Judith W. Rhue and Steven Jay Lynn, "Fantasy Proneness,

Hypnotizability, and Multiple Personality" in *Human Suggestibility,* John F. Schumaker, ed., (New York: Routledge, 1991), 201.

6. John Arnott, Discovery Church, Orlando, Fla., 29 January 1995, audiotape.

7. Vance L. Shepperson, "Hypnotherapy," in David G. Benner, *Psychotherapy in Christian Perspective* (Grand Rapids, Mich.: Baker Book House, 1987), 164.

8. Robert W. Marks, *The Story of Hypnotism* (Grand Rapids, Mich.: Prentice-Hall, 1947), 190.

9. Ibid., 191.

10. Charles Baudouin, *Suggestion and Autosuggestion* (London: George Allen and Unwin, 1954), 80.

11. Marks, *Story of Hypnotism,* 193.

12. Ibid., 195.

13. A full description of this event appears in chapter 22, "The Altered State of Consciousness."

14. Baudouin, *Suggestion and Autosuggestion,* 82.

15. George Abell and Barry Singer, eds., *Science and the Paranormal* (New York: Scribners, 1981), 193–94.

16. Norman Geisler, *Signs and Wonders* (Wheaton, Ill.: Tyndale House, 1988), 121.

Epilogue

1. R. A. Torrey, *The Power of Prayer* (Grand Rapids, Mich.: Zondervan, 1981), 123–24.

2. John Blanchard, comp., *Gathered Gold* (Durham, England: Evangelical Press, 1984), 231.

3. Ibid., 218.

4. As noted by Barry Liesch, "Two basic views on the terms exist: They describe and emphasize either (1) the full range of style employed or (2) three different forms." Barry Liesch, *The New Worship: Straight Talk on Music and the Church* (Grand Rapids, Mich.: Baker Book House, 1996), 35.

5. Liesch, *New Worship,* 20. Liesch's internal quote reference is to Kenneth A. Myers, *All God's Children and Blue Suede Shoes: Christians and Popular Culture* (Westchester, Ill.: Crossway Books, 1989).

6. The original Shaker composition was immortalized in Aaron Copeland's ballet "Appalachian Spring" and is familiar to many from its adaptation as the theme music to the popular tabloid television program *American Journal* and in an Oldsmobile ad. The lyrics embrace both of the Shaker distinctives: simplicity and physical "enthusiasms." The lyrics read: "'Tis the gift to be simple,/'Tis the gift to be free,/ 'Tis the gift to come down where we ought to be,/And when we find ourselves in the place just right/It will be in the valley of love and delight./ When true simplicity is gained,/ to bow and to bend, we will not be ashamed/ To turn, turn, will be our delight,/'Til by turning, turning, we come round right." Shaker heresies and practices are discussed in part 4, "Slain in the Spirit."

7. Kathryn Riss, "New Winos Drinking Song Number One," in e-mail communication new-Wine@grmi.org, 9 September 1995. Kathryn Riss communicated that she was "not a songwriter, neither the son of a songwriter" but that the Lord had given her these lyrics. She said that the e-mail should be forwarded to my attention with her comment, "Pass it on to Brother Hank . . . just tell him it beats forty years of depression."

8. Charles Swindoll, *Growing Strong in the Seasons of Life* (Portland, Ore.: Multnomah Press, 1983), 78.

9. Blanchard, *Gathered Gold,* 37.

10. Ibid., 39. Hugh Latimer (1485–October 16, 1555) was an English Reformer who was imprisoned, tried, and sentenced to burn at the stake by the Catholic Queen Mary Tudor. As he and his fellow Reformer Nicholas Ridley were set afire he proclaimed, "We shall this day light such a candle, by God's grace, in England as I trust shall never be put out."

11. This statistical illustration, while pertinent, is not intended to convey that every person who is evangelized will in fact become a true believer or that supernatural conversion can be reduced to a statistical formula.

12. Philip Yancey and Tim Stafford, *The Student Bible: New International Version* (Grand Rapids, Mich.: Zondervan, 1992), "Insight" note at Mark 4:41, 892.

Appendix A

1. Originally appeared in the *Christian Research Journal* (November–December 1997): 54.
2. James Beverley, "Counterfeit Critique," *Christianity Today,* 1 September 1 1997, 59–60.
3. Attributed.
4. James Beverley, *Revival Wars* (Toronto: Evangelical Research Ministries, 1997), 10–11.
5. Letter from Tom Stipe to Michael Maudlin (managing editor, *Christianity Today*), 29 August 1997.
6. Personal fax to Hank Hanegraaff from Tom Stipe, 27 August 1997.
7. Beverley, "Counterfeit Critique," *Christianity Today,* 59.
8. See Hank Hanegraaff, *Counterfeit Revival* (Dallas: Word Publishing, 1997), 104–5. I have retained the exact wording in this expanded edition (see pp. 118–19).
9. Beverley, "Counterfeit Critique," 60.
10. Fax to Hanegraaff from Stipe, 27 August 1997.

Appendix B

1. Adapted from my article, "The Counterfeit Revival (Part Three): Separating Fact from Fiction on the Pensacola Outpouring," *Christian Research Journal* (November–December 1997): 15.
2. Hank Hanegraaff, *Counterfeit Revival* (Dallas: Word Publishing, 1997).
3. See Michael L. Brown, *Let No One Deceive You: Confronting the Critics of Revival* (Shippensburg, Pa.: Destiny Image Publishers, 1997), 248–58.
4. Hanegraaff, *Counterfeit Revival* (1997), 83–101. See pages 97–115 in this updated and expanded edition.
5. Michael Bowman, e-mail message to Debra Bouey (forwarded to CRI 29 July 1997, CRI files).
6. Brown, *Let No One Deceive You.* Brown had told me personally that he would pull from his book the appendix titled,

"Counterfeit Criticism: A Review of Hank Hanegraaff's *Counterfeit Revival.*" Unfortunately, no edition yet exists without this appendix and as the updated and expanded edition of *Counterfeit Revival* goes to the printer, Brown continues to sell the original version including the aforementioned appendix through his own ICN ministries in Pensacola, Florida.

7. Brown, *Let No One Deceive You,* 242–243.
8. Hanegraaff, *Counterfeit Revival* (1997), 106. See p. 120 of this updated and expanded edition.
9. As quoted in Hanegraaff, *Counterfeit Revival* (1997), 47. See p. 46 of this updated and expanded edition.
10. Hanegraaff, *Counterfeit Revival* (1997), 106. See p. 120 of this updated and expanded edition.
11. Hanegraaff, *Counterfeit Revival* (1997), 106. See p. 120 of this updated and expanded edition.
12. For example, R. W. Schambach's books are featured on Hinn's Web site at www.bennyhinn.org (retrieved 31 January 2001).
13. Brown, *Let No One Deceive You,* 244.
14. Brown does acknowledge this qualifying portion of my statement in an endnote, only to falsely dichotomize my single point into two seemingly unrelated ones (see Brown, *Let No One Deceive You,* 290, n. 19).
15. These points, in addition to numerous others, concerning Brown's indictment of *Counterfeit Revival* were brought to my attention through a very thoughtful analysis written by Shawn Paul Sauve. Many who have undertaken the arduous effort of analyzing Brown's arguments have highlighted similar issues.

Appendix C

1. "The State of the Church 2000," Barna Research Online, 21 March 2000 at http://216.87.179.136/cgi-bin/PagePressRelease.asp?PressReleaseID=49&Reference=E.

Appendix D

1. This statement originally appeared in the "A Message from Hank Hanegraaff" column of the *Christian Research Newsletter*, March–April 1998.

Select Bibliography

Books

Abell, George, and Barry Singer, eds. *Science and the Paranormal.*
New York: Scribners, 1981.

Alt, A., O. Eissfeldt, P. Kahle, and R. Kittel, eds. *Biblia Hebraica
Stuttgartensia.* Stuttgart, Germany: Deutsche
Bibelgesellschaft, 1984 edition.

Ankerberg, John and John Weldon. *Encyclopedia of New Age
Beliefs.* Eugene, Ore.: Harvest House Publishers, 1996.

Arnott, John. *The Father's Blessing.* Orlando, Fla.: Creation
House Publishers, 1995.

Aune, David E. *Prophecy in Early Christianity.* Grand Rapids,
Mich.: William B. Eerdmans, 1983.

Baudouin, Charles. *Suggestion and Autosuggestion.* London:
George Allen and Unwin, Ltd., 1954.

Bedell, George C., Leo Sandon Jr., and Charles T. Wellborn.
Religion in America. New York: Macmillan Publishing Co., Inc.,
1975.

Benner, David G. *Psychotherapy in Christian Perspective.* Grand
Rapids, Mich.: Baker Book House, 1987.

Beverley, James A. *Holy Laughter and the Toronto Blessing.* Grand
Rapids, Mich.: Zondervan Publishing House, 1995.

Beverley, James A. *Revival Wars*. Toronto: Evangelical Research Ministries, 1997.

Blanchard, John, comp. *Gathered Gold*. Durham, England: Evangelical Press, 1984.

Blumhofer, Edith. *Aimee Semple McPherson: Everybody's Sister.* Grand Rapids, Mich.: William B. Eerdmans Publishers, 1993.

Bright, Bill. *The Coming Revival*. Orlando, Fla.: New Life Publications, 1995.

Brown, Michael. *From Holy Laughter to Holy Fire*. Shippensburg, Pa.: Destiny Image, 1996.

Brown, Michael. *Let No One Deceive You*. Shippensburg, Pa.: Destiny Image, 1997.

Bruce, F. F. *The Spreading Flame*. Grand Rapids, Mich.: Eerdmans, 1958.

Buckingham, Jamie. *Daughter of Destiny*. Plainfield, N.J.: Logos, 1976.

Buranelli, Vincent. *The Wizard from Vienna*. New York: Coward, McCann & Geoghegan, Inc., 1975.

Burgess, Stanley M., and Gary B. McGee, eds. *Dictionary of Pentecostal and Charismatic Movements*. Grand Rapids, Mich.: Zondervan Publishing House, 1988.

Carson, D. A. *Showing the Spirit: A Theological Exposition of 1 Corinthians 12–14*. Grand Rapids, Mich.: Baker Books, 1987.

Castaneda, Carlos. *The Art of Dreaming*. New York: Harper Collins, 1993.

Chevreau, Guy. *Catch the Fire: The Toronto Blessing—An Experience of Renewal and Revival*. London: Marshall Pickering, 1994.

Coleman, Robert. *The Coming World Revival*. Wheaton, Ill.: Crossway Books, 1995.

Colson, Charles. *Against the Night, Living in the New Dark Ages*. Ann Arbor, Mich.: Servant Books, 1989.

DeArteaga, William. *Quenching the Spirit*. 2nd ed. Altamonte Springs, Fla.: Creation House Publishers, 1996.

Delitzsch, Franz. *Isaiah*. Volume 7 of *Commentary on the Old Testament in Ten Volumes*. Grand Rapids, Mich.: Eerdmans, 1976.

DeVoto, Bernard. *Mark Twain in Euroption*. San Francisco: Harper & Row Publishers, 1922.

Douglas, J. D., Philip W. Comfort, and Donald Mitchell, eds. *Who's Who in Christian History*. Wheaton, Ill.: Tyndale House Publishers, 1992.

Draper, Edythe. *Edythe Draper's Book of Quotations*. Wheaton, Ill.: Tyndale House Publishers, 1992.

Edwards, Jonathan. *The Works of Jonathan Edwards*. Carlisle, Pa.: Banner of Truth Trust, 1992. Reprint of 1974 edition, first published in 1834. Volumes 1 and 2.

Ellis, E. Earle. *Prophecy and Hermeneutic in Early Christianity*. Grand Rapids, Mich.: Baker Books, 1993.

Elwell, Walter A., ed. *Evangelical Dictionary of Theology*. Grand Rapids, Mich.: Baker Book House, 1984.

Epstein, Daniel Mark. *Sister Aimee: The Life of Aimee Semple McPherson*. New York: Harcourt Brace Jovanovich, Publishers, 1993.

Fant, Clyde E., Jr., and William M. Pinson Jr. *A Treasury of Great Preaching*. 13 vols. Dallas, Tex.: Word Publishing, 1995.

Fee, Gordon. *God's Empowering Presence*. Peabody, Mass.: Hendrickson, 1994.

Fisher, G. Richard, and M. Kurt Goedelman. Rev. ed. *The Confusing World of Benny Hinn*. St. Louis: Personal Freedom Outreach, 1996.

Forbes, Christopher. *Prophecy and Inspired Speech*. Peabody, Mass.: Hendrickson, 1997.

Geisler, Norman. *Signs and Wonders*. Wheaton, Ill.: Tyndale House Publishers, 1988.

Green, Jay P., Sr. *The Interlinear Hebrew-Aramaic Old Testament*. Peabody, Mass.: William Hendriksen Publishers, 1985.

Green, Michael. *Evangelism in the Early Church*. Grand Rapids, Mich.: Eerdmans, 1970.

Green, Michael. *I Believe in the Holy Spirit*. Rev. ed. Grand Rapids, Mich.: Eerdmans, 1989.

Grudem, Wayne, ed. *Are Miraculous Gifts for Today? Four Views*. Grand Rapids, Mich.: Zondervan, 1996.

Grudem, Wayne. *The Gift of Prophecy in the New Testament and Today*. Rev. ed. Wheaton, Ill.: Crossway, 2001.

Grudem, Wayne. *Systematic Theology*. Grand Rapids, Mich.: Zondervan, 1994.

Guinness, Os. *Fit Bodies, Fat Minds*. Grand Rapids, Mich.: Baker Book House, 1994.

Hagin, Kenneth E. *I Believe in Visions*. 2nd ed. Tulsa, Okla.: Rhema Bible Church, 1989.

Hagin, Kenneth. *Why Do People Fall under the Power?* Tulsa, Okla.: Kenneth Hagin Ministries, 1981.

Hanegraaff, Hank. *Christianity in Crisis*. Eugene, Ore.: Harvest House Publishers, 1993.

Hardman, Keith J. *Seasons of Refreshing*. Grand Rapids, Mich.: Baker Book House, 1994.

Harrell, David Edwin, Jr. *All Things Are Possible: The Healing and Charismatic Revivals in Modern America*. Bloomington, Ind.: Indiana University Press, 1975.

Hill, Clifford. *Prophecy: Past and Present*. Ann Arbor, Mich.: Servant Publications, 1989.

Hillstrom, Elizabeth L. *Testing the Spirits*. Downers Grove, Ill.: InterVarsity Press, 1995.

Hinn, Benny. *The Anointing*. Nashville, Tenn.: Thomas Nelson Publishers, 1992.

Hinn, Benny. *Good Morning, Holy Spirit*. Nashville, Tenn.: Thomas Nelson Publishers, 1990.

Hollady, William L. *A Concise Hebrew and Aramaic Lexicon of the Old Testament Based upon the Lexical Work of Ludwig Koehler and Walter Baumgartner*. Grand Rapids, Mich.: William B. Eerdmans Publishing Company, 1988.

Howard-Browne, Rodney. *The Coming Revival*. Louisville, Ky.: RHBEA Publications, 1991.

Howard-Browne, Rodney. *Flowing in the Holy Ghost*. Louisville, Ky.: RHBEA Publications, 1991.

Howard-Browne, Rodney. *Fresh Oil from Heaven*. Louisville, Ky.: RHBEA Publications, 1992.

Howard-Browne, Rodney. *Manifesting the Holy Ghost*. Louisville, Ky.: RHBEA Publications, 1992.

Howard-Browne, Rodney. *The Touch of God*. Louisville, Ky.: RHBEA Publications, 1992.

Hunter, Charles and Frances ("The Happy Hunters"). *Holy Laughter*. Kingwood, Tex.: Hunter Books, 1994.

Johnian, Mona. *The Fresh Anointing*. South Plainfield, N.J.: Bridge Publishing, 1994.

Joyner, Rick. *The Harvest.* Pineville, N.C.: MorningStar Publications, Inc., 1990.

Keil, C. F. and F. Delitzsch. *The Pentateuch.* Vol. 1 of *Commentary on the Old Testament.* Reprint. Grand Rapids, Mich.: William B. Eerdmans Publishing Company, 1976.

Kelsey, Morton. *The Christian and the Supernatural.* Minneapolis, Minn.: Augsburg Publishing House, 1976.

Knox, Ronald A. *Enthusiasm: A Chapter in the History of Religion.* Notre Dame, Ind.: University of Notre Dame Press, 1950.

Liesch, Barry. *The New Worship: Straight Talk on Music and the Church.* Grand Rapids, Mich.: Baker Book House, 1996.

MacNutt, Francis. *Overcome by the Spirit.* Grand Rapids, Mich.: Chosen Books, 1990.

Marks, Robert W. *The Story of Hypnotism.* New York: Prentice-Hall, Inc., 1947.

McConnell, D. R. *A Different Gospel.* Rev. ed. Peabody, Mass.: Hendrickson, 1995.

McPherson, Aimee Semple. *This Is That.* Los Angeles: Echo Park Evangelistic Association, Inc., 1923.

Moll, Albert. *Hypnotism.* New York: DaCapo Press, 1982.

Moriarty, Michael. *The New Charismatics.* Grand Rapids, Mich.: Zondervan, 1992.

Mounce, Robert H. *The Book of Revelation.* Grand Rapids, Mich.: William B. Eerdmans Publishing Company, 1977.

Murray, Iain H. *Jonathan Edwards: A New Biography.* Carlisle, Pa.: Banner of Truth Trust, 1987.

Myers, Kenneth A. *All God's Children and Blue Suede Shoes: Christians and Popular Culture.* Westchester, Ill.: Crossway Books, 1989.

Needham, Nick. *Was Jonathan Edwards the Founding Father of the Toronto Blessing?* Welling, Kent, England: Nick Needham (self-published), 1995.

New Bible Dictionary. Wheaton, Ill.: Tyndale House Publishers, 1983.

Noll, Mark. *The Scandal of the Evangelical Mind.* Grand Rapids, Mich.: William B. Eerdmans Publishing Co., 1994.

Oropeza, B. J. *A Time to Laugh.* Peabody, Mass.: Hendrickson, 1995.

Packer, J. I. *Hot Tub Religion*. Wheaton, Ill.: Tyndale House
Publishers, 1987.

Passantino, Bob. *Fantasies, Legends, and Heroes*. Costa Mesa,
Calif.: Answers in Action, 1990.

Reid, Daniel G., Robert D. Linder, Bruce L. Shelley, and Harry S.
Stout, eds. *Dictionary of Christianity in America*. Downers
Grove, Ill.: InterVarsity Press, 1990.

Riss, Richard M. *A History of the Worldwide Awakening of 1992–
1995*. 11th ed. (e-mail source address): self-published, October
15, 1995.

Riss, Richard M. *Impression of Morningstar Conference from Kent
McKuen*. (e-mail source) April 24, 1996.

Roberts, Dave. *The Toronto Blessing*. England: Kingsway Publications Ltd., 1994.

Ryle, James. *A Dream Come True*. Orlando, Fla.: Creation House,
1995.

Ryle, James. *Hippo in the Garden*. Orlando, Fla.: Creation House,
1993.

Schlafer, Dale. *Becoming an Agent of Revival: Revival Primer*.
Denver, Colo.: Promise Keepers, 1997.

Schumaker, John F., ed. *Human Suggestibility*. New York:
Routledge, 1991.

Smith, David L. *A Handbook of Contemporary Theology*. Wheaton,
Ill.: Victor Books, 1992.

Springer, Kevin. *Power Encounters*. San Francisco: Harper & Row
Publishers, 1988.

Sproul, R. C., John Gerstner, and Arthur Lindsley. *Classical
Apologetics*. Grand Rapids, Mich.: Zondervan, 1984.

Swindoll, Charles. *Growing Strong in the Seasons of Life*. Portland, Ore.: Multnomah Press, 1983.

Synan, Vinson. *The Holiness-Pentecostal Movement in the United
States*. Grand Rapids, Mich.: William B. Eerdmans Publishing
Company, 1971.

Tart, Charles, ed. *Altered States of Consciousness*. Garden City,
N.Y.: Doubleday/Anchor Books, 1972.

Thomas, Larry. *No Laughing Matter*. Excelsior Springs, Mo.:
Double Crown Publishing, 1995.

Torrey, R. A. *The Power of Prayer*. Grand Rapids, Mich.:
Zondervan Publishing Company, 1981.

Warner, Wayne E. *Kathryn Kuhlman*. Ann Arbor, Mich.: Servant Publications, 1993.

White, John. *When the Spirit Comes with Power.* Downers Grove, Ill.: InterVarsity Press, 1988.

Wimber, John with Kevin Springer. *Power Evangelism.* San Francisco, Calif.: Harper & Row Publishers, 1986.

Woodworth-Etter, Maria. *A Diary of Signs and Wonders.* Tulsa, Okla.: Harrison House, 1916.

Wyckoff, James. *Franz Anton Mesmer.* Englewood Cliffs, N.J.: Prentice-Hall, Inc., 1975.

Yancey, Philip and Tim Stafford. *The Student Bible: New International Version.* Grand Rapids, Mich.: Zondervan Publishing House, 1992.

Articles

Advertisement for Good News New York crusade with Rodney Howard-Brown. *Charisma* (April 1999): 81.

Allman, John W. "Revival Prays to Raise an Infant from the Dead." *Pensacola News Journal* on-line archive at www.pensacolanewsjournal.com (September 20, 1998).

Allman, John W. "Revival Revises Routine." *Pensacola News Journal* on-line archive at www.pensacolanewsjournal.com (March 7, 1999).

Arnott, John. "Moving into Increasing Anointing." *Spread the Fire* (May–June 1995): 2.

Beverley, James. "Counterfeit Critique." *Christianity Today* (September 1, 1997): 59–60.

Boring, M. Eugene. "Prophecy (Early Christian)." In *The Anchor Bible Dictionary,* vol. 5., ed. New York: Doubleday, 1992, 495–502.

Bouy, Debra. "Accusers of the Brethren or Good Bereans?" www.geocities.com/Heartland/Plains/4948/accuser.html (n.d.).

Brown, Michael. "Pensacola: God or Not?" *Destiny Image Digest* (winter 1997).

Brown, Michael. "Revival in Brownsville?" *Destiny Image Digest* (winter 1997).

Brown, Mick. "Unzipper Heaven, Lord." *Telegraph Magazine* (December 3, 1994): 26–30.

The Canadian Press. "TV Evangelists Forced to Recant Claims of God's Divine Dentistry: An Honest Mistake." *National Post* online at www.nationalpost.com (May 12, 1999).

Cannon, Steve. "Kansas City Fellowship Revisited: The Controversy Continues." *The Quarterly Journal,* Personal Freedom Outreach 11, no. 1 (1991): electronic version.

Cannon, Steve. "Old Wine in Old Wineskins, A Look at Kansas City Fellowship." *Personal Freedom Outreach* 10, no. 4 (October–December 1990): 1, 6–12.

Chambers, Joseph R. "False Brags and Real Facts." *The End Times and Victorious Living* (March–April 1997): 7.

Crann, Alice. "Pastors Orchestrated First Revival." *Pensacola News Journal* (November 19, 1997): front page.

"Did You Know?" *Christian History* 14, no. 1, 45 (1995): 2.

Duin, Julia. "An Evening with Rodney Howard-Browne." *Christian Research Journal* (Winter 1995): 43–45.

Duin, Julia. "Praise the Lord and Pass the New Wine." *Charisma* (August 1994): 20–28.

Farnell, F. David. "The Current Debate about New Testament Prophecy." *Bibliotheca Sacra* (July–September 1992): 277–303.

Farnell, F. David. "Does the New Testament Teach Two Prophetic Gifts?" *Bibliotheca Sacra* 150 (January–March 1993): 62–68.

Farnell, F. David. "Fallible New Testament Prophecy/Prophets? A Critique of Wayne Grudem's Hypothesis." In *The Master's Perspective on Contemporary Issues,* Robert L. Thomas, ed. Grand Rapids, Mich.: Kregel, 1998, 31–53.

Farnell, F. David. "The Gift of Prophecy in the Old and New Testaments." *Bibliotheca Sacra* (July–September 1992): 387–410.

Farnell, F. David. "When Will the Gift of Prophecy Cease?" *Bibliotheca Sacra* 150 (April–June 1993): 171–202.

Fisher, G. Richard, and M. Kurt Goedelman. "The Murky River of Brownsville: The Strange Doctrine and Practice of the Pensacola Revival." *The Quarterly Journal,* Personal Freedom Outreach (April–June 1997).

Fisher, G. Richard, Stephen F. Cannon, and M. Kurt Goedelman. "Benny Hinn's Anointing: Heaven Sent or Borrowed?" *The*

Quarterly Journal, Personal Freedom Outreach 12, no. 3 (July–September 1992): 1, 10–14.

Galli, Mark. "Revival at Cane Ridge." *Christian History* 14, no. 1, 45 (1995): 8–14.

Ganaway, George. "Historical versus Narrative Truth." *Journal of Dissociation* 2, no. 4 (December 1989): 205–220.

Goetz, David L. "Trendsetters in the Religious Wilderness." *Christian History* 14, no. 1, 45 (1995): 26–29.

Goodman, Walter. "About Churches, Souls, and Show-Biz Methods." *New York Times* (March 16, 1995): B4.

Good News on-line at www.goshen.net/gnm/hill.htm (July–August 1996).

Grady, J. Lee. "Laughter in Lakeland." *Charisma* (August 1995): 61–62.

Grady, J. Lee. "When God Interrupts Your Agenda: An Interview with the Leaders of the Brownsville Assembly of God." *Ministries Today* (November–December 1996).

Grant, Cincilla. "'Holy Water' Triggers Healing Revival." *Charisma* (June 1996): 21–23.

Hagin, Kenneth. "Rejoice! This Is the Day Which the Lord Hath Made!" *The Word of Faith* (July 1996): 14–17.

Hanegraaff, Hank. "The Counterfeit Revival Revisited." *Christian Research Journal* 21, no. 4 (1999): 54–55.

Hanegraaff, Hank. "The Counterfeit Revival (Part Three): Separating Fact from Fiction on the Pensacola Outpouring." *Christian Research Journal* (November–December 1997): 10–20, 42.

Hanegraaff, Hank. "Frauds, Fictions, Fantasies, and Fabrications." *Christian Research Journal* (Winter 1996): 35, 54–55.

Hill, Steve, "Heart to Heart, with Evangelist Steve Hill." *Destiny Image Digest* (Winter 1997).

"The Hunger before Revival." The Remnant at www.theremnant.com (n.d.).

Joyner, Rick. Untitled Article. *Morning Star Prophetic Bulletin* (May 1996): electronic version.

Joyner, Rick. "Azusa Street: The Fire That Could Not Die." *The Morning Star Journal* 6, no. 4 (1996): 61–72.

Kring, Stephen. "The Nature of New Testament Prophecy: An Examination of Wayne Grudem's Position." *The Fellowship for

Reformation and Pastoral Studies 26, no. 4 (1997) on-line at www.netrover.com/dontheo/264.htm.

Lynn, Steven Jay, and Judith W. Rhue. "Fantasy Proneness." *American Psychologist* (January 1988): 35–44.

Maudlin, Michael. "Seers in the Heartland." *Christianity Today* (January 14, 1991): 18–22.

Orange County Register (March 13, 1997): Metro 1.

Ostling, Richard. "Laughing for the Lord." *Time* (August 15, 1994): 38.

"People and Events: Yonggi Cho Changes His Name." *Charisma* (November 1992): 80.

Rabey, Steve. "Pensacola Outpouring Keeps Gushing." *Christianity Today* (March 3, 1997).

Reid, Gail. "Joy on the Other Side of Offense." *Spread the Fire* (March–April 1995): electronic copy.

Ruthren, John. "They Called Jesus a Counterfeit, Too." *Charisma* (July 1997): 61–62.

Sightler, Carl. "Results from the Revival." Brownsville Revival Testimonies Web page at www.brownsville-revival.org/testimon.html (n.d.).

Stalcup, Elizabeth Moll. "Glory Dust from Heaven?" *Charisma* (November 1999): 78.

Stalcup, Elizabeth Moll. "It Happened before Our Eyes." *Charisma* (November 1999): 80.

Stalcup, Elizabeth Moll. "When the Glory Comes Down." *Charisma* (November 1999): 77.

"The State of the Church, 2000." Barna Research Online (21 March 2000) at www.barna.org.

Tart, Charles T. "Transpersonal Potentialities of Deep Hypnosis." *The Journal of TransPersonal Psychology* 1 (1970): 27–40.

Taylor, Mike. "What Happened Next?" *Evangelicals Now* (February 1995): 1, 8.

Trott, Jon. "The Grade Five Syndrome." *Cornerstone* 20, no. 96: 16–17.

Watanabe, Teresa. "Struck by 'Golden Miracles.'" *Los Angeles Times* on-line archives at latimes.com (January 25, 2000).

Woodward, Kenneth, Jeanne Gordon, Carol Hall and Barry Brown. "The Giggles are for God." *Newsweek* (February 20, 1995): 54.

Audiotapes

Arnott, Carol. "Receiving the Spirit's Power." (Together for the Kingdom '95.) Toronto: Toronto Airport Vineyard, April 20, 1995. Tape 793C.

Arnott, John. Untitled Message. Toronto: Toronto Airport Vineyard, December 16, 1994.

Arnott, John. Untitled Message. Orlando, Fla.: Discovery Church, January 29, 1995.

Arnott, John. "Catch the Fire." Midland and Wales, U.K.: Toronto Airport Vineyard, February 2, 1996.

Arnott, John. "Dynamics of Receiving Spiritual Experiences." Toronto: Toronto Airport Vineyard, November 18, 1994.

Arnott, John. "Go for the Kingdom." Toronto: Toronto Airport Vineyard, n.d.

Arnott, John. "The Love of God." Mission Viejo, Calif.: Vineyard Christian Fellowship, July 17, 1995. Tape 621.

Arnott, John. "Understanding and Responding to the Movers of God Conference." Toronto: Toronto Airport Vineyard, April 25, 1996.

Arnott, John. "Valuing the Anointing." Toronto: Toronto Airport Vineyard, October 15, 1994.

Arnott, John, and Guy Chevreau. Untitled Message at Pastors' Conference. Toronto: Toronto Airport Vineyard, October 19, 1994.

Bickle, Mike. "An Interview with Bob Jones by Mike Bickle." Kansas City, Mo.: Kansas City Prophets, 1989.

Bickle, Mike. "Regional Pastors' Conference" (Session 2G). Newport Beach, Calif.: Vineyard Christian Fellowship, 1989.

Bickle, Mike, and Michael Sullivan. "Understanding the Phenomena That Accompany the Spirit's Ministry."

Cain, Paul. "God Speaking the Second Time." (Leadership Conference, General Session.) Grandview, Mo.: Grace Ministries, 1990.

Cain, Paul. "Prophecy for the Vineyard." Anaheim, Calif.: Vineyard Christian Fellowship, February 1989. Tape 3.

Campbell, Wes. Untitled Message. Toronto: Toronto Airport Vineyard, October 14, 1994.

Campbell, Wes. "Spiritual and Physical Manifestations of the Holy Spirit." Toronto: Toronto Airport Vineyard, October 15, 1994.

Clark, Randy. "Questions and Answers." (Pastors' Conference.) Toronto: Toronto Airport Vineyard, October 14, 1994.

Clark, Randy. "Test Me Now . . . I Will Back You Up." (Catch the Fire Conference.) Toronto: Toronto Airport Vineyard, 13 October, 1994.

DeArteaga, William. "What Is Heresy?" Toronto: Toronto Airport Vineyard, October 13, 1994.

Deere, Jack. Untitled Message. Toronto: Toronto Airport Vineyard, November 20, 1994.

Deere, Jack. "Intimacy with God and the End Time Church." Denver, Colo.: Vineyard Christian Fellowship, 1989.

Duplantis, Jesse. "Close Encounters of the God Kind." New Orleans, La.: Jesse Duplantis Ministries, 1988.

Dupont, Marc. "The Father's Heart and the Prophetic." Toronto: Toronto Airport Vineyard, November 16, 1994.

Dupont, Marc. "Prophetic School, Part 3." (Pastors' Meeting.) Toronto: Toronto Airport Vineyard, November 16, 1994.

Hanegraaff, Hank with Oliver Wilder-Smith. *Bible Answer Man.* Rancho Santa Margarita, Calif.: Christian Research Institute, 15 May 1997.

Hanegraaff, Hank with Michael Brown. *Bible Answer Man.* Rancho Santa Margarita, Calif.: Christian Research Institute, 20 March 1997.

Howard-Browne, Rodney. Untitled Message. Lakeland, Fla.: Carpenter's Home Church, 9 March 1993.

Howard-Browne, Rodney. Untitled Message. Jacksonville, Fla.: New Life Christian Center, November 10, 1994.

Howard-Browne, Rodney. Untitled Message. Anaheim, Calif.: Melodyland Christian Center, January 16, 1995.

Howard-Browne, Rodney. Untitled Message. Anaheim, Calif.: Melodyland Christian Center, January 17, 1995.

Hunter, Todd. "Revival in Focus." Mission Viejo, Calif.: Vineyard Christian Fellowship, October 23, 1994.

Jones, Bob. "The Shepherd's Rod." Belper, Derbys, England: Banner Ministries, October 1989. Tape 160.

Jones, Bob, and Paul Cain. "Selections of the Kansas City Prophets."
  Belper, Derbys, England: Banner Ministries. Tape 155C.

Joyner, Rick. "The Heart of David: Worship and Warfare."
  (Conference Report.) April 18, 1996.

Randolph, Larry. "Renewal and Revival Today." Toronto: Toronto
  Airport Vineyard, November 18, 1994.

Ravenhill, David. "Understanding Prophecy and Its Fulfillment:
  Introduction to the Prophetic." Grandview, Mo.: Metro Vineyard Fellowship, September 17, 1989. Tape 90917.

Ryle, James. "The Beatles' Anointing Story: The Sons of Thunder
  (A New Generation of Worshipping Warriors)." Pineville, N.C.:
  MorningStar Publications, June 21, 1990.

Steingard, Jerry. "Handling Objections to Manifestations." (Catch
  the Fire Conference.) Toronto: Toronto Airport Vineyard,
  October 13, 1994.

Wimber, John. "A Biblical Approach to Fallen Leaders." Anaheim,
  Calif.: Vineyard Ministries International, 10 November 1991.

Wimber, John. "The Business of Laughing: What the Spirit Is
  Saying—Volume 1." Anaheim, Calif.: Anaheim Vineyard, May
  1, 1994.

Wimber, John. "History and Vision of Vineyard Christian Fellowship." Placentia, Calif.: Vineyard Ministries, Int'l, May 18,
  1980.

Wimber, John. "Spiritual Phenomena: Slain in the Spirit—
  Parts 1, 2, and 3." Anaheim, Calif.: Vineyard Christian Fellowship, 1981.

Wimber, John. "Speaking on Paul Cain and the Office of the
  Prophet." Anaheim, Calif.: Vineyard Christian Fellowship,
  February 19, 1989.

Videotape

Copeland, Kenneth, and Rodney Howard-Browne. Untitled Message. (Southwest Believers' Convention.) Fort Worth, Tex.:
  Kenneth Copeland Ministries, August 5, 1993.

Crouch, Paul. *Praise-a-Thon.* Santa Ana, Calif.: Trinity Broadcasting Network, April 2, 1991.

Crouch, Paul. *Praise the Lord.* Santa Ana, Calif.: Trinity Broadcasting Network, September 10, 1999.

Donahue, Phil. *The Phil Donahue Show.* Chicago: Phil Donahue Productions, September 19, 1995.

Ely, Maul. Brownsville, Fla.: Brownsville Assembly of God, 16 March 1997. Audio.

Hill, Stephen. Brownsville, Fla.: Brownsville Assembly of God, May 30, 1996.

Hinn, Benny. "Double Portion Anointing, Part 3." Santa Ana, Calif.: Trinity Broadcasting Network, April 7, 1991. Audio.

Hinn, Benny. "PTL Praise-a-Thon." Santa Ana, Calif.: Trinity Broadcasting Network, April 2, 2000.

Hinn, Benny. *Praise the Lord.* Santa Ana, Calif.: Trinity Broadcasting Network, November 8, 1990. Audio.

Hinn, Benny. *Praise the Lord.* Santa Ana, Calif.: Trinity Broadcasting Network, April 12, 1991. Audio.

Hinn, Benny. *Praise the Lord.* Santa Ana, Calif.. Trinity Broadcasting Network, June 12, 1996. Audio.

Hinn, Benny. *Praise the Lord.* Santa Ana, Calif.: Trinity Broadcasting Network, July 8, 1996. Audio.

Hinn Benny. "This Is Your Day." Santa Ana, Calif.: Trinity Broadcasting Network, March 29, 2000.

Howard-Browne, Rodney. "Manifesting the Holy Ghost." Orlando, Fla.; Orlando Christian Center, 1990.

In Times Like These. Pensacola, Fla.: Brownsville Assembly of God, n.d.

Jennings, Peter. "Peter Jennings Reporting: In the Name of God." New York: An MPI Home Video presentation of an ABC News Production, 1995.

Kilpatrick, John. Brownsville, Fla.: Brownsville Assembly of God, June 18, 1995.

Kilpatrick, John. "God's Ears." Brownsville, Fla.: Brownsville Assembly of God, April 6, 1997.

Matthews, Allan, director, producer. "Rumors of Revival." Milton Keynes, England: Nelson Word, Ltd., 1995.

Osbourne, T. L. *Praise the Lord.* Santa Ana, Calif.: Trinity Broadcasting Network, June 19, 1989.

Rajneesh, Baghwan Shree, in *Fear Is the Master*, San Bernardino, Calif.: Jeremiah Films, 1986.

"Toronto Blessing," *60 Minutes-Australia*, June 18, 1995.

Web Sites

Barna Research Online (www.barna.org)
Brownsville Revival (www.brownsville-revival.org)
Global Resource Ministries (www.grmi.org)
Los Angeles Times (latimes.com)
National Post Online (www.nationalpost.com)
Reapernet chat (chat.reapernet.com)
Toronto Airport Christian Fellowship (www.tacf.org)

Scripture Index

Subject Index

A

A Dream Come True (Ryle), 81
Abraham, "slain in the spirit"
    claim, 201–3
Acronyms
    APES, 232
    FLESH, 13–17
    WOW, 17
Adam, "slain in the spirit" claim,
    200–201
Agabus, 90–91
Airport Vineyard.
    See Toronto Airport Vineyard
Allen, A.A., 15, 147–50, 173
Allen, Lexie (wife of A.A.), 150
Altered states of consciousness
    (ASC), 237–45
Altered States of Consciousness
    (Tart), 238–39
Anaheim Vineyard, 241–42.
    See also Mother's Day
    phenomenon; Wimber, John
Ananias, 101
Andrews, Lynn, 239
Angelo, Tony, 3–8
"Animal magnetism" concept,
    234, 235
Animal noises
    as manifestation, 42, 242

John Arnott's response, 53
APES acronym, 232
Arianism, 104
Arius, 316n
"Army of seers", 89. *See* Prophecy
"Army of the Lord" concept, 166–67.
    See also "Joel's endtime army"
Arnott, Carol, 47, 49, 51, 128–29
    and Benny Hinn, 107
    and Stephen Hill, 57
    before Toronto Blessing, 46
    on Holy Spirit, 125–26, 321n
Arnott, John, 47–51, 95, 99, 128,
    188, 239, 241, 244–45, 251, 276
    and Benny Hinn, 46, 107
    and Claudio Freidzon, 46–47
    and Randy Clark, 44–45
    and Rodney Howard–Browne, 46
    before Toronto Blessing, 46
    gold fillings claim, xix–xx
    on current revival, 103
    on dangers of caution, 8, 50–51,
        248–50
    on God "throwing party", 52–53
    on Jesus Christ, 118
    on Jonathan Edwards, 95–97
    on manifestations, 242
    on Sarah Lilliman, 74–75
    response to critics, 54–56

367

alleged sign of Holy Spirit, 9
Azusa Street, 143
Second Great Awakening, 135–37.
See also Manifestations
Speaking in tongues, 158–59
Azusa Street, 143–45
hoaxes, 171–73
vs. Pentecost, 171–73.
See also Manifestations
"Spiritual drunkenness" concept, 29
Spirituality. *See* Pagan spirituality
Spriggs, Agnes, 186
Stipe, Tom, ix–xviii, 271–72, 274
and Mother's Day phenomenon,
215, 218–19
Stone, Barton W., 135, 323*n*
Stone, Jean, 159
Story of Hypnosis, The, 253–54
Strader, Karl, 28–29, 31, 33, 38
Suggestion, 234–36, 255–60
hypersuggestibility, 255–56,
257–58
subtle suggestion, 256–57.
See also Hypnotism
"Super apostles and prophets"
concept, 9, 160, 161–69, 175–78
"Sweeping the sanctuary", xxiv–xxv
Synan, Vinson, 142, 144, 171

T

Tart, Charles, 237
Tetzel, Johann, xviii
"They Called Jesus a Counterfeit,
Too", 67
Thiessen, Elmer, xxi
Thiessen, Willard, xxi
"Thoroughly blasted" concept, 57
"Thrown by the spirit" claim, 207–8
Time Magazine, 9
Tongues. *See* Speaking in tongues
Toronto Airport Christian Fellowship,
299*n*.
See also Toronto Airport Vineyard;
Toronto Blessing
Toronto Airport Vineyard, 47–51,
242–43
DeArteaga's influence, 96

Kristy's story, 75–78
manifestations, 51–54
name change, 299*n*.
See also Toronto Blessing
Toronto Blessing, 113
beginnings, 47–51
"gold fillings" claim, xix–xxi
origins, 44–45
Pensacola as outcome, 59–60.
See also Pensacola Outpouring
Sarah Lilliman claims, 74–75
Torrey, R.A., 262
Trance states, 240–41. *See also*
Altered states of consciousness
(ASC); Hypnotism
Twain, Mark, 225–30, 247, 255, 260

U/V/W

Unity, 265–67
Vineyard. *See* Anaheim Vineyard;
Association of Vineyard Churches;
Toronto Airport Vineyard;
Vineyard Christian Fellowship
Vineyard Christian Fellowship,
213–21
Vitolo, Joseph, 253–54
Wagner, Peter, 160
Waltrip, Burroughs A., 185–86
Ward, Alison, 64
Ward, Elizabeth, 64
Warner, Wayne E., 185
Wesley, John, on manifestations,
195–96, 287
White, John, 273
on Mother's Day phenomenon,
217–18
Wigglesworth, Smith, 38
Wilder–Smith, Oliver, 71
Williams, Mrs. Alvester, 148
Wimber, Carol, 273
on Mother's Day phenomenon,
215–16, 218
Wimber, John, 16, 160, 174, 239,
258
as Quaker, 124

Mother's Day phenomenon, 213–21
on Paul Cain, 161, 164–65,
175–76
on Scripture, 123
on "slain in the spirit", 199–211
Witnessing, 267–69
Woodworth–Etter, Maria Beulah,
181–84
Worldwide Church of God, 286

Worship choruses, 263–64
repetition, 237–39, 257–58
Worship, 262–65
WOW acronym, 17

X/Y/Z

Zeal in religion, 108–9
Zechariah, 91

About the Author

Hank Hanegraaff answers questions live as host of the *Bible Answer Man* broadcast, heard daily throughout the United States and Canada. He is president of the world-renowned Christian Research Institute headquartered in southern California and author of the best-selling Gold Medallion winner *Christianity in Crisis*.

As author of Memory Dynamics, Hank has developed memorable tools to prepare believers to effectively communicate: (1) *what* they believe, (2) *why* they believe it, and (3) *where* cults deviate from historic Christianity. He has also developed fun and easy techniques for memorizing Scripture quickly and effectively.

Hank is a popular conference speaker for churches and conferences worldwide. He resides in Southern California with his wife, Kathy, and their eight children: Michelle, Katie, David, John Mark, Hank Jr., Christina, Paul, and Faith.

For further informaton on Memory and Personal Witness Training materials address your request to:

Hank Hanegraaff
Box 80250
Rancho Santa Margarita, CA 92688-0250
or call (714) 589-1504

Counterfeit Revival Tape

You've seen the documentation. Now, you can hear how the leaders of the Counterfeit Revival define and defend doctrines that have more in common with the kingdom of cults than the kingdom of Christ. These landmark audiotapes provide a powerful tool for reaching loved ones ensnared by the preaching and practices of the Counterfeit Revival.

What can Heaven's Gate, Waco, and Jonestown have in common with a church near you?

As incredible as it may seem, the very principles used by leaders of cults are today employed in literally thousands of churches worldwide. Tactics once relegated to the ashrams of cults are now replicated at the altars of churches—as Christians worldwide ape the practices of pagan spirituality:

- Pensacola, Florida—In the emotionally charged atmosphere of the 10 o'clock Sunday morning worship of an Assemblies of God church, a woman works herself into an *altered state of consciousness* as she jerks her head violently from side to side for more that 2½ hours.

- Oklahoma City, Oklahoma—Benny Hinn Healing Crusade—Ella Peppard dies from complications suffered after someone who succumbs to the power of *peer pressure* is "slain in the spirit" on top of her.

- London, England—Holy Trinity Brompton—An Anglican vicar *exploits the expectations* of parishioners to such an extent that they become "drunk in the Spirit." Designated drivers and taxi cab services are recommended for those too spiritually inebriated to leave on their own.

- Toronto, Canada—Vineyard Christian Fellowship—A pastor employing the *subtle power of suggestion* manipulates a crowd into acting "like lions, oxen, eagles, and even warriors." Though deeply frightened, they are duped into believing their experiences are divine rather than demonic.

Socio-psychological manipulation tactics such as **A**ltered states of consciousness, **P**eer pressure, **E**xploitation of expectations, and **S**ubtle suggestions **(A-P-E-S)** are so powerful they can cause human beings to "behave like beasts or idiots and be proud of it." No one is immune—once an epidemic of hysteria is in full force, it can make black appear white, obscure realities, enshrine absurdities, and cause people to die with purple shrouds over their corpses. (See page 232 and following.)

How do you **know** that Christ was **raised** from the dead?

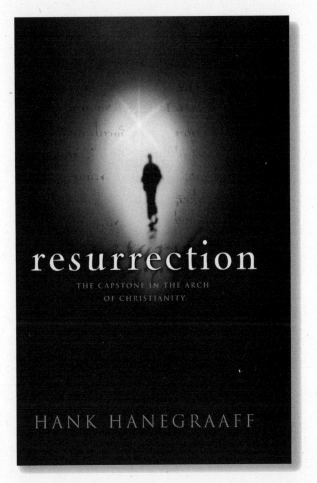

resurrection

THE CAPSTONE IN THE ARCH
OF CHRISTIANITY

HANK HANEGRAAFF

Christian apologist Hank Hanegraaff unveils the mystery and misunderstanding surrounding the historicity of the physical resurrection of Christ, as well as our own future physical resurrection. Biblical truths are revealed, equipping readers with a way to readily defend the faith.

WORD PUBLISHING